The Parson's Boys

The Parson.

The Parson's Boys

By

ROBERT CASEY, A. M.

WASH-DRAWINGS AND PEN SKETCHES, -	-	BY A. DOROTHY CESSNA
CHARACTER SKETCHES, - - -	-	BY L. C. PHIFER
MARGINAL EMBELLISHMENTS, -	-	BY LUCILE KLING

DENVER, COLORADO
THE PARSON'S BOYS PUBLISHING COMPANY
1906

PRESS OF THE METHODIST BOOK CONCERN, CINCINNATI, OHIO

To Every

SON OF A PARSON

THIS VOLUME

Is Fraternally Dedicated

BY THE AUTHOR

"Children, obey your parents in the Lord, for this is right."—Eph VI, 1.

———

"And ye fathers, provoke not your children to wrath, but nurture them in the chastening and admonition of the Lord."—Eph. VI, 4

———

"Love endureth long and is kind."—1 Cor XIII, 4.

FOREWORD.

Affidavit.

State of Colorado ⎤
    City and   ⎬ ss.
County of Denver ⎦

On this First Day of April, 1906, before me personally came Nathan Bangs Flint and William Asbury Flint, being of lawful age and sound minds, and made affidavit as follows, to-wit:

That they, being the acknowledged sons of a Methodist preacher, were in nowise worse than other youths of their own ages, circumstances and previous conditions of latitude.

Furthermore, they solemnly affirm on oath that, to the best of their knowledge and belief, they were very much <u>better</u> than most of the boys of their acquaintance who had not the distinguished honor of being born of Methodistic and ministerial lineage.

The above deposition was subscribed and sworn to before me on the day and date above set forth.

(Signed)   ANANIAS LIEBOLD,

Notary Public.

My commission expires when I do.

After this solemn affidavit we trust that the scandalous indictment above set down will be quashed, and never more heard of. Should the Court still have doubts, however, He is respectfully referred to the inside evidence we present.

TABLE OF CONTENTS.

CHAPTER VII.

WILLIAM BECOMES A LIFE MEMBER.

CHAPTER VIII.

BIRDS OF A FEATHER.

CHAPTER IX.

MOTHER'S WAY.

CHAPTER X.

NEW SCENES.

CHAPTER XI

THE PARSON'S YARN.

CHAPTER XII.

TWO KINDS OF GAME.

CHAPTER XIII.

FARM LORE.

CHAPTER XIV.

"THE ROD OF CORRECTION."

CHAPTER XV.

SOME FOOLISHNESS.

CHAPTER XVI

MORE FOOLISHNESS.

CONTENTS.

4

6 *CONTENTS.*

LIST OF ILLUSTRATIONS.

WASH DRAWINGS
By Miss A. Dorothy Cessna.

PEN SKETCHES.

7

8 *LIST OF ILLUSTRATIONS.*

· 2

MARGINAL EMBELLISHMENTS
By Lucile Kling

The Parson's Boys.

LAYING OUT THE TASK.

The Parson's Boys.

CHAPTER I.

A SATURDAY'S TASK.

"O WILLIAM!"

It was the Parson who called. He was busy dragging hickory poles and gnarly oak limbs from a huge, tangled wood-pile, and putting them in a place by themselves.

"O William!"—this time louder.

With hands in his trousers' pockets, a boy about eleven years of age stood by ruefully watching the proceedings, the toes of his bare feet burrowing in a heap of sawdust at the end of a rickety, scarred old saw-buck. As the Parson tugged

13

away, and the pile of selected wood grew larger, the discontented look upon the boy's face became deeper, and a cloud of gloom seemed to shadow him.

"O William!"—this time quite savagely.

"Yes-sur; I 'm a-comin'," a voice replied.

As the now perspiring Parson glanced over the lot fence toward the parsonage, a second youth nearly two years younger than the one already mentioned made his appearance around the corner of the back porch, and came slowly through the gate to the scene of operations. He had scanty eyebrows, a very freckled face, and washed-out blue eyes with sparse lashes scattered lonesomely along the lids. His hay-colored hair was surmounted by an apology for a straw hat out of the brim of which some hungry cow had chewed a large crescent. While coming reluctantly at the Parson's call, he was busily munching a slice of bread, through the pores of which sorghum molasses dripped in long, amber beads.

"Why do n't y' answer when ye 're called?" demanded the impatient Parson with a look of stern reproach.

"I *did* answer, every time," replied the boy, swallowing the last mouthful of bread and wiping his sticky fingers on the saw-buck. Then he picked up the bottom of a tin-can and sailed it at a rooster that had found a beetle close by, and was calling loudly to his harem of hens.

The missile was not well aimed, but at the last of its

CLIPPED A FEATHER

flight it took a queer twist, and clipped a long curving feather from the tail of the chattering fowl. As he glimpsed the moving shadow of the tin, the rooster uttered a warning "h-a-a-w-w-k!" but when it struck his stern timbers he gave a hoarse squawk and jumped a yard from the ground on his way to a place of safety. Both the boys laughed, but not the exasperated Parson. He clicked his jaws and made a quick pass at the side of William's head, which that watchful urchin adroitly dodged.

"What are ye always tryin' to destroy somethin' for?" asked the Parson angrily. Then as no answer came from the culprit he said warningly, "You jist let that be the very last!"

After a pause to allow this admonition to sink deep into the boy's mind he continued:

"Now I 'm going away, to be gone over the Sabbath; and I 've laid out a pile of poles and limbs here, for you and Nathan to manufacture into fire-wood. See that ye do n't cut it too long; and I want to find the job all done when I git back Monday."

With these words he strode away to the house Shortly reappearing with a pair of saddle-bags on his arm, he mounted a horse that had been stamping at the gate for half an hour, and with a cluck and a kick, rode away to one of his preaching places.

꙰ ꙰ ꙰

By all standards which he held as of any value, Parson Flint was a good man. The only boy in a family of seven children, and left an orphan at an early age, he had been brought up to share the hard work and pinching poverty of a fatherless household. For several generations his ancestors had been Methodists of the strictest type; and when yet a very young man he himself had entered the ministry of the church, becoming one of those itinerants who every year or two were moved to new charges, having here no abiding city.

Parson Flint was tall, raw-boned, big and austere. His hair was still black, his face rugged and stern featured, with keen gray eyes under heavy brows. He wore a beard, but no moustache; and when he set his firm upper lip upon its nether, two deep grooves slanted from the nose to the corners of his mouth, so that when aroused to indignation his face set and hardened as if carved in iron.

There was a strain of Scotch blood in his veins, and as he grew up the stern spirit of the old Covenanters seemed to crop out in his disposition. His early education had been scant, but his great and aggressive energy served him well among the people to whom he ministered, and who shared his fervent faith.

One curious fact about him is worthy of notice. When talking with his family, or mingling casually with his parishioners, his speech was usually that of the back-woods where he had been born and reared; it was rude and ungrammatical, though often forceful. But when in the pulpit or upon the platform, or whenever religiously moved and exalted much of this uncouthness seemed to fall away from him, and by some strange inspiration he could rise into another tongue. Then he became Biblical, sometimes stately, and very often thrillingly eloquent. His ministerial work had thrown him among strange peoples, and he was wont to call himself an "Apostle to the Gentiles."

Piety was the one great business of Parson Flint's life, and he worked at his trade with tireless industry. His hatred of all things wicked touched at times upon fanaticism; thus he sometimes failed to make necessary distinctions, and was prone to include the sinner with his great abhorrence of sin. He was much given to old saws, and pious or Scriptural adages. His favorite quotation to the boys was from Solomon:

"Foolishness is bound in the heart of a child; but the rod of correction shall drive it far from him."

And it must be confessed that he showed his great faith in this remedy by using it on all occasions. The dreams, pranks and impulses of his own youth had long been put aside; and he firmly believed that the right method for keeping boys out of mischief was to "correct" them often, giving them afterwards plenty of hard, disagreeable work to do.

So as upon this Saturday he strode away to his duties, he felt sure that the task he had laid out for the two urchins would be enough to keep them busy, and prevent them from "sitting in the seat of the scornful or standing in the way of sinners."

❧ ❧ ❧

As the Parson disappeared from view down the street, the boys, who had been doggedly hacking away at their task, flung down ax and saw, uttering a loud whoop of satisfaction.

William even went so far as to turn a summersault, but came down on a big chip, when he quickly scrambled up again, with a wry face and a vigorous rub of the hurt place.

The rooster had recovered from his fright, and they now spied him in a neighboring fence corner, lying on his side and scratching dust over his heated body. In another second the unsuspecting fowl was astonished by a bombardment of chips. With a hoarse note of terror he sprang up and tried to creep through a hole in the fence; but it was too small for him, and he suddenly backed out, doubtless intending to run for it. But alas! Just as he withdrew his head from the hole a sharp-edged chip hit him square and hard. He gave one tremendous flop, and the next second was lying on his back, his wings feebly moving and his expiring legs kicking the June air. The missile had broken his neck!

When the boys realized what they had done, there was a gasp of dismay, and they felt the bitterest remorse. Who would have dreamed of such an outcome to a little sport? They knew well what the reckoning for it would be when the Parson returned. A dark scheme suggested itself; they thought of sneaking the dead rooster away and burying him. But when inquiry was made they knew the truth would out, and so that deception was abandoned. They talked it over for some time, and then with many futile regrets Nathan took the dead fowl and went to tell his mother. She was working in the kitchen, and when she saw what the weeping boy carried in his hand the truth was easily guessed.

"Now what have you done?" she asked reproachfully.

"Oh ma," Nathan blubbered, "we did n't mean to kill him; really and truly we did n't. We was only havin' some fun, and tryin' to scare him off; but he got in the way of a chip, an' it killed him. But we never once thought of doin' such a thing;" and sincere tears attested his grief.

"Ah my son," replied Mrs. Flint sadly, "you never stop to think until it 's too late. My best rooster, too! What will your pa say when he gets back?"

Nathan guessed only too well what it would be, and gave way to renewed tears as he thought of "the judgment to come." After snuffling, and trying hard to explain for several minutes he returned dismally to the wood-pile, and with William set to work in earnest at his task.

They toiled hard for nearly an hour, but at the end of that time there was not a very great difference in the size of the stint laid out by the sturdy Parson. Nathan eyed the remainder gloomily.

"We can't git it done in a week," growled William savagely. He had been watching the black expression on his brother's face.

But Nathan suddenly had an idea. "Jist you wait," he said.

Then climbing on top the main wood-pile, he threw off a large quantity of the lighter stuff, and with William's help put about a third of the amount laid out for them to cut in the hole thus made, covering it over with the limbs he had displaced. After accomplishing this fatiguing task the boys sat down to rest.

"Do n't ye wisht we had a million dollars?" asked William when he had got his breath again.

A million was William's idea of the extreme limit of wealth. In all his life he had never owned more than five cents at a time. This desirable sum he occasionally earned by "catching white hairs." The process was as follows:

Often on a warm day the Apostle would take his Bible or a volume of Wesley's sermons and retire to the shade of a tree in the yard to read. Here, tipped back in his chair, he would soon become drowsy, closing his eyes, dropping his head, and holding the book loosely in one hand with a finger between the leaves to keep the page. This restful occupation he called "meditating;" and during such sleepy spells, liking to have his head fumbled, he would say to William:

"Now, my son, see if ye kin find fifty white hairs on yer daddy's head, and if do I'll give ye a five-center."

William would seize upon this chance for wealth with great avidity Such occasions were not frequent, however. The Parson was wonderfully economical, and he usually made the terms of payment impossible Thus he would stipulate as the condition of the reward that William should find a gray hair of a given length,—say a half inch or an inch longer than any kind of hair on his head

But if the Parson sought to be shrewd, William in his turn was guileful This white-hair industry was his only source of revenue, and he couldn't afford to fail So he would slyly smuggle into his pocket a few hairs of the required length from the white tip of the old cow's tail. Then having extended

The White-Hair Industry.

"I'd a good deal rather have an Aladdin's lamp," said Nathan as William paused in his rapt recital.

"Could ye do more with that than with a million dollars?" asked William doubtfully.

"Shucks! I sh'd think ye could! W'y all ye have to do is jist to rub the lamp, and a great big jinny-i pops up and says,—'What would'st thou? I'm ready to obey thee as thy slave, and the slave of all that holds the lamp in their hands:' and when ye tell him to do it he brings ye money, and fine clothes and di'monds; and if ye're hungry he fetches a big table with silver dishes loaded down with pound-cake and fried chicken and gravy and flaky biscuits like mother makes when company comes, and butter and honey, and everything ye want!"

While his brother was describing these marvels William had risen to his knees; his eyes were suffused, and the water was coming to the corners of his mouth. As Nathan finished, William sank back on his heels in a kind of trance, and exclaimed with intense longing:

"My o-h-h! *Don't* ye wisht we had one?"

Just at this juncture Mrs. Flint called from the back porch: "Oh William, bring mother an armload of stove-wood: be quick about it, the fire is nearly out."

William sprang up instantly to obey. Longings for another bread and sorghum lunch spurred him greatly. He gath-

STEPPED ON A SMALL HOOP.

ered up the wood and started for the kitchen; near the porch, however, he stepped on a small hoop which flew up and whacked him viciously across the shins. Tripping, he lunged forward and brought up against the cistern curb, his armful of wood flying in every direction.

The clattering noise and William's screech brought Mrs. Flint hurriedly to the rescue. She helped the boy to his feet, and after picking up the wood again he limped tearfully into the house, where he was quickly comforted by a large slice of bread and molasses.

"Do try to be more careful, my son," said Mrs. Flint as she handed it to him. Then preparing a second slice she directed him to give it to Nathan.

William started for the wood-pile once more; but before turning the corner of the porch he made a careful survey of the two slices of bread. His own was a fourth eaten; so he nibbled the edge off square, and upon reaching the lot, soberly handed this to his brother, keeping the whole slice for his own use. Then they sat down, and for a few minutes were too busy to speak. After the last crumb had been put away, William said with a sheepish grin:

"Mother's picked the rooster, and she's a cookin' some of it, I guess. Somethin' smelled like it, anyhow."

While Nathan was cutting a caper at this welcome news he spied the calf lying in a fence-corner, waggling its big ears, and beating its tail up and down in drowsy efforts to keep off the flies. Slipping behind the sleepy animal, he seized it by the busy tail. The calf scrambled to its feet in a fright and

3

started for the barn; but finding the door shut it turned again and raced down the fence, Nathan clinging tightly and going ten feet at a jump.

"B-a-a-a!" bawled the flying calf; and Whitey, the old cow that was grazing not far away came bellowing and shaking her head threateningly at the tormentor of her offspring. Finally in an attempt to turn suddenly in a corner the calf slipped and came down on its side with a terrible thump, running its hind legs through the lower crack in the fence. There it lay, panting and rolling its big eyes as if utterly exhausted.

Nathan looked up apprehensively and saw his mother with one of the girls watching him from the back porch. He was now badly frightened lest the awkward brute had done itself some serious injury. His scare was not lessened as his sister called sharply:

"You little torment! I'll lay you've hurt that calf, and maybe killed it Pa'll larrup you good when he gets back!"

Nathan hurriedly pulled the calf's legs free from the fence, and then tried to coax the animal to its feet; but the effort was of no use. Bossy was discouraged; he sullenly refused to stand up, but putting his nose to the ground grunted as if the breath had been knocked out of him.

Seeing at last that his efforts availed nothing, Nathan returned again to the wood-pile and set remorsefully about his task When conscience hurt him worst he always soothed it by working harder than ever

After a while he lifted a long, hard hickory pole upon the

saw-buck, but found that it would not balance, teetering up and down so it was impossible to use the saw. When numerous exasperating efforts to conquer the thing had been tried, he propped up the long end of the pole with a stick of stove-wood, and the difficulty seemed to be mastered. But by this time all the "set" had been taken out of the saw, and it could scarcely be drawn through the wood. Finally in an angry attempt to jerk it through, the prop under the pole fell down; this caught the saw-blade against the side of the buck and snapped it in two.

Surely it was a day of calamity! It seemed that every-thing combined to get the boy into trouble. He gazed at the broken saw in despair, and ruefully went to show it to his mother and explain how it happened.

Kind as they were, there was little comfort to the afflicted boy in her motherly words and at last he returned to the lot, where he and William took turn about hacking at their task with the ax. This was hard, slow work; the ax was both heavy and dull, so presently they quit the wearisome job, slipped away to the barn, climbed over the back fence and went to seek more interesting employment. It was not long before they came across Dick Patterson, one of their schoolmates with whom William played a game of "keeps." Dick was a past master at that kind of sport, and quickly won every marble William had. Even his favorite "taw" had been forfeited, but Dick generously allowed him to retain this on condition that he would pay interest in the shape of a glass marble the next time he got a new supply.

It was late in the evening when they returned home, furtively entering the lot in the same manner they had gone; for it must be known that the Parson never allowed them to wander from the parsonage premises when he was at home. They got back in time to help their mother do the milking, it being their part to pull off the calf and halter him when he had got a fair share of supper: and Nathan was greatly rejoiced to find that the unruly brute had not really suffered any serious injury in its fall. After supper they greased their shoes, took a bath and went to bed, where in a short time all the troubles and vexations of that eventful Saturday were forgotten in a maze of dreams

CHAPTER II.

"LAYING UP MORE WRATH."

SUNDAY morning dawned with a flood of golden June sunshine. Everywhere was a Sabbath stillness; not a wandering breeze stirred the leaves, but a delicious languor wrapped Nature, which seemed reluctant to be roused from its final beauty nap. Earth was weltering in a bath of dew; and when the warm sunshine spilled over an eastern hilltop and ran down its side, every grass-blade was fringed with diamonds, and the sweet morning-glories gurgled liquid pearls in their delicate white throats.

The Parson was ever given to early rising, and had trained his family to the same thrifty habit. So Mrs. Flint was up betimes, watching the light grow and glow as she went about her morning work, singing the while an old-fashioned Methodist hymn.

Tired out with their previous day's work, the boys slept as if their eyelids had grown together. Mrs Flint seemed to know how delightful early morning sleep is to growing youths, so she did not disturb them until breakfast was nearly ready.

"Wake up, my boys!" she called cheerily at their bedroom door; "I 'm going to bake you some nice pan-cakes, and you must be ready to eat them while they are good and hot."

27

The boys were always hungry, but nothing less tempting than pan-cakes could have stirred them just then. They crawled slowly out and sat on the edge of the bed, rubbing their sleepy eyes and yawning with many gasps and grunts. Finally putting on shirts and trousers they got a wash-pan, soap and towel from the kitchen, went out to the cistern, and there sat down on the platform to rest.

Near by was a "Dominicker" pullet with sun-burned skin, having no feathers to speak of save on its neck, wings and tail. It was jumping up and pecking at flies that basked in the sunshine on the side of the house; but the insects were wary, and, after missing a number, the chicken gave up the attempt, shook its head, poked one leg out behind and stretched a scantily covered wing down over it, at the same time gaping prodigiously. The example was wonderfully contagious, and the boys promptly imitated it. Old Tabby came through the lot gate from the barn, carrying a fat mouse and uttering a smothered "maow" to her numerous family, that with tails up came racing from every direction.

The sunshine was deliciously soothing, and everything was so still that William leaned back against the cistern curb, closed his eyes and came near falling asleep once more. But as he fetched a jaw-cracking yawn, Nathan suddenly stuck a corner of the cake of soap in his mouth, and in turn got a crack over his own head with the wash-pan.

Mrs. Flint's voice stopped this sky-larking. "Hurry along, boys," she called to them. "Breakfast is on the table."

At this they sprang up, dashed water over their heads and

Sat Down on the Platform to Rest.

faces, gave their front hair a stroke or two with the comb and hastened eagerly to the feast they knew to be awaiting them. Mother's pan-cakes were always delicious, and the hungry boys ate as long as possible. It was not worth while to stop, even when Ruth, their youngest sister made sarcastic remarks about the tangles they had been too lazy to comb out of their hair.

When breakfast had been despatched, they returned to their bed-room and donned their Sunday clothes, heartily wishing that they could dispense with shoes on such a warm day. Then after submitting to have Eunice, the oldest sister, comb their hair properly, they sat down to learn a lesson in the catechism. This was a task concerning which the Parson was very strict on Sunday. Nathan acted as questioner and William tried to answer him.

CATECHISM.

"Who made you?"

"God," replied William promptly.

"What is God?" Nathan continued.

"An unkerrated (uncreated) sperret," William responded. Then without waiting for further questions he asked:

"Say, Nathan, what is a sperret? Is it a ghost?"

"I dunno," Nathan replied; "but the book says God's one. I wonder what He looks like!"

"I know," William rejoined, proud to settle at least one puzzle for his older brother. "He looks like Uncle Tommy."

"Shucks!" sneered Nathan loftily. "You ain't got half gumption. What do you know about how God looks?"

"Jist looky here," said William indignantly, picking up "The Singing Pilgrim," their Sunday-school hymn book and pointing to the back of it. "Here's a picture of God settin' on His throne with a ring above His head, and all the angels flyin' around like 'skeeters. Do n't that look like Uncle Tommy, now?"

"Suppose it does," returned Nathan stubbornly. "I do n't believe God looks like that. Who took His picture?"

This shrewd question was a poser for William; but he was the Parson's son, and already quick to defend his cherished theology. With final and lofty rebuke he said:

"Ye see the picture, do n't ye? I guess the men what made the book knowed more about God than you do. You never seen God."

Before such argument as this it was Nathan's turn to feel worsted. He made no reply, and after a few minutes' musing they went on with their catechism until Mrs. Flint entered the room, ready for Sunday services. It was not the Parson's day to preach in town, and on such vacant Sabbaths "class-meeting" was held instead

When Mrs Flint and the boys entered the somber old church it was almost time for the services to begin. The urchins followed their mother up to the front, where all three sat down in the "amen corner," as the seats on each side of the pulpit were called in the Parson's family Thirty or forty people were present, all staid, somewhat elderly, and sitting in decorous silence Besides themselves no other young people were there, and the boys felt rather lonesome.

As ten o'clock struck, a grave, white-headed brother who was known as the "Class-leader" arose, put on his spectacles and opened the big Bible. Then in a solemn but earnest voice he read the chapter from St. John's Gospel,—"Let not your hearts be troubled." Following this reading he lined out a hymn,

> "How tedious and tasteless the hours
> When Jesus no longer I see."

This being sung, the leader asked all to kneel in prayer, and in pleading voice he called down the blessing of the Lord upon the little flock committed to his care and counsels.

"LET NOT YOUR HEARTS BE TROUBLED."

During this somewhat lengthy exercise the boys grew quite tired of the hard floor, but at last the brother reached his "amen," and the kneeling group again seated themselves, a few minutes of impressive silence following. Then the old class-leader stood up and began to give in his personal experience.

"Brethren and sistern," he said with a deep sigh, "it is now goin' on forty years since I give my heart to the Lord and felt his savin' grace. My pathway has not all been strowed with roses, and sometimes I 've had to 'rastle mightily with the Evil One. My one regret is that I 've been but a weak and feeble servant in the Master's vineyard. It is owin' to the boundless mercy of God that it has n't been said of me as it was of the barren fig-tree,—'cut it down, why cumbereth it the ground!' But though my sins hev been many, the mercy of the Lord endureth forever; and by the grace of God I shall yet triumph over sin, sorrer and Satan, and land my bark safe on the happy shores of Canaan. Do n't fergit me when y' kneel at a throne of grace."

A sympathetic murmur went up from the devout listeners, and all received the speaker's words with hearty good-will and approval. After wiping a tear from his eye, the class-leader then walked up to a brother sitting in front of him and said kindly:

"Brother Snedecor, can you tell us this morning what great things the Lord has done for your soul?"

The brother thus addressed arose, and in a constrained manner recited his many hopes, fears and short-comings, saying that he felt himself to be very unworthy and imperfect, but was nevertheless determined to fight the good fight of faith, and at last wear a crown of glory at God's right hand.

When he had sat down, the leader spoke a few words of pious encouragement to him, afterwards passing on to the next member.

Now the boys had long been familiar with class-meeting exercises, and in most instances they could tell pretty nearly what each member of the group would say. So as the routine progressed, William ceased to be very greatly interested, and became quite restless. He squirmed about on the seat, relieved several itching places on his nervous body, and finally began to amuse himself by indenting the top of the pew in front of him with his teeth, afterwards counting the marks thus made.

But for some reason that did not appear, Nathan remained solemn and upright in his seat. A pious purpose was working in his mind, and it made his heart thump with great fear, which seemed to grow upon him as the class-leader came closer to where he was seated. Mrs. Flint was the last of his flock to whom the good old man addressed himself. She spoke briefly and sat down. When the leader had given her his usual words of advice he stepped before the two boys and said in a tone of fatherly interest:

"My sons, can't you say a word for the Lord this morning? Youth is the time to give your hearts to God."

William was greatly abashed, and sat far down on the small of his back, gnawing at his handkerchief which he had rolled into a ball and held tightly in a fist. But to his unutterable stupefaction and fright Nathan arose in his place, took a desperate grip upon the top of the pew in front, swayed feebly back and forth, and said:

"Brethren and sistern, I-feel-t'-say this morning'-that I'm thankful-t'-God-that-it's-as-well-with-me-as-what-it-is. I-know-I-often-do-many-things-I'd-ought-not-t'-do, an'-leave-undone-many-things-I'd-ought-to-do; but-pray-fer-me-that-I-may-hold-out-faithful-an'-at-last-meet-you-all-on-'tother-shore!"

Having reeled this all off in a breath, and in a shaking voice that died out to a whisper and gasp toward the close, he sank limply back into his seat. When he got up to speak, the eyes of all present were turned upon him in pious approval and sympathy. A hearty and loud "amen" followed his words, and the class-leader said feelingly:

"Praise the Lord, my son! You've taken up yer cross to follow Him. That's right. The Good Book says: 'Remember now thy Creator in the days of thy youth.' May the Lord bless and keep you for His name's sake. Go on in the good way, and you shall find reward at last."

Then a tearful sister started in a high, cracked voice the well-known hymn,—

"From every stormy wind that blows"

William sat open-mouthed and stunned, while Nathan was quite overcome until Mrs. Flint reached out a tender arm and clasped him, weak and trembling, to her side.

A final earnest prayer followed, sprinkled with loud "amens" and other pious ejaculations from many lips; then the meeting was over, and the gathering dispersed. The boys returned to the parsonage with their mother, Nathan very sober, and William feeling deeply awed in the presence of his suddenly pious brother. It might be, however, that the dead rooster and the broken saw had something to do with Nathan's remarkable and unexpected attack of religion.

By the time they had reached the house, Nathan's heart had got down out of his throat into its proper place again, and some of his scare had left him. Yet the solemnity of the step he had taken still bore heavily upon his spirits. To feed his pious cravings, he went to the Parson's library and picked out "Deathbed Scenes," which he sat down to read William watched him with wondering eyes, and lying down on the floor at a little distance tried hard to attract his attention by sundry grunts and *sotto voce* remarks But it was all of no use; the reader's thought was wrapped in mournful contemplation, and he refused to listen Finally William became discouraged,

turned over on his stomach, and began to sing in a doleful
voice,—

"How tejis an' tas'cless the hours!"

The situation became dreadfully strained, and it is doubtful how long either urchin could have endured it; but at last
the spell was broken by the voice of Mrs. Flint, calling them
to dinner.

The slaughtered rooster had been cooking since early
morning, and was as tender as a peach. When the boys took
their places at the table, the savory mess smote their nostrils
with great joy, and they almost ceased to regret the untimely
death of the fowl. So good was it that Nathan passed his plate
for a third helping, asking for "a drum-stick
this time." Then Louise, who had been
watching him with critical eyes for some
minutes, spoke tartly, saying:

"I should think you'd choke on it,
you little wretch. If I'd killed the poor
thing as you did, I couldn't eat a
mouthful."

A DRUM-STICK.

Her tone was intensely provoking, and it so angered
Nathan that he forgot all about his class-meeting testimony,
and fell from grace. Puckering up his countenance into a
horrible grimace, he stuck out his tongue at Louise and
said, "Yah, yah, yah, yah," for which she promptly slapped
him.

Nathan choked and spluttered with rage, and was about
to strike back, but the voice of his mother made him drop his

raised hand. He looked savagely at Louise, however, and said threateningly:

"Smarty! I 'll get even with you fer that! See if I do n't!"

The provocation was certainly great; but it must be confessed that when Nathan realized what he had done, conscience hurt him sorely. For a long time he felt very miserable, and was the more aggrieved at the uppish Louise that she had caused him so soon to backslide.

The dull Sunday afternoon wore away at last, having no further incident to mar the peace that belonged to it. When dusk fell, two young men called to spend the evening with Eunice and Louise. The girls met them with smiling cordiality, and ushered them into the parlor.

It was nine o'clock when the boys went to bed, but for a long time sleep refused to come. After tumbling about for an hour Nathan crept out of bed and quietly pulled on his trousers

"Whachu goin' to do?" whispered William.

"Never you mind," was the surly reply. "I 'm a-goin' to show Louise that she can't pound me over the head every time she wants to "

"I 'm goin' along," exclaimed William, jumping up to put on his clothes

They crept softly down stairs into the kitchen and purloined the big dish-pan Then sneaking out with it to the wood-pile, Nathan found a pole six feet in length and about three inches thick. Noiselessly making their way to the front door, the urchins perched the pan on top the pole and leaned it against the door, so that when the visitors left, the pan and pole together would fall into the house.

Having fixed this nasty trap to their satisfaction, the wicked boys slipped back up stairs to bed, chuckling in glee as they imagined the surprise waiting for the girls a little later. In order to enjoy it to the full, they tried to keep awake until the event came off, but as time passed they found it very hard work.

About half-past ten o'clock, however, they were brought out of a doze by a scream from Louise and a loud clatter of the dish-pan.

"They 're jist goin' away," whispered William excitedly. "I wonder what they thought of it!"

"Mebbe Louise 'll ta'nt me, and bang me over the head some more," replied Nathan, sitting up to listen.

But they heard nothing more, and as time passed, some-how the trick did n't seem as brilliant as they had at first thought it. And when next morning Louise appeared at break-fast with eyes red and swollen from hours of bitter crying, the thing was no longer funny.

For some reason breakfast did n't taste good; and after enduring the reproachful eyes of their mother as long as they could, the culprits betook themselves to the wood-pile, where they began to chop, turn about, on the hardest hickory pole they could find.

4

FLEW TO OPEN
THE GATE.

CHAPTER III.

"THE JUDGMENT TO COME."

THE boys worked like beavers until eleven o'clock, though the sun grew very hot. Their industry was a desperate attempt to atone in some measure for their sins, and the time was growing short. But, by picking out small sticks they got along quite fast, and made large additions to the ancient chip-pile,—that ugly monument of their numberless trials and sorrows. The stack of stove-wood became a high heap, and was still rapidly growing, when in a low voice William suddenly exclaimed:

"Yonder comes the 'Postle!"

Nathan quickly straightened up to look, and about thirty rods down the dusty road he saw the old bay horse coming along with a gait between a fast walk and slow trot. The Apostle was dangling the reins in his left hand, while the right held the stub of a switch with which he constantly pecked at the old horse's withers. Every two or three rods this pecking was aided by a few sharp clucks, which the boys imagined they could hear, even at that distance. The rider's crooked elbows rose and fell with every jog of the horse, as

38

if he might be practicing the motions of flying in order to save future time.

As the Parson rode up, Nathan flew to open the gate, and tried to appear greatly rejoiced at the home-coming; but do the very best he could, he was only able to screw his face into a look of adoring apprehension. Without speaking the Apostle rode into the lot, and immediately cast his eyes upon the fruits of the boys' industry. He was surprised: the rigid lines in his face quite relaxed, and in a jolly, approving voice he exclaimed: "Hooray me brave boys! I tell ye what, this looks as if somethin' was comin' to pass!"

But alas, this was what the uneasy boys themselves secretly thought, and they feared that the coming event might not be pleasant! The Parson's kindly tones sent a great thrill of delight through their hearts and down their spines, but it was quickly changed to a feeling of remorse and dread.

However the Parson really had cause for unwonted good-humor. It had been "Quarterly Meeting Sabbath,"—one of those oases in the desert of a Methodist preacher's year, when a portion of his usually meager salary is paid in. On this occasion he had received a goodly amount of "quarterage," and had the promise of more to follow soon.

Dismounting stiffly, and with a touch of lumbago, he unbuckled the well-worn saddle-bags and threw them across his arm. One side held his Bible and hymn-book, together with sundry articles of clothing; the other contained a mess of lamb's-quarter greens, which some well-disposed sister had done up neatly in a newspaper and sent to Mrs. Flint.

As Nathan started with the tired horse to the barn the Apostle called after him to say:

"Teck the saddle off 'n him, and see if he'll drink; then put him in the stall an' give him ten yeers of corn with plenty of hay."

It was at all times the Parson's habit to give minute instructions when he required anything of the boys.

"All right, I'll tend to him," said Nathan obediently. Then followed by William he led the animal away to the barn. This building stood at the far end of the lot on a slight rise of ground . Beyond it was a copse, part of a woods-pasture be-- longing to a neighbor. As Nathan removed the saddle, William put him a question which he was secretly anxious to have settled:

"D 'ye think he'll give us a lickin'?"

"I *bet* he will when he learns about that rooster," replied Nathan gloomily.

Then as the aggravation of it impressed him, he exclaimed, "Dag-*gon* the luck! What *did* the old idiot pull his head out of that hole for jist at the wrong time?"

William had no time to speculate on this puzzling problem; the horse wanted to take a roll in the dirt Leading him out of the shed, Nathan held his halter, and Daniel squatted in a heap, dropping stiffly on his side. Then he wallowed about, trying to turn over, the while kicking his bony old legs in the air, and groaning as if tortured with rheumatism. Yet he really enjoyed the exercise immensely, and kept at it so long that William grew tired of waiting, and hit him a resounding crack on the forehead with a cob. This brought him quickly to his feet, and after allowing him to drink, Nathan led him into a stall. Here the old fellow seemed to think his weekly troubles were over, and blew out a long sigh of rest and satisfaction.

"But pleasures are like poppies spread," and previous experience might have taught the old charger to expect more difficulties. When Nathan had tied him securely to the manger rail, that wicked youth reached slyly around and prodded the unsuspecting brute in the short ribs. With a wince, Daniel laid back his ears and made a savage snap at his tormentor's arm; but the boy was looking out for this, and met the fierce attempt with a vigorous slap on the animal's nose, which caused him to lunge to the further side of the stall, and snort with vast indignation.

William now joined in the attack, and began to tickle the angry old fellow with a switch, making him writhe, shake his skin and look furious. Presently in desperation he delivered a kick that knocked the instrument of torture out of his enemy's hand; but just then Nathan appeared on the other side, and had sharpened the end of his prod. The victim of this unkind treatment became greatly enraged. He pawed furiously, switched his long tail, and shook his head as if a cloud of gadflies were after him. In his vigorous efforts it finally happened that he plunged one forefoot over the manger-rail, where it was caught and held fast by the calks of his shoe. At this he struggled noisily, and was in great danger of doing himself some serious injury.

The wicked boys were by this time as badly scared as the horse, and they began to agonize, lest the Parson might hear the racket and make his appearance before they could set things right. After trying several times to release himself, Daniel paused a second to take breath. Nathan promptly grabbed the hoof and lifted it clear of the rail. Daniel gave a quick jerk, catching the urchin's knuckle against the manger-top, and peeling off a large flake of skin. He clapped the wounded member into his mouth with a grunt, but just then was struck chilly by the sight of the Parson's frigid face at the stable door. Glaring at the two young rascals sternly for a few minutes, the angry observer stepped in and rasped out:

"What on earth possesses ye to always be a-wantin' to torment somethin'? H'ain't the old horse hed enough to do without that?"

Then nervously opening and shutting his hands several times he added with sharp menace, "*Move* yerselves out of here, 'fore I 'frail ye!"

The abashed culprits had no excuse to offer for their misconduct, and upon being ordered out, sneaked furtively by the Parson, expecting to feel the palms of his twitching hands on the sides of their heads. But upon emerging from the stable door they perceived the reason for his unusual forbearance. Brother Ratcliffe, a jovial old farmer at whose house William first ate "manarvelins," had arrived with a wagon load of corn, and was halting just beyond the lot-gate. This timely incident meant respite for a few more hours. The boys knew that the final "reckoning" as the Parson called it would be postponed until this visitor had gone home. It was most unexpected good-luck, and their spirits rose once more.

" 'Light! 'light, Brother Ratcliffe," called the Parson in far sweeter tones than he had last used to the boys. "How do you do, and how is Sister Ratcliffe to-day?"

"Oh, fair to middlin', Brother Flint; how are you and yourn gettin' along?" was the reply.

"Nothin' to complain of, I believe," returned the Apostle. "Drive in," he added, opening the lot gate.

"Skik, skik!" clucked the farmer. "Git up there, Bally!" And at the same time he brought a long hickory down upon the back of an ugly, big-footed horse, whose head was hung low in an attitude of utter de-jection. Awakened by the sting of the gad, Bally lifted his neck and began to lean forward, which action seemed to lengthen him greatly. Meanwhile a saucy looking mule—the second mem-ber of the team—stepped off minc-ingly, and the wagon rolled into the lot.

"Skik, Skik! Git Up, Bally."

Brother Radcliffe now alighted from his wagon, and in the whole-souled fashion of a happy farmer greeted the Parson. Then the latter called the boys, who had lingered in the shed at the barn. The visitor's powerful grip made their fingers tingle, but they did n't mind this, being sure the Parson had some work for them.

"You git into the crib," said the Apostle, "and throw all

the white corn up to the front, and the yeller yeers to the back—"
waiting to hear no more the boys jumped to obey, but the Parson
stopped them :—

"Here! Say, will ye wait till I 'm done?"

"Yes-sur," was the subdued reply.

"When ye 've got the corn throwed to its place, git a rake
and clean out all the shucks; put 'em into the manger fer the
horse to pick at, and then see how much of this load ye kin
throw into the crib by the time we git back."

When these minute instructions had been delivered, Brother
Ratcliffe drove the wagon under the opening of the bin, put
on the brakes, and with the Parson went down town.

To the boys this was a chance for an hour's unmixed fun.
In a jiffy they were in the crib, pelting each other with nubbins
and making the corn fairly fly. While cleaning out the shucks
they uncovered several mice's nests, and William raced away to
borrow a bench-legged ratter, owned by one of their neighbors;
this lively animal made short work of the thieves in the Parson's
barn   By the time Brother Radcliffe and the Parson got back,
a large part of the wagon-load had been cribbed, and with a
scoop-shovel the farmer quickly threw in the balance. A bag
of luscious June apples, hidden in the load greatly rejoiced the
boys   When visitors came they were always required to wait
second table, and so they planned a raid on this fruit while the
rest of the family were eating dinner.

Brother Ratcliffe drove the empty wagon around to the
front of the barn, where he unhooked and left it standing upon
the side of the sloping ground, near the garden fence   The

Apostle took Daniel out of his stall, put in the visitor's team and gave them a liberal bait of corn. He tied Daniel to one of the front wheels of the empty wagon, and threw some hay into the bed for him to nibble at. But the horse merely tossed the hay about with his nose, being desirous of getting at the shattered corn that lay on the bottom beneath it.

When the Parson and his visitor had gone into the parsonage, the boys went to the smoke-house and picked out two large apples, with which they returned to the lot and climbed into the wagon. Nathan put the seat-board across the back end of the bed, and the two urchins perched themselves upon it to enjoy themselves while there was yet time.

While gnawing at his apple, Nathan picked up some grains of corn and shot one at the horse. Daniel had his nose buried in the hay; he was licking up the shattered corn lazily, perhaps enjoying it more because he could get so little at a time. William saw Nathan shoot the kernel with his thumb, and exclaimed meaningly:

"Wait till I get our snap-guns!"

With this he sprang over the end of the wagon and scudded into the barn, quickly returning with two stiff pieces of whalebone, which had doubtless been filched from one of his sisters. Each now took one of these instruments and began a siege upon the old horse.

Meantime dinner had been served. Brother Ratcliffe and the family, with the exception of Ruth, the youngest girl, sat down to eat It was Ruth's duty to keep flies from the table by means of a peach-tree bough, whose pendant leaves made a

very good brush. When all were seated a solemn pause ensued;
then the Parson looked at his guest and said:

"Brother Ratcliffe."

The brother understood   He bowed his shaggy head and
asked a most fervent blessing upon the meal, to which the Parson
responded with a deep "Amen!"   Then seizing a large buck-
horn handled knife and fork, he proceeded to carve a lusty
chicken that lay before him in a ring of dumplings, and looked
a very savory, tempting object.

In the task at hand the Parson was a born artist. He knew
to a hair where to hunt for joints, and in three minutes the
young cock which had that morning been making hoarse attempts to crow was dismembered and scattered to the four corners of the table.

During this interim Ruth's briskly swinging fly-brush had
deposited several leaves in the butter and gravy. This annoy-
ance caused Louise to go into the back-yard for a fresh bough,
and while there she spied the boys shooting corn at Daniel and
hugging themselves to keep from laughing too loudly at his
antics

In those days Methodists never laid aside their religion;
so as the meal proceeded it was enlivened by spiritual conversation, and congratulatory remarks about the quarterly meeting
of the previous day

"As I was sayin', Brother Ratcliffe," said the Parson, "I 've
seldom seen a greater outpourin' of the sperret than we hed
visterday   It reminded me of the day of Pentecost, when the
disciples were gethered together."

"About three sups, sister," mumbled the brother, handing his coffee cup to Mrs. Flint, and shoveling a dumpling into his roomy mouth. "Yes," he added, in reply to the Parson's remarks; "the Lord was mighty gracious, and on the givin' hand. We'd orter prostrate ourselves at a throne of grace for a revival in this part of the moral heritage. It's needed bad."

"Amen! The Lord grant it," responded the Parson, fervently.

Just at this moment there was a sharp rattling of the wagon to be heard, mingled with excited shouts from the boys. The Parson and his visitor sprang up and hurried out to see what had happened.

Upon reaching t h e b a c k porch, they saw the wagon rolling down hill. Its tongue, held up by a stick thrust under the hounds, was wagging about in a quick, jerky fashion, and the double-trees were w h a c k i n g Daniel viciously on the legs. Tied as he was the frightened horse was plunging

SAW THE WAGON ROLLING DOWN HILL.

around in a semi-circle, and with every turn of the wheel his head bobbed up and down. Nathan was rushing frantically about, snatching first at the wagon-tongue and then at the halter, while William, looking as if the crack of doom had sounded, tottered to and fro upon the seat.

The running men had not reached the lot, when, with a sudden swerve, the wagon plunged its tongue through the garden

fence, knocking down a whole panel, and scaring Daniel silly.
He gave one desperate wrench that jerked him head down and
turned him heels up on his back, but the halter strap fortunately
broke in time to save his neck. Scrambling up he looked about
in a dazed manner, and then careered off to the farthest corner
of the enclosure, where, facing about, he uttered a loud snort.
Then, with elevated tail, he trotted gingerly around, seeking
for some place of escape. Nathan quickly caught him, however,
and while leading him to the shed, exclaimed for the benefit of
the astonished Parson:

"What's the matter with ye, y' old fool? Ain't ye got no
sense?"

But the suspicious Parson was not to be greatly misled by
such an artifice. He felt morally certain that some trick of the
boys was at the bottom of the affair, and eyed them surlily.
Not knowing what to conclude just then, however, he pulled
away the wagon with the farmer's help, and set up the displaced
panel to keep the calf out of the garden, after which he and the
visitor went back to finish their meal.

"Was the horse hurt much?" asked Mrs. Flint, anxiously.

"I reck'n not," replied the Parson, gruffly. "It's a thousand wonders he did n't break his neck, though; or cripple hisself for life. I do n't understand what ailed him."

"I know," put in Louise, quickly. "Those trifling boys were
shooting corn into his ears and eyes with whale-bones they stole
from me;" and heedless of her mother's imploring looks she
went on wrathfully, "they have been perfect torments ever since
you went away; killing the chickens, breaking the saw and dis-

gracing the whole family. If you do n't take them in hands pretty soon, there 'll be no living in the house with them."

It was all explained now; the fright of the boys, the accident to the wagon, and the urchins' unusual industry. As Louise rattled off her story the Parson's face lengthened gloomily. But if his heart grew heavy, his stomach remained cheery, and when the eaters arose from the table, the chicken was a total wreck, most of its bones being piled in two plates.

The boys were now called in; but as they glanced at the table and guessed the amount of chicken left for them, the one sustaining hope of that awful morning seemed utterly eclipsed. It was too much; they were on the point of breaking down in despair, when Mrs. Flint came in from the kitchen with a plateful of dumplings, in which were hidden a gizzard, liver and several other choice tidbits. The boys sprang up and hugged her on the spot, Nathan around the neck and William about the waist from behind. She kissed each with a sad smile and went back to her work. Left alone, the boys then gorged themselves until it was physically impossible to go any farther, and William looked at the remaining scraps with a sigh. As they were stowing away the last bites Louise passed through the dining-room, and looked at them with a cruel triumph in her eye as she said, tauntingly:

"Just wait, you little wretches; you 'll not feel so good when the dessert comes on."

With this she entered the kichen, and shortly the boys overheard her saying spitefully to their mother, "I do n't care; they deserve all they 'll get, and more too!"

Then they felt their hearts fail them, and their knees knock together. In gloomy anticipation of the judgment to come they wandered disconsolately out to the wood-pile, and not even waiting for their dinners to settle, began taking turn about, chopping on the hardest, knottiest pole to be found.

After an hour's talk with the Parson about the church and the general condition of Zion, Brother Ratcliffe hooked up his mule and horse to go home. When he had driven away the Apostle returned to the house, where he learned from the irate Louise every detail of the boys misconduct, and it was painted bad enough. Presently the miserable culprits saw him coming around the corner of the house with hands behind his back; and there was a grim conviction of duty in his eyes, which the boys could plainly feel without close examination. He came up, leaned on the fence near by, and for a few dreadful moments looked at them in utter silence.

William had the ax in hand, and chopped desperately, while Nathan never before felt such a longing for something to work with. He

CROSS EXAMINATION:

actually thought he could hug the dullest ax in the world if he had it just then.

"Where's the saw?" at length asked the Parson.

"It's broke," replied Nathan weakly.

A long pause, during

which an agony of suspense racked the minds of the waiting urchins.

"And what broke it?" asked the Parson solemnly, just as
if he did n't already know.

"I was a-sawin' an' the pole was too long; it kept a-teeterin'
so I could n't do nothing. I put a stick of stove-wood under
the end to keep it up, an' it fell down an' broke the saw an'
mashed my sore foot," replied Nathan, in a voice that seemed
to stick in his throat.

"And was that what was the matter with the rooster?"
asked the Apostle, after another sinister pause.

William hacked at the pole with the energy of despair,
and Nathan thought the Parson's question the most senseless
thing he had ever heard.

"Why do n't ye answer me?"—with a slight elevation of
voice. "Was that what was the matter with the rooster, and the
horse ye was shootin' corn at, tryin' to put out his eyes?"

"No, sir," blubbered both the boys, for the tears would
flow under the prolonged pumping.

"Was that what was the matter with the calf, and the pole
ye set up, to fall down and knock people's brains out and dis-
grace the hull fam'ly?"

By this time the victims were past replying. Life had lost
its savor, and was not worth living. They felt the bitterness
of despair, as looking up, they saw the sorrowful face of their
mother at a window, the tears falling fast down her cheeks.

The Parson seemed to have closed his cross-examination
with most satisfactory results. He walked solemnly through

the lot, climbed over the back fence and disappeared in the copse beyond. The boys sat down on a log, waiting miserably and wishing they were dead, or had an Aladdin's lamp to whisk them off to the moon or some other far spot until the Parson should go off to preach again.

But as for the Apostle, he walked along a narrow trail until he reached a bending tree, at the foot of which lay a small, worn piece of plank. It was his place of secret prayer. Here he knelt and prayed long and earnestly, during which exercise he groaned, and seemed to wrestle much, occasionally rubbing his great hand over his face, or tugging at his heavy beard. At last he arose, took out his knife and cut two long, slim hickory sprouts Stripping off the leaves, he drew them through his hand to try their flexibility, walked gloomily back to the barn, opened the door and called ominously:

"Boys, come here!"

It sounded like the trump of Gabriel, summoning them to their accounts. Their tears broke forth anew, and they moved as if each step was the last.

The Parson's great strength of arm always made his punishments severe enough; but when they were dragged out in such dismal preparations, sensitive imagination added yet greater dread and weight of misery to the ordeal. The unhappy culprits reached the place of execution, and leading them into an empty stall, the avenger said grimly:

"I shell jist hev to whip ye, there's no other course to pursue; teck off yer coats."

At these decisive words the boys broke forth into wailing,

and pulled at their garments as if the jackets were frozen to them. From a neighboring stall old Daniel peered wonderingly through a big crack, and with William's grief mingled a fancy that the knowing old charger was actually pitying them.

Whack! Whack! Whack!

The snuffling cries changed into an agonized yell.

Whack! Whack! Whack! Whack!

Then there was the sound of a muffled break-down, performed with bare feet, and an imploring voice could be heard crying:

"Oh, pa, do n't, do n't! I will be good; I *will* be good! I did n't go to kill the rooster! Oh Ow! Ow! Wow! Do n't, ye 're killing me," and then the noise sounded smothered, as if the executioner had twisted the victim's head under his arm.

The same solo, with but trifling variations was repeated by William, and finally the voice of the Parson could be heard in solemn questionings, mingled with the lugubrious sound of their weeping:

"D' ye think this 'll be the last time ye 'll hev to hev it?"

("Ye-ye-ye-ye-e-es-s-sir!")

("Ye-ye-ye-ye-e-es-s-sir!")

"And d 'ye think ye 'll mind what I tell ye, and not be a-disgracin' the hull fam'ly by yer outragis conduct?"

("Ye-ye-ye-e-es-s-sir!")

("Ye-ye-ye-e-es-s-sir!")

And so on, until the number of virtues those boys promised to practice would have translated them forthwith, had it not

5

been that they had been similarly converted at least twenty times that same year.

When it was all over the Parson once more knelt, made them do so, and offered up an earnest petition in their behalf. They needed it; but owing to immediate causes they occupied the time by slyly rubbing their smarting legs, and knuckling the hot tears from their inflamed eyes.

At last release came, and the ordeal was over. Then they wandered back to the wood-pile, that final destiny of their lives. Supper was little better than a sham, and after family prayers they crept sullenly off to bed, brooded an hour over their heavy woes and finally fell into a sobbing slumber.

Yet before sleep became an oblivion, Nathan dreamed that his dear, patient mother stole softly into their room, knelt by the bed and prayed for them; and when finally she tenderly kissed them, it seemed as if her cheeks were all wet with tears.

Ever blessed are such precious dreams to wayward childhood!

CHAPTER IV.

A BIT OF DIPLOMACY.

A STORM always purifies the air, and it was just so with the tempest in Forgot to Untie Their Tails. the domestic sky at the old parsonage. The boys would "lay up wrath against the day of wrath" until the measure of their iniquity was full. Then the thunder-cloud of the Parson's anger would discharge itself in lightning strokes of justice, and a few days of real sunshine would follow.

True, the boys never really intended to do wrong, but somehow their efforts at fun were sadly unfortunate. The innate perversity of things was attributed to them. If in sport they threw a stone or chip at a chicken, it seemed always to hit; whereas if they threw at a legitimate mark the missile went wide every time. If they tried to have some fun with the calf the

55

awkward brute was sure to get himself mixed up with something. He would run against the fence, or try to plunge through a half-shut door, catch himself by the shoulders and peel the hide off his carcass in a frightful manner. But once let the reprobate get his stomach full of milk, and he would race all over the lot with tail up and never come in contact with a single obstacle.

To the boys this evidence of willful depravity on the part of the calf was very plain; but the purblind Parson could never see it, and he never tried to figure it out.

Yet had he remembered the incidents of his own youth, perhaps he might have been inclined to mitigate the severity of his oft-inflicted penalties The boys treasured many a tale of mischief he had related to them in times of extraordinary good humor One episode in particular they had laughed over many times It was an attempt on the Parson's part to break a team of six-months old calves to the yoke.

After yoking them up, he tried to make them pull a sled; but the brutes would persist in running their rear-ends around in opposite directions, in which position they would struggle, in great danger of breaking their necks To overcome this difficulty the Parson had lapped their tails about eight inches, and tied them firmly together with strong cord. This expedient was a decided success and all progressed finely But when the lesson in breaking was over, the youth unyoked the animals and forgot to untie their tails They ran off together a few yards, and then tried to separate, but the "tail holt" was too strong. With set hoofs they strained vigorously, and uttered a loud baa! It seemed as if they would loosen each other's back bones.

Realizing his mistake too late, the frightened Parson had tried to cut the cord that bound the straining calves; but no sooner did he approach than they took fright and sped away towards a wood-pasture where they were in the habit of grazing. Here, in an attempt to pass on opposite sides of a tree, they became separated; but one carried two tufts on his tail, and the other's was bare as a rat's.

Yet such incidents, so funny in the Apostle's youth, were never recalled when he sat in judgment upon the pranks of his boys; they were judged by different standards.

After the chastisement recorded in our last chapter, the cloud of dread that had hung over the parsonage for three days was dissipated, everything becoming serene. And when the Parson learned of Nathan's testimony in class-meeting he felt deeply gratified, and determined that such sporadic piety should be encouraged. Accordingly, he bought a brand new saw in fine condition, had the ax sharpened to a keen edge, made a second buck to keep up the long end of poles, and in many other ways tried to further the work of grace in the boy's heart.

The piles of wood he laid out for them to chop were not less, but occasionally he took the ax in hand himself, and in the midst of his powerful blows asked the urchins if they had ever seen a man chop so fast he could n't see his own head for the chips.

Stimulated by these extra attentions, in the next three days the boys piled up an astonishing amount of stove-wood; so much in fact, that had not idleness been such a sin in the Parson's eyes they need not have cut any further supply for a month. However, experience had taught them that there might be some kind of climax to the Parson's good humor, and they wished to hasten the event if possible. For this reason they did not always stop with the stints he set them, but acted very industriously on their own hook.

Friday morning following their correction Parson Flint arose very early and called the family. The boys were dead sleepy, but the anticipation of something good soon caused them to throw it off While Mrs. Flint was preparing breakfast the Apostle said:

"Nathan, you and William run over to Brother Sisson's and ask him to lend me his plow. Find out too if I can have his spring-wagon to-morry Meck haste and see how quick ye kin git back; jist lay yer legs to the yeth!"

With his first sentence the boys' hopes withered, and their eager faces soured They knew it meant a day's hard work in the broiling sun, and nothing could cause them greater chagrin. However, no choice was left but to obey, but they failed to lay their legs to the earth very fast; the facetious sally of the Parson seemed to them a taunting sham. In about a quarter of an hour they returned with the plow, and reported that the Parson could use the spring-wagon until noon the following day.

Prayers and breakfast being over, the Parson put some old harness on Daniel, secured two big rusty hoes from the barn, summoned the boys and went out to an acre lot that adjoined the premises Here planting a pole at either end for guides,

he began to throw up some long ridges with the plow. After
completing three he said:

"Now, my sons, teck yer hoes and work these ridges all
up nice fer late sweet-pertaters. Scrape the dirt from both sides,
and pulverize it fine. If ye git the job done in time, we'll go
a-fishin' down at Big Bend to-morry."

Nathan and his brother had been watching their father's
proceedings with doleful feelings, and faces forlorn with
blighted hopes; but at the Parson's final words they suddenly
brightened amazingly. Seizing the hoes they went eagerly to
work, while the Apostle drove to the other side of the enclosure
to plow some corn.

The boys toiled along for a quarter of an hour, and then
stopped to survey their task. It looked very discouraging; the
ridges were so long they had a perspective; but there were only
three of them, and the workers took comfort in the fact that
they were not six. As they began again William spied an earth-
worm, and was seized with a brilliant idea.

"I'll tell ye what we'll do," he exclaimed eagerly to Nathan. "Le's git a can and pick up all the bait we see. It'll
save us a lot of time to-morry morning."

"That's bully," replied his brother; "jist wait."

Flinging himself over the fence he sped to the house, and
shortly returned with a half-gallon fruit can, in which they
deposited every worm, bug and grasshopper that came in their
way.

Manfully they tugged along in the scorching sun, blister-
ing their hands, and getting the back-ache from so much

stooping. Meanwhile they could hear the Apostle scolding
Daniel.

"Yahh! *Git* up there! Keep yer huff off'n that corn, 'fore
I larrup ye. Skik, skik, skik!"

Old Daniel was humping along, bobbing his head, and
weaving about in such a way as to demolish all the corn possible; when a particularly tall stalk came in his way, he took the
top of it along for lunch, and for this the Parson frequently
gave him sounding slaps along his sweaty sides with the lines.

Occasionally while the horse was blowing, the Parson visited the boys to see that they were doing their work as he had
told them. He was reeking with perspiration which trickled
down his face and dripped from the end of his nose.

By noon the boys had scarcely finished half their task, but
they had got their second wind and fallen into the knack of
the work, so felt encouraged. It was deep dusk when the last
ridge was completed, and as William expressed it, they were
"tired all over and more too."

However, they had found scores of worms of all sizes,
and that gave them a deal of comfort. Supper over, they hunted
up their fishing tackle, all meager and home-made. After sort-
ing out and arranging it with great care they went to bed to
dream of coming sport.

Next morning the Parson took Daniel over to Brother
Sisson's, and in a short time brought back the spring wagon.
Putting in a hatchet and the big ax he called the boys and set
off for Big Bend The excited urchins were in high glee, but
grew very impatient with Daniel's slow pace This they tried

to increase by numerous hints to the driver, and remarks that the fish always bit early in the day. But Daniel was not to be hurried. He had long before acquired a gait of his own, out of which he seldom varied. The Parson would cluck to him continuously for a dozen yards, but the jogging animal paid no attention to it, unless it was to slow up a trifle when the clucking ceased. Then the Apostle

ON THE WAY TO BIG BEND.

would hit him a sounding whack along his keel with the whip, and thus reproduce the average speed, but no more.

For nearly two miles the road wound along the top of a low wooded ridge, and during this part of the trip the boys had a good time. They jumped from the wagon to chase squirrels, or to follow a snake-track that creased the dust of the highway. Plenty of fine fishing-poles grew all along the route, some large enough, William remarked, to land a whale. At one place Nathan ran to ask the Parson for the ax with which to cut one, but he only said, gruffly:

"Never mind about that. Ye 'd both better git into the wagon, and not go skivin' about like a couple of Injins."

There was no real command in his tones, however, and the boys knew they were not expected to follow his advice. Presently one of their digressions from the road caused them to fall quite a distance behind, and upon racing away to catch up, they saw that the wagon had stopped, so hurried the faster to see what had happened. Then they made a most unexpected discovery, and were led to believe that the whole promise of a fishing trip was only a gigantic fraud. The Apostle had driven to one side of the road and tied Daniel to a sapling. He himself was sitting upon a log, and sharpening the hatchet with a small piece of whetstone.

"Whachu stopt for?" asked William, anxiously.

"To cut some pea-sticks," replied the Parson, coolly. "The peas are spilin' fer want of stickin'. You cut down them hazel bushes, Nathan, an' William may bring 'em to this log fer me to sharpen."

"I thought we wuz goin' fishin'," said William, astonished.

"You 'll hev plenty of time fer all the fish you 'll be likely to ketch when this work 's done," returned the Parson, contemptuously.

"Yes, an' then the sun 'll be so hot the fish won't bite," cried Nathan, indignantly "You 've said yourself that early morning is the best time to fish"

"Jist don't ye let me hear any more like that," said the Parson, sternly, "or I 'll teck and wear out one of these sprouts on ye!"

This closed the argument Nathan took the ax and began to hack down brush It was not by any means easy or pleasant work; the bushes were tough and springy, causing the big ax to glance in most exasperating fashion But the work went doggedly on, and in the course of an hour the Parson said they had enough. Peeling some hickory bark he tied the sharpened pea-sticks into several bundles, which were set up against the log to be taken in upon their way back.

When they believed the long-deferred sport once more near at hand the boys regained some of their cheerful spirits. They got into the wagon again almost in a good humor.

"Can't we leave the ax here?" asked William.

"No," replied the Parson. "It might be stolen; and besides I want it to cut the poles."

Sure enough; they had forgotten that use for it. In a little time they were driving down a long hill into the river-bottoms. These were a half-mile across, and covered with slim undergrowth. The river was soon in view, and the boys caught sight of the broad lake-like ford, where silver-sides were jumping out of the water after flies. The pea-stick disappointment was wholly forgotten, and both the urchins sprang from the wagon for a race to the Bend.

"Hold on! Jist wait a spell: I want to cut them poles," called the Parson loudly.

"But maybe there's some poles on the bank," William replied.

"I don't mean fishin' poles, but *bean* poles," replied the Parson.

The boys were furious in a second.

"You told us we wuz goin' a-fishin' I jist think it's rotten mean," roared Nathan in a rage, while at the shock of it William fairly jumped up and down.

The Apostle had alighted from the wagon, and was tying
Daniel to a tree; but at Nathan's words he whirled sharply
about, and every line in his stern face seemed cut in iron. With
open mouth he eyed the boy for a moment, and then said in
rasping tones:

"Let me hear another word like that out of ye, an' I'll
'frail ye till yer hide won't hold shucks!"

Then in vast, indignant rebuke:

"You pore triflin' child! A little work hurts you about the
wust of anyone I ever see. You'd git somebody to breathe fer
you if ye could, I reckon!"

That ended all parley. The angry boys choked down their
wrath as best they might, but by this time it was impossible to
hold back the acrid tears. They followed the Parson about
through the bottoms, picked up the poles he selected, and carried them sullenly back to the wagon. It took the better part
of another hour to do it, and then in his glummest manner the
Parson said:

"Go and fish awhile now, if ye want to."

The boys received his permission in silence, took their half-
gallon can of worms, and once more started for the bend. The
Parson got out his pocket Bible, which was always with him,
and reclined against a log to study his Sunday sermon. When
the boys were out of ear-shot, Nathan looked back and growled
savagely:

"Dern'd old stick-in-the-mud; to tell us such a lot of whacks
as that, jist to git us to work!"

"I thought somethin' wuz up when he stuck that ax into

William Gets Caught.

the wagin," said William sympathetically. "Might a-knowed
he could never let *us* have a good time. It 'ud be a marvel!"

But these bitter reflections were soon forgotten in the excitement of the well-earned sport. They found some excellent
poles upon the bank, and began to fish. Presently Nathan got
a bite. He gave a jerk that would have broken the jaw of a
steel-trap; it did not hook the fish, but wound his line about
twenty times around the limb of a tree near by, and he had to
climb up to get it loose. This took a provokingly long time
and when it was done he found that his only good hook was
broken, and he had to substitute one almost big enough to catch
a dolphin. Having tied it on, he baited it with a worm to cor-
respond and cast again. But it was a failure; the minnows
nibbled off the bait, but could not get the hook into their mouths.

During these misfortunes, however, William was having
better luck. He caught two fair-sized perch, and was highly
elated. Just as Nathan threw in his big hook, William caught
a fine cat-fish, and ran up the bank to take it off. While he
was engaged in this task, Nathan felt another tremendous bite.
Again his line swished through the air, with a sound like a
rocket. The nibbling fish was not caught, but William was.
While he was stooping to unloose his prize Nathan's line swiped
round him and the sharp hook picked up about a quarter of
an inch of flesh on the calf of his leg He set up a loud screech
that brought the Apostle on a run to see what ailed him.
Neither of the boys could swim, he knew Their visits to the
river had not been frequent enough for them to learn that useful art.

When he found what the trouble was, the Parson's reaction from his scare greatly exasperated him. He comforted William by snorting in a tone of deep disgust:

"Why do n't ye yell! I thought ye might be hevin' a leg sawed off, or somethin'."

However it was not so easy to remove the hook as he had thought. It had passed through beyond the barb; and after several rough attempts, which were interspersed by shrieks and clog-dances on William's part, the Parson got out his knife and began to whet it on the sole of his boot, preparatory to a surgical operation But just here Nathan suggested that he had better break the shank of the hook, and pull it out the other way. This was soon done and the Parson shut his knife with a snap saying decisively, "Come, let 's go home "

To him dozing over the subject of "Regeneration" the time had passed very slowly; but to the excited boys only a few minutes seemed to have elapsed

"Oh le's stay jist a little while longer," pleaded William through his tears "I got a bully good bite jist now; and we hain't got half a mess yet."

"It 's now a little after eleven o'clock," rejoined the Parson as he strode away "We must git back by noon. Come on!"

The boys rebelled, and as soon as he was out of sight began fishing again; but they had not been at it long before the Parson had got Daniel hooked to the wagon and shouted:

"O Boys!"

They fished on, and presently the call was repeated with more emphasis; but a most promising nibble held them to the spot.

In the meantime the Parson was getting a number of bites himself; some lusty "Gallinippers"—so called, the victim had explained to the boys because at each "nip" they took a "gallon"—were trying to puncture his bronzed skin. By extra drilling one or two had succeeded, only to be wrecked for all time by a slap of his broad palm. He grew very impatient, and in a voice that sounded like a cross-cut saw among splinters, called to the delaying urchins a third time:

"Air you *comin'*, or will I hev to fetch you?"

They knew what this last suggestion meant, and got up to go. "Confound the onery luck to Guinea!" exclaimed Nathan in a rage as he wound up his line. "This is a pretty way to take a feller fishin'! I'll be-diddle-de-diddled-de-daggon if I do n't wish a cattymount 'ud bite his dern'd leg off!"

But as he uttered this frightful wish it must be confessed that the memory of his testimony in class-meeting the Sunday before came back to him, and his conscience ·rebuked him bitterly. Yet the provocation was more than most boys could bear.

When they reached the wagon, the Apostle was ready to go, and seeing their expression, did not press his rebuke. The boys walked up the long hill, put in the pea-sticks, took an uncomfortable seat upon the load, and Daniel jogged homeward. The dew was gone, and he raised a great cloud of dust that kept him coughing and sneezing all the way.

A deep gloom overshadowed the boys; they did not cut any capers or race about through the woods this trip. The Parson sang and made sundry facetious remarks to Daniel,

6

ON THE WAY HOME.

but the disappointed youths would not be beguiled, keeping a wordless silence which even the artful Parson felt was but natural. William's leg was now smarting; he took it upon his knee and managed to squeeze out a few pathetic tears over it. When they reached home Nathan opened the lot gate; the Parson drove in, piled his load of pea-sticks and poles in one corner of the acre patch, and then took the wagon back to its owner.

The boys entered the house through the back porch, and encountered their mother in the kitchen. She saw at a glance that something had gone wrong, but asked in a cheerful voice if they had a good time and caught lots of fish.

"Naw!" bawled Nathan, who was boiling over. "He told us we was goin' a-fishin' and made us work like niggers to git to go; and then before we got there, he made us cut pea-sticks and bean-poles fer two hours. Then jist as we'd begun to git some good bites he made us come home. I wisht I was dead!"

His violent grief touched Mrs. Flint to the heart; but she could not seem to reflect upon her husband's conduct; so she said kindly:

"Never mind, boys; mother has made you a turnover apiece. If you'll try to be good, I'll get you something nice before long."

This meant a certainty of some treasure prized by boys,

for they knew the promise was good as gold; but their feelings could not be subdued all at once, so they continued to snuffle until in a low voice Mrs. Flint said:

"Hush, boys; there comes pa!" Then they stopped.

In due time the turnovers appeared, and hunger made them taste all the more delicious. Two weeks later, upon Mrs. Flint's return from Benton, where she had gone to "trade," each of the boys got a brand new top and a dozen glass marbles. They felt rich. William carefully concealed his treasures until he had paid off Dick Patterson by playing "keeps" with a small, potato; it will be remembered that he had already forfeited his "taw."

The loving mother had bought these simple presents for the boys with money saved on the price of a pair of shoes for herself, but for a long time afterward the boys did not know it.

O tender-hearted, sweet-souled mothers! Surely heaven must be peopled largely with such as you!

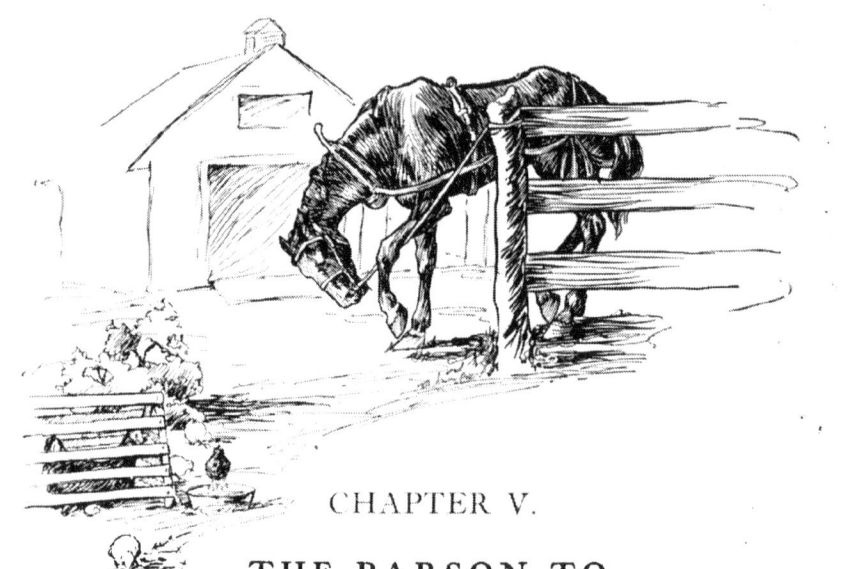

CHAPTER V.

THE PARSON TO THE FORE.

WITH FOOT UP AND HEAD DOWN.

WHEN Parson Flint returned the borrowed wagon he found Brother Sisson in the barn, mending a set of old harness. It was now high noon, and the hot sun caused wavering heat to dance everywhere, making the perspiring Parson long for a quiet "meditation" somewhere in cool shade.

Brother Sisson was a very kind-hearted, but sad-appearing man. He had come to the place several years before, where by hard labor and great frugality the family had built up a neat, pretty home. But as will appear, the light of his life had gone out forever, leaving him and his broken wife in the shadow of a great sorrow.

The brother helped Parson Flint to unhook Daniel, after which he invited the preacher to sit down with him and have a talk. Soon their conversation turned upon religious topics;

for in those good old days Methodists felt it their "bounden
duty to let their conversation be of heavenly things."

"Do you know, Brother Sisson," said the Parson impress-
ively, "that I think the missionary cause is one of the grandest
features of our Church? Away off there in them benighted
lands of Chiny, Afriky and In'jy, where the gracious influence
of Christianity has never been felt heretofore, the pore heathen
has begun to wake up and become concerned. Our reports
show an increase of conversions that's astoundin', and I never
read 'em without thinkin' of the Apostle's words; 'they that
sow sparingly shall reap sparingly.' It does seem to me a cryin'
duty fer us to contribute as much as we can spare of our substance to support them that take their lives in their hands and
go forth to preach the everlastin' gospil."

Now, Brother Sisson and his wife were childless. They
had lost three sweet children, all within a few days of each
other by that dread disease, diphtheria. This terrible calamity
had shed a profound melancholy over both their lives, but
especially that of the lonely father. Himself, he dearly loved
all boys; perhaps that was because he had never been tormented
by them as had the Parson. But he had noticed the preacher's
stern methods of discipline; and it made his soft old heart ache
to see the youngsters dodging about like frightened rabbits to
avoid their father's watchful eyes.

The brother was likewise a very thoughtful man, and did
not always blindly follow the Parson's ideas The Apostle knew
that he had never seemed warmly enthusiastic over the missionary cause, which was his own special hobby. In a few days

the annual "Missionary Meeting" of the church was to be held, and it was one of the Parson's great ambitions to report large collections. Thus it will be perceived that the introduction of this topic was not without its object; the Parson was a "fisher of men." It is little wonder then that he was somewhat piqued by Brother Sisson's reply to his shrewd appeal.

"I am inclined to think, Parson, that we have n't done all we can at home yet," rejoined Brother Sisson evasively. "It seems to me that money spent here in Walnut Hill would be a better investment than to send it away, nobody knows where. Our young people need help in many ways; and if we could devise some good means of cultivating their social as well as their religious natures, instead of letting them wander off into sin and folly it would be a mighty acceptable work in the Lord's sight Do n't you think so?"

In a half-hearted way the Parson admitted that there might be something in the idea, but quickly added:

"You know, Brother Sisson, that the natural tendency of the young and giddy is to evil, and that continually. And I think we 'd ought to discourage all these night gatherin's unless of course it 's a young people's prayer-meeting or the like. W'y only jist last week I passed the house of a man that used to be a bright and shinin' light in the church; he had a houseful of boys and gals, and there was the sound of a fiddle goin' and the noise of feet, ca-lum', ca-lum', ca-lum'! It 's a direct violation of the discipline, and I shall hev to bring his case up before the quart'ly conference fer it"

"Yes, yes," replied the parishioner, smiling at the Parson's imitation of the dancing feet, "but it won't do to hold our young folks with too tight a rein. If we do, when they grow older they're likely to resent it, and give us trouble. Give them no amusements that are right, and they'll be sure to seek them that are wrong. I do think that if our parents would give this subject more attention, we should have a better set of boys and girls. Just think! It ain't been such a long time ago, Parson, when you and me were youngsters, and liked our fun as well as any of 'em."

But this was pupil teaching teacher, and when he remembered his own family and position, the Parson's ministerial dignity somewhat bridled at it. He arose to go, and found that in trying to reach a forbidden bunch of grass old Daniel had got one foreleg over his halter strap. With foot up and head down he was standing in a very uncomfortable, apprehensive kind of way, much like all that belonged to the Apostle. After relieving and untying him the preacher said:

"Well, I must be gittin' back and seein' after things. I'm a thousand times obleeged to ye fer the loan of the wagon, Brother Sisson."

"Not at all! Not at all!" was the cheerful reply. "Won't you stop in and take dinner with us? It must be nigh ready."

It was not often the Parson refused an invitation to dine, but being near at home he did so this time. He bade his parishioner good bye and led Daniel away.

By the time he had reached the parsonage and stabled Daniel his own meal was ready, and the family sat down to table. William's fish had been fried, and as he helped himself

to one the savory odor reminded the Apostle of a ditty he had
learned in boyhood:

"There was a minner in the brook,
The daddy caught him with a hook;
The mammy fried him in a pan,
The daddy ate him like a man."

But the boys were glum and unresponsive; they did not
even smile at this sally, but looked with sober longings at the
apple-dumplings.

When dinner was finished, the Apostle took the two urchins
to the acre-patch, and gave them careful instructions about

sticking the peas. He showed
them how the sticks must be
crossed, how far apart they
should be set, and just how
deep into the ground to thrust
them. The boys were in a
mood to rebel, but knowing
how useless that would be they

PEA-STICKING.

went doggedly to work. The Parson saw how sullen they were,
and after watching them a short time with rebuke written large
on his countenance, he went to take an afternoon "meditation."

Left to themselves the boys were not nearly so careful
in following the Parson's directions as he had been in giving
them; they did not measure the distance between sticks, nor use
very great force in pushing them into the ground, thus getting
along much faster than it was intended they should. Whenever they found a particularly long, lithe hazel it was laid aside
for reasons that will appear.

About the middle of the afternoon their work was finished, and they went to reconnoiter. The Apostle was seated on the shady side of the house, tipped back in a chair, a foot upon a rung, and one leg crossed over the other in a sound nap.

Finding him thus oblivious, the boys skulked off to a ravine some distance away, where they worked up a batch of tough clay into a stiff cake and smuggled it into the buggy shed. Next preparing their hazel switches, they rolled up small pieces of clay, stuck them on the ends of the sprouts and began to throw them. This was evidently no new sport, for they were very expert. Shortly the pellets were directed toward a neighbor's house, which soon exhibited the appearance of incipient chicken-pox; and when Dick Patterson climbed over the back fence and joined them, the disease rapidly grew worse. Presently the spat of the mud-balls upon the house brought a woman to the door to see what was going on; but upon her appearance the boys would dodge into the buggy-shed and chuckle wickedly until she had retired.

THROWING CLAY BALLS.

At last the Parson interfered with this vile sport. Awakened by the fall of his book and not seeing the boys he set out to find them. Striding up in high dudgeon he jerked the sprouts from their hands and quickly turned the siege upon the besiegers at short range and with clubbed guns. At the first sign of danger Dick Patterson beat a hasty retreat, stopping at a safe distance to see the end of the affair. When the Parson had completely routed the foe he looked sternly at Dick and said in his most forbidding tone:

"Teck yerself off, young man; and do n't let me see ye round here any more, sir!"

But Dick was not the least abashed. He sat down impudently in the middle of the road, and began to pile dust over his bare feet.

When the smoke of conflict had drifted away the Parson set the boys to hoeing corn; and as each started upon a row he sent after them the words:

> "Satan finds some mischief still
> For idle hands to do."

A THUMP OF THE HOE.

Nathan heard it, and bursting a clod with a vicious thump of his hoe muttered under his breath that he "did n't give a dern."

It was night-fall before the boys were called to supper, and they felt that this horrible day had been one of the most miserable hoaxes in all their lives. Its piled-up disappointments seemed more than any ordinary boys could bear. At family prayers William laid his tired head in his mother's lap and snuffled; but Nathan sat bolt upright, looking as ugly as possible. The Apostle read a selection beginning, "He that being often reproved hardeneth his neck, shall suddenly be destroyed, and that without remedy."

Of course the boys knew that this was intended especially for them, but Nathan wickedly felt his neck, hoping to find it growing harder. The Parson was very impressive and dismal in these exercises, reading in a deep, deliberate tone the better to burn the warning into the hearts of his degenerate sons. His words sounded as might those of some stony judge, about to pronounce the death-sentence upon a prisoner at the bar.

When at last he had finished the Scriptural reading, he took his chair a little way toward the wall, knelt upon one knee and offered up the evening petition, pleading for all that mercy, tenderness and forgiveness which he somehow failed to show the boys.

They crept away to bed in silent bitterness. Through the leaden murk of their grief there came one final ray of hope at last. The Fourth of July was only a few days off!

CHAPTER VI.

FOURTH OF JULY.

IN all the country there was not a more patriotic man than Parson Flint. He was known as a "red-hot abolitionist" who was enthusiastic and outspoken on every occasion. He believed in the observance of all National services and holidays, particularly that of the Fourth of July. When, therefore, on the Monday following the events of our last chapter the boys asked if they might collect old iron to get money for the coming celebration, he gave a hearty consent. The plan pleased him well because it would involve no outlay of his own scanty means.

Highly elated at the prospect, the boys went eagerly to work at once. There had been several wrecks of old stoves abandoned by former occupants of the parsonage, and to these the boys quickly added every scrap of metal they could find. One of the flat-irons was discovered with a side of its handle loose; and for some occult reason the other side quickly gave out, rendering the article unfit for further use, so it was added to their store. They drew every nail in reach, inspected all the buggy bolts, and even went so far as to try old Daniel's shoes to see if they were on tight. During this operation Daniel evidently thought some new attack was about to be made upon his ribs, so he reached around and gave Nathan a sharp nip where it would do the most good.

On the afternoon of the third, they procured a wheelbarrow, and took their collection to a blacksmith's shop, where it sold for sixty cents. This was more money than they had ever owned before, and they regarded it as a large factor in the million dollars William always coveted. Long before this they had determined what to buy; accordingly they purchased a Roman candle, two fair-sized sky-rockets, and had ten cents left to spend upon the celebration grounds. On the way home they invited every boy they met to come and witness their fireworks, and went to bed in a fever of excitement over the coming sport.

TOOK THEIR IRON TO A BLACKSMITH'S SHOP.

Booming cannon and snapping fire-crackers awoke them betimes the following morning. The Parson had forbidden them to leave the parsonage grounds, but they were quickly dressed and perched upon the fence to see what was going on.

The day's celebration was to take place at the fair-grounds, a mile from town, and several magnates were expected to speak. Soon from all directions straggling crowds of country people began to arrive. There were sway-bedded wagons, full to their utmost capacity. There were jaded women, some with a baby on one hip, and a youngster or two clinging to their skirts. Rural swains

PERCHED ON THE FENCE.

strolled about, often holding a sweetheart's hand, looking as bashful and awkward as possible. Then there were farmers in shirt-sleeves and blue-jeans, some of them already boisterous with too much whiskey.

About nine o'clock a long, motley procession strung out down the main street of the village, and headed for the fairgrounds. It was preceded by a horrible brass band, and flanked with skylarking small fry of every description. The boys wanted to join this noisy cavalcade, but the Parson forbade it, saying they would go later when the dust had settled.

Once having arrived at the celebration grounds, the boys managed quickly to elude the Parson's watchful eye, and wandered about among the stands and booths at their own sweet will. They were full of admiration and open-mouthed wonder. Among the many novel objects that attracted them a "wooden nigger" and a hand-organ interested them finally more than anything else. The former image with a pipe in its mouth was set up before a piece of canvas: its proprietor had a score of short clubs, and anyone throwing so as to break the pipe received, so the owner loudly declared, a fine cigar.

The price of a trial was one dime, but as William had already spent their ten cents for bologna sausage, the boys had to stand and watch others make the trial. Each felt sure, however, that if the image were only a live rooster he could hit it every cast.

After watching these proceedings for a long time, they wandered off to a lemonade stand and gazed at the thirsty crowd that thronged about it. Presently the jovial voice of Brother Ratcliffe hailed them.

"Hello, boys! You a-celebratin', too? Come along and have a glass of lemonade with me!"

No second invitation of this kind was needed, and soon each of them was provided with a tall tumbler of the refreshing beverage. After drinking and asking where their father was, Brother Ratcliffe gave them each a dime and strolled away. Such unexpected good fortune made them wriggle with delight, and they hastened at once to purchase a throw at the wooden nigger.

For a wonder Nathan smashed the pipe at the first cast, and according to the terms already mentioned, received from the grinning proprietor a "fine Havana cigar." It was really a vile thing with a Lincoln green wrapper. The boy took it sheepishly, for neither he nor William had ever before so much as handled one. They quickly retired from the main crowd, and sat down upon a log to examine their prize. Finally they concluded to light it, but before doing so, William went through elaborate motions of smoking. He held the cigar between his thumb and finger, put it nearly to his lips, took an imaginary pull and gave a very artistic puff. Then he spat smack on a bumble-bee that was hanging to a clover-blossom near by, and handed the cigar to Nathan.

Producing some matches he had carried for a fortnight in anticipation of the fireworks, Nathan lighted one, stuck the cigar between his teeth and tried to smoke, but a choking whiff of sulphur was all he succeeded in getting. However, William

informed him that he must bite off the end of the cigar before
it would draw, and having attended to this, he had better success upon the second trial. The acrid smoke rolled in a white
cloud out of his mouth and nose.

"Gosh!" he exclaimed, when he had got his breath again;
"I do n't like it. The onery thing tastes like the measles."

When William had tried it he fully agreed with this ver-
dict, and made a wry face at the nasty weed.

"I 'd a good deal rather have bologna," he remarked, in
disgust, and threw the cigar into the grass.

With the remaining dime they bought a box of prize-candy
at a confection stand. This package was said to contain beside the full money's worth of sweetmeats, a valuable piece
of jewelry Seizing this new treasure, they quickly went aside
and sat down under a tree to examine it.

Nathan placed his hat upon the ground and poured the
contents of the box into it: these were a dozen bits of candy
about the size of worm-lozenges, together with the prize,
wrapped in tissue paper. William stood before his brother
with hands on his knees and a look of intense expectancy upon
his face When the paper was unrolled, both gave a grunt of
genuine delight; the prize was a piece of brazed tin stamped
into a figure of a locomotive, something they had very seldom
seen With bated breath they gazed at it, examining each
detail of cab, bell, sand-box, cow-catcher, smokestack and all.
Then they turned it over to see what was on the reverse side,
and found a pin to attach it to one's coat.

It was finally arranged that they should wear it alternately, William to have the first turn. He fixed it to the breast of his roundabout and strutted through the crowd, certain that everybody must notice and admire the novel ornament.

It was a trifle after noon when the speaking was finished and dinner announced from the grand-stand. The boys were by this time ravenously hungry, and were not missing when there was eating to do. They sampled everything in reach, and when finally each received a large slice of jelly-cake, it seemed as if they had reached the delectable land. William wished fervently that the day would never end.

But "no man can tether time or tide." Late in the afternoon the Apostle hunted them up, coming upon them near a stand where some noisy men were drinking beer. Noticing their absorbed interest in this sight, the Parson asked them solemnly if they "hed been teckin' a glass with the others." William ruefully replied:

"No; we hain't got no money."

"What did ye do with the money ye got fer the iron?" asked the Parson at this. To tell the truth his conscience reminded him of how little he had himself aided them to celebrate.

"We spent that fer Roman candles and things," replied Nathan.

Upon learning this the Parson felt much better, and satisfied his qualms with a promise of some powder for a "fluff" to go with the fireworks that evening. A "fluff" was merely the flash of ignited powder, laid on a chip.

The boys were greatly tickled with this prospective addition to their coming fund of amusement; and William whis-

7

pered to Nathan that they could make some cob-cannon when they reached home. After returning to town and doing their evening chores, they set about making the cob-cannon, and soon had two fine ones completed. Darkness seemed to be a long time coming, and in their impatience they brought out and arranged their assortment of fireworks before it was deep dusk.

Neither of them understood the mechanism of Roman candles, so Dick Patterson, who had come around at their invitation, acted as their instructor. The candle they had bought would shoot three times, and it was arranged that each boy should hold it in turn. Dick lighted the fuse and whirled the thing about in a great shower of sparks. Presently out popped a red fire-ball, upon which he promptly handed the sputtering article to William, who got burned and dropped it on the ground with a yelp. However, Nathan seized it and very dexterously fired his shot against the side of the house, when the shell alone remained, an empty emblem of patriotism. William asked Dick it if could n't be made to shoot some more, but that expert said no, the "spondulicks" were all out of it.

By this time it was quite dark, and they tackled the rockets, setting up a yell of delight as the wonderful thing went swishing off toward the sky, leaving behind a dying trail of sparks

This last performance exhausted their supplies, and Dick said he must run down town to see what was going on there. Of course the boys were forbidden this treat, so they had to content themselves with what they could witness from the top of the smoke-house.

In a little time they recalled the Parson's promise of powder for a fluff, and ran to get it. The Apostle poured them about a tablespoonful on a piece of paper and handing it out said:

"Now be careful, and don't blow yerselves up. Here's enough powder for twenty fluffs."

Out to the lot they raced with a whoop, and Nathan soon had a cob-cannon heavily loaded. Lighting the end of a switch, he got behind a tree to touch it off, while William peeped nervously from the barn-door a dozen yards away. The explosion was tremendous; and the Apostle opened the door to call anxiously:

"What air ye doin' out there? Fust ye know ye'll be blowin' yer heads plumb off!"

But Nathan explained that they were only having a new kind of fluff, and set to work to reload the cannon. The previous success had made him very bold, so he stood from behind the tree in the open, and when the explosion came the cob burst into a dozen pieces, one of which knocked a patch of skin about the size of a nickel from the rash youth's forehead, just above his left eye. He jumped back and felt anxiously to find if his brains were not oozing out.

William poured the remaining powder on a large chip, and tried to set it off with a live-coal; but after several fruitless efforts he dropped upon his knees to learn what ailed it. This brought his face too near the treacherous stuff; it suddenly flashed up and scared him out of his wits, at

THE COB FLEW INTO A
DOZEN PIECES.

the same time singeing off most of his eyebrows and sparse
eye-lashes. When he got up his face looked as sooty as the
wooden nigger's at the fair-grounds.

They made a trip to the kitchen, where Nathan covered
his wound with tallow, and William bathed his disfigured countenance with buttermilk.

This ended their memorable Fourth of July. It had been
full of incident and accident, and they were sorry it was over.
After family prayers they went to bed, too tired to dream. But
the next morning William awoke with the colic, and Nathan's
swelled forehead looked as if he might be sprouting a horn
like a calf.

CHAPTER VII.

WILLIAM BECOMES A "LIFE-MEMBER."

DURING the next few days nothing of any special interest occurred at the parsonage. The excitement of the Fourth died out, and under its reaction neither the Parson nor the boys felt much energy.

However, upon the next Saturday and Sunday came the great "Annual Missionary and Sunday-school Convention." Delegates from all over the county attended this notable gathering, and one or two of them were entertained by the Parson's family. In preparation for the event the girls swept and garnished the house, the while imparting to Nathan and William much private instruction as to how they should behave. But none of their iron-clad rules of conduct could improve William's bald countenance from which the skin had begun to peel, nor cure Nathan's forehead, which showed signs of gangrene.

A month before the convention took place Parson Flint had distributed among the Sunday-school scholars of Walnut Hill several "Juvenile Missionary Cards." These slips were designed for subscriptions to the cause, and were very pretty, containing upon the margins various Scriptural quotations:

"Cast thy bread upon the waters."

"The Lord loveth a cheerful giver."

"He that soweth sparingly shall reap sparingly," etc.

When by soliciting with one of these cards the collector had raised five dollars, he was then entitled to a missionary certificate.

This prize was a parchment about fifteen by eighteen inches in size, and upon it was stated that the holder was thereby constituted "A Life Member of the ———— Conference Missionary Society of the Methodist Episcopal Church."

Besides this inscription it had in one corner the picture of a very fat bull around which some people were kneeling, while the animal glared at them with wondering eyes as if to inquire what ailed them. At the top were the figures of two men who seemed to have just been awakened from sound sleep by a spook which was pointing toward a town upon the far horizon. Printed underneath was a sentiment which said spook was supposed to be uttering:

"Come over into Macedonia and help us."

When the Parson distributed collection cards among the scholars he had held up and explained one of these marvelous prizes with an eloquence that fired several boys and girls with a consuming ambition to become "A Life Member." They did not know exactly what it meant, but all fancied there must be some great honor and possible profit to result from its possession.

Now, William had been entrusted with one of the cards, and in the meanwhile had exerted himself to obtain subscriptions; but the great day had come and he had unfortunately secured only four dollars and seventy-five cents It made him feel very

William Becomes a Life Member.

sad to come so near glory and yet miss it by "two bits." On his way to church, however, Brother Sisson overtook him and asked kindly:

"What makes you look so glum, my boy?"

"Cause I hain't got enough money," replied William ruefully, exhibiting his collection card.

Brother Sisson examined the subscription list, and then without putting his own name down handed William a quarter, which made that youth rejoice with exceeding great joy.

At last the auspicious moment came. There before all the delegates and a dense crowd of spectators William stood upon the pulpit platform, nearly swooning to find himself the only boy among five saucy, giggling girls. His closely cropped hair bristled; his sun-burned hands seemed to weigh forty pounds apiece, and he tried to hide them in his trousers' pockets. His lean balls of knees smote together, and his onion-like eyes looked wild and glaring without their lonesome lashes. It was unspeakably mortifying when Sis Pickle whispered loud enough to be heard several pews off:

GAVE WILLIAM A QUARTER.

"You look perfectly awful! What's the matter with you, and why ain't ye got no eye-winkers?"

Silas Durham, William's most detested enemy, overheard these pert questions, and when the terrible ordeal was over upon the platform did not spare William his gibes and ridicule.

When with appropriate remarks he had bestowed the coveted certificates, Parson Flint requested the sufferers to recite the

Twenty-third Psalm together, which they did, William's voice being a trembling quaver, a half-octave higher than any other.

The glory-crowned six were now "Life-Members." They were seated upon the mourners' bench, and several people of the convention were requested to speak in favor of the Missionary Cause. Among those who responded was one of the guests from the parsonage. His speech was quite interesting, and in the course of his remarks told a pretty story about "Little Atung," a poor China boy, who lived in a far heathen land. This waif "was converted to Christianity by a good missionary; he abandoned his idols, and because he could not speak plainly afterwards prayed to Je Chlist."

Then the speaker paid a very hearty tribute to the noble half-dozen seated before him. He told them that all the money they had collected would be sent to the heathen to instruct their minds, convert their souls, thus making them "fit meat for the Master's use." William listened wonderingly to all this. The speaker stood right in front of him, and when he uttered the words "fit meat for the Master's use," the boy wondered if converted heathen were good to eat.

Brother Van Bunthusen was a great curiosity to the new "Life-Members." He had a full moon-face, a short, chubby body, and a wonderful flow of language, but the strangest kind of gestures. These were made entirely from his elbows, which were planted in his sides. His forearm seemed to be all ball-and-socket joints, particularly loose at the wrist. During one sentence he would twirl his hands around from the outside towards his stomach, and in the next would reverse this motion.

But as odd as were his appearance and motions, the brother's

speech was very earnest and well received. Before sitting down
he said he was very sorry to find that but one he-lamb of the
fold had been working for the good cause: and while saying
it he suspended his circular gestures long enough to reach out
and lay a fat hand on William's head. It startled him to find
how much that youth's bristles resembled the feel of a hair-
brush. Perhaps William was a Mexican lamb.

After several others had spoken, much in the same strain,
the now restless assembly sang "From Greenland's icy moun-
tains," and were dismissed until the afternoon session.

On his way home William was very much annoyed by
Silas Durham, who taunted him meanly, yelling aloud such
awful epithets as "preacher," "owl," "bald-face," until the victim could stand it no longer. He struck one, and in a second
the pugnacious couple had clinched. In utter disregard of
the day, Sunday suits or dread of the Apostle's wrath, they engaged in a lively fisticuff right in the middle of the dusty road.
William managed to trip his enemy and then caught him with
both hands by the shock of hair, which soon brought cries for
mercy.

"Will ye ever call me preacher ag'in if I let ye up?" Silas
said he would n't.

"Well, this ain't a patchin' to what I'll give ye if ye ever
call me names ag'in," said William as he arose.

He was a sight to see, covered from head to foot with dust;
and in the very worst plight possible he was seen by Louise who
was walking home with Brother Van Bunthusen. Silas Durham cleared the dust from his eyes and ran away; but at a safe
distance he turned round and yelled spitefully at William:

"The delegate's a-sparkin' yer sister! Preacher! Preacher! Bald-face! Wall-eye!"

"I 'll lick him good and plenty before the week's out; you see if I do n't," said William savagely.

"Yes," replied Nathan; "and I reckon if Louise tells pa what you been doin' he 'll take a hand in it, too."

"I do n't keer," said William resolutely; "I jist ain't goin' t' let him call *me* preacher!"

And he meant it, too; for of all the epithets with which Walnut Hill youths taunted the Parson's boys, that of "preacher" was regarded by both Nathan and William as the most insulting.

But William had not long to wait for revenge. During the afternoon session of the convention he got even with Silas by bending and planting a pin under him while the congregation stood up to sing. When Silas dropped upon it he straightway rose again in great haste, while he reached round and pulled out the instrument of torture with a most gratifying expression upon his freckled face. William stuck out his tongue, looked as much like a frost bitten apple as possible, and whispered, "Goody, goody!"

Of course the expected "settlement" with the Parson came duly upon the following day; but owing to the honors gained by William in "Life Membership" the exercises were much easier than usual. When the threshing had been administered Parson Flint talked long to convince William that to be called "preacher" was by no means insulting, but rather a great honor. William, as in duty bound, listened to his arguments attentively, but he was by no means convinced.

CHAPTER VIII.

"BIRDS OF A FEATHER."

THE Parson quoted nothing oftener to Nathan and William than the old adage, "Evil communications corrupt good manners;" and because of his great faith in this proverb he strove hard to keep them "unspotted from the world." But alas for his efforts! The boys seemed to draw inspiration for mischief from the very air. As the Apostle often expressed it, they were "as prone to evil as the sparks are to fly upward."

But Parson Flint was not a man to be discouraged in any good cause, and especially in the matters of family discipline. He hedged the boys about with threats and commands, striving with pious zeal to make them feel a foretaste of "the wrath to come" when they went astray. The limits of their playground— when indeed they ever had time for sport—were the parsonage fences; notably those of the barn-yard. If they ever strayed beyond these it was when the Parson was off on his circuit; and as he was frequently absent, the boys enjoyed far more liberty than he would otherwise have permitted.

True he had sometimes ridden upon them thus outside the "deadline" of his wrath, and always "laid it on" heavily for their disobedience; but although they bawled loudly, promising with wails and tears "never to do so again," they seemed to forget with marvelous ease. Theirs was a case of "birds of a feather flocking together;" and the stern Parson, failing to see it in the light of a natural law, was much vexed and troubled in spirit.

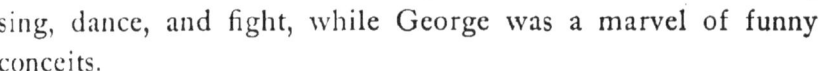

The boys had two boon companions, who sought them and whom they in turn sought at every opportunity. These cronies were Dick Patterson and George Harris. Such playmates were all that any reasonable boy could desire. They had the entire village for a playground, and knew everything that was going on.

Besides Dick was the very embodiment of high spirits, and George was a veritable clown. Neither of them went to church often, and they were totally ignorant of Class-meetings and Life Memberships. But Dick could whistle, sing, dance, and fight, while George was a marvel of funny conceits.

"TOMP-TELY-TOMP-TILY."

George and Dick were their "really and truly" names as William expressed it; but they were seldom called by these titles. Dick was known as "Tomp-tely-tomp-tily" and George responded to the remarkable nick-name of "Muckemtady." To all but the boys themselves of course these ridiculous names were Greek. "Muckemtady" had no traceable origin, but Dick's title came about as follows:

We have said that this youth could sing. When in good luck he always did so, and with his few wants this was very often. He would accompany his vocal exercises by a double shuffle of his grimy feet, the soles of which in summer were tough and leathery. Dick had no great variety of songs. In fact he had but one, of which we quote the only stanza.

> "Tomp-tely-tomp-tily, tomp-tompe-tomp-tomp,
> Tomp-tely-tomp-tily-tomp-tompe-tomp-tomp;
> Tomp-tely-tomp-tily, tomp-tompe-tomp-tompe,
> Tomp-tely-tomp-tily, tomp-tompe-tomp-tomp."

This remarkable ditty expressed all the sentiments of Dick's joyful heart, and he seldom tried any other. Of course it was from it that the boy had derived his nick-name.

Such a care-free, jolly companion as "Tomp-tely tomp-tily" perfectly fascinated the Parson's boys; and with the exception of his marvelous luck in playing "keeps" he shed sunlight upon their paths.

"Muckemtady" too was versatile beyond anything. He was always "acting the fool" as the Parson disgustedly said, and doubtless this habit was what rendered him a chum after the boys' own hearts. He had been cut out for the chief clown in a circus, but the narrow limits of his village life had somewhat dwarfed the pattern.

Among Walnut Hill youths about this time there was in vogue a new dialect called "goose-latin." Muckemtady learned it first and afterwards taught it to the entire juvenile fraternity. It was very simple, the only feature being the addition of *vis* to the syllables and ends of ordinary words. When Muckemtady wished to ask, Do you know what I am saying? he would put it, "Dovis youvis knowvis whavis Ivis avis sayvisivis?"

MUCKEMTADY.

The very "foolishness" of this word-butchery found instant response in the hearts of the Parson's boys. The first time the Parson heard them jabbering it he asked in huge disgust:

"Why do n't ye talk like a couple of ediots?"

Among his many other wonderful arts Muckemtady could entirely reverse the natural way of doing things. He could walk on his hands like an acrobat; could look "cross-eyed" beyond anything ever heard of; could do back handsprings; could drink nearly a quart of water, and then rattle it in his capacious stomach like a horse; could squat, lock his hands across his knees and turn over twenty times in any direction. And stranger than all he could talk, and mostly did talk while drawing in his breath instead of doing it in the usual way. At the same time he would pick up a nip of skin on his throat and shake his Adam's apple until his own mother could hardly have recognized his tremolo tones.

Nothing made him happier than to exhibit these tricks to the Parson's admiring boys, and they in turn were constant in the practice of them all.

When the Apostle was at home, however, he never permitted either Dick or Muckemtady to come about the premises, and in his absences this deprivation made their presence all the more welcome to Nathan and William. It was useless to lecture upon the depravity of human nature, and the villainy of George and Dick in particular; they were positive poles to the Parson's negatived offspring, and the attraction was all but irresistible.

As time went by this perpetual battle against evil caused

the Parson great worry. The "rod of correction" seemed to have lost some of its reputed virtue; and while the Parson used this old-fashioned remedy freely and prayed much, somehow he must have been weak in faith, since the cause of his wrestling did not grow less. Finally he began to look forward towards the close of his ministerial year with secret satisfaction. He was meditating a great plan.

Before becoming a preacher he had owned a good farm in the then thinly settled portion of Jefferson county. This property he had sold for two thousand dollars, and the amount had been put out at good interest. As we shall see, the Parson was now to find use for it.

One Saturday about the middle of August he divided the wood-pile into halves, and in addition laid out for the boys much agricultural job-work in the acre-patch, announcing that he expected to go away and not return for a week. That afternoon Nathan drove him to Frankfort, where he was to preach on the following day, and the boy was sent back home with the horse and buggy. Frankfort was seven miles from Walnut Hill, and Nathan was delighted to go, for the trip would give him a chance to see the cars, one of the seven wonders of the world to Walnut Hill youths.

In all their lives the Parson's boys had seen the cars but three times, and they talked about them for days afterwards William spent much time trying to construct a locomotive out of the big wooden churn and some stove-lids; but failing in this attempt he finally converted the churn into a cannon by driving a nail through the side for a vent. No one but his mother

8

ever knew of this damage to the old family butter-mill, and she filled the hole with a rag, keeping the discovery to herself for obvious reasons.

In point of mystery and wonder, the boys regarded a locomotive as next to an Aladdin's lamp, and the sight of a railroad always filled them with a sort of awe. The telegraph lines they did not at all understand. Upon his first sight of them, William mistook their use and asked "how people ever hung their clothes that high."

When the Apostle decided to have Nathan drive him to Frankfort where he was to take the train for his intended journey, William pleaded earnestly that he might go along; but the shrewd Parson very promptly refused him. He knew better than to allow the young reprobates two hours together when they were not under the eyes of some older person, so Nathan alone was permitted to accompany him. But that exulting urchin counted his fortune too soon. When he and the Parson had reached the suburbs of Frankfort, the latter stopped and headed Daniel towards home, saying coolly:

DROVE A NAIL.
THROUGH THE
SIDE.

"Now see if ye can git back and attend to yer work I laid out for ye. Let the horse take his time, and feed him well when ye git home."

Thus it happened that Nathan did not see the cars at all, and he was most bitterly disappointed. He forgot all about the Parson's parting words, and reached home in something more than an hour, with Daniel in a lather of sweat.

CHAPTER IX.

MOTHER'S WAY.

"COME now, boys," said Mrs. Flint cheerily, as Nathan got in from stabling the horse, "put in and get all your work done; then you can have the rest of the time for your own. If you get through by Tuesday I'll take you somewhere."

"Git it all done by Tuesday!" exclaimed Nathan in a spasm of bitterness and disgust. "W'y, we couldn't finish it by Christmas! He's laid out half the woodpile, an' told us to hoe the whole acre-field besides."

"Oh, no; not so bad as that. You can get it all done if you work hard," said his mother encouragingly. "Just lean to it and see how much you can do to-day. I've got something real nice in store for you if you are industrious."

Of course they began to tease to know what this treat was, but she shook her head with a knowing smile. It excited their hopes to such a pitch that they fell to work with a zeal that they had not shown since the day before the Apostle's pea-stick hunt. This time they entirely reversed the usual order of attack, beginning with the biggest, hardest sticks first, so as to have the smaller ones to taper off on. Despite dull ax and saw they made a very hopeful beginning, and were still "leaning to it" when the voice of Brother Sisson hailed them from the road.

99

"Go for it, boys!" he exclaimed in kindly tones. "That's the way I got my start." Then perceiving Nathan's labored efforts, he asked, "What 's the matter with your saw?"

BROTHER SISSON.

"It 's dull and got all the set out," was Nathan's reply.

"Let me see it a minute," said Brother Sisson.

The tool was handed him over the fence, and after sighting down the blade and rubbing his broad thumb over the teeth he said:

"Well, I should think so! Just let me have it for awhile; I'll put it in better shape. Come over for it in half an hour."

When, after the allotted time, Nathan went after it, Brother Sisson had put the saw in fine condition, and the boy's evident delight seemed to please him greatly. Thanking the good man very earnestly, Nathan started home, but spied a huge maul lying by the gate. After eyeing it for a minute he asked diffidently:

"Can I borry yer maul a little while, Mr. Sisson? I'll bring it back this evening if you want it."

"Take it right along," was the amused reply; "but you 'll find it more than you want to tackle I guess."

Nathan had conceived a great idea, however, and shouldering the unwieldy prize, he trudged off home.

"Whachu goin' to do with that?" asked William in great astonishment, as his brother pitched the maul over the lot fence and climbed nimbly after it.

"I'll show you," replied Nathan knowingly. "You jist take and cut that pole half-way in two all along, and then give it to me."

William set about this, while Nathan plied his newly sharpened saw with genuine delight. When finally the notched pole was ready he put a chunk of wood under one end, and brought the maul down upon the notch next to it. To William's great satisfaction the stick broke off with a loud snap, flying high in the air. Thus the device saved much hard chopping.

About four o'clock a cautious

BROKE WITH A SNAP.

whistle from the barn electrified the industrious boys. They
ran to see who it was, and found "Tomp-tely-tomp-tily" am-
bushing outside.

"Whacher doin'?" he asked cautiously.

"Choppin' wood; whacher reckkon?"

"Where 's yer dad?"

" He 's gone off, an' won't be back for a week."

"Whacher choppin' wood fer then?"

"Cause we got to; and besides if we git all our work done
by Tuesday ma 's a-goin' to take us somewhere. She said so."

"Whereto?"

"We dunno yet; but it's somewheres. Mebby to a picnic."

"Say, lemme go 'long."

"If ma says you may."

"You go an' ast her. I 'll help you chop wood if y' will."

Nathan hurried away; but his mother looked troubled at
the request and said irresolutely:

"Your pa would n't want that boy around here, Nathan."

"But that 's jist fer playin', ma," pleaded Nathan earnestly.
"Tomp-tely-tomp-tily will help us do our work; we jist can't
git it all done by ourselves."

This settled the question. His mother gave her consent.
but felt almost guilty as she recollected the Parson's commands.
However, when the delighted Nathan went whooping out to
his work with three big apples she gave him, she felt almost
justified in thus breaking the Parson's strict rules.

"Come on!" shouted Nathan loudly. "Ma says you
may."

The two waiting boys came racing up, and Dick received his apple with the usual song and dance. When they had eaten the very cores, an attack was made upon the wood that left little doubt about their mother's promised reward.

Sunday came and went in unusual quiet. When the sun was almost setting, Mrs. Flint took the boys for a walk, and went to the Parson's familiar place of prayer in the copse. Here where none could see them she poured out her soul to heaven. Her heart seemed to be saddened by some strange, dread forecast of the future that rendered life a burden grievous to be borne. It was not because her lot was one of toil; in spite of its dreary round, work was a comfort. It was a deep pathos; an undercurrent of the poetic melancholy which found voice in the prophets and Psalmist of old. She prayed from the depth of a sorrow-laden spirit, and lifted her streaming face to the darkening skies above her, that infinite "home of the soul" toward which countless eyes gaze when hearts ache, and earth seems a desert to the panting toiler. There was little thought for herself; it was all for her loved ones. She was not her own, but "bought with a price." Her talk with the kneeling boys at her side seemed all love, and her piety was a sweet exhalation of soul.

When mother prayed the boys repented in detail of every sin they could remember. Her tender arms pressed each repentant head to her bosom; and as they knelt in the rustling leaves, while katydids creaked in the trees and whip-poor-wills sounded mournful accompaniments, they wept, saddened, yet uplifted by her sweet devotion.

On Monday morning the boys were up bright and early to complete their task before the sun grew hot. When it was all done, they piled the wood up in a great rick, and looked with pride upon such a monument of honest toil. Then they seized their hoes and went to the acre-patch. To their intense satisfaction they found this a much less formidable job than it had seemed. Working rapidly, by night the ugly barrier raised by the Parson between them and leisure was completely broken down. They had, as they believed, six whole days ahead before his frigid face would chill their warm impulses and his harsh commands sound in their ears.

During frequent visits to the cistern for water, they noticed that Mrs. Flint was unusually busy. She was baking pies, cookies and doughnuts, while something that smelled a great deal like chicken was boiling in a pot. With their knowledge of her ways, they naturally connected all this with her promise. Up to this time, however, she had not told them anything definite of her plans; but they were not uneasy; many a time before they had trusted to her goodness of heart and had never been disappointed. That night she said to them kindly:

"Wash your feet, boys, and go to bed soon. You are tired, and might have to get up early to-morrow morning."

In a little time they kissed her good-night and went to bed, too tired from their hard day's work to dream. At daybreak next morning they were wakened by her voice at the bed-room door:

"Come, my little men, jump up. Breakfast is nearly ready, and you must feed the horse *if you want to go fishing!*"

This was her secret. The boys raised a regular war-whoop
and jumped out of bed in a tangle. While Nathan hopped about
with one foot in his trousers' leg, William threw a pillow at
him and knocked him over a chair. They flew to the barn and
fed Daniel, who greatly to his vexation was made to paw twice
for every mouthful of corn he got.

Mrs. Flint had already milked old Whitey, and she was
grazing industriously upon the commons. They went back to
the house "half-hammon" and bolted breakfast, hardly stopping to chew. Meanwhile they discussed as well as they could
the wonderful things to be done during the day. Their mother
was packing a large lunch-basket with the previous day's cooking, so the boys knew they would remain at the river until
evening. Then, too, she had bought them new hooks and lines,
"real store tackle," and they nearly smothered her with hugs
and kisses.

While Nathan hitched Daniel to the two-seated carriage,
William set off at a gallop to warn Dick Patterson. They soon
came back together, Dick eating a chunk of corn-pone and a
slice of bacon as he loped along. In the presence of Mrs. Flint
he was a trifle shy at first, but her motherly way soon reassured
him; so he began to sing his familiar song, and danced the ac-
companiment until he ran a splinter into his great toe and
stopped for repairs.

Daniel did not lag this time; and while swinging his bony
legs along the dusty road, urged occasionally by a keen switch,
he probably wondered what on earth had happened to demand
this unusual speed. But when at last he drew up near the

Bend, and was tethered where he could eat his fill of sweet, dewy grass, he sighed in great content.

Mrs. Flint knew the rare art of letting joy alone. She had no fretful cautions to give, and the boys were not detained by any unexpected jobs. In a trice they had fixed everything snugly and set off shouting for the Bend, where but a few weeks before they had been so bitterly disappointed.

AT BIG BEND AGAIN.

"Tomp-tely-tomp-tily" was an adept at angling, and soon taught the boys many things about it they had never known. Everything went delightfully. Fish—big ones, too—bit greedily, and the eager boys were kept busy. They set two or three poles with long lines to reach the middle of the channel; here Dick told them the big catfish lay, and soon one of the rods began to sway under the weight of a ten-pounder. When this struggling prize was landed the boys were fairly wild.

By half-past eleven o'clock they were ravenously hungry. Two dozen fine fish had rewarded their sport, and they concluded to go back and hunt up Mrs. Flint. She had found a cool, grassy spot under a wide-spreading oak, and built a fire. Upon this she cooked enough of their fish "to fill them up to the neck," as William said, and they had a feast that would have shaken the habits of a stoic.

Of course it was the sweeter for their surroundings. They were out in the glorious forest; all about them rain-crows were "chorking," wood-peckers drumming, and staid king-fishers might sometimes be seen perched on a bough overhanging the river. Occasionally one of these watchful fellows would dart down with noisy chatter after some hapless minnow that turned its silvery side up to the sun. Their hearts were brimming with the fresh spirit of the woods, and every sense was sharpened. Not less did the boys enjoy it because their mother was there; for her dear face was alight with the happiness which overflowed the chattering urchins.

"Tomp-tely-tomp-tily" got his full share of everything, and ate as if he never expected to get another meal as long as he lived. When dinner was over and the things put away, the boys lolled about in the shade for an hour and listened to some very entertaining stories of Mrs. Flint's life down at Puncheon

Camp. This was then a wild country, full of all kinds of game that delight a hunter's heart. Then they threw some lines in the deep-river channel, and leaving Mrs. Flint to watch them, set off on a mile tramp up the river. During the excursion they saw at one point something that looked

LOLLED ABOUT IN THE SHADE.

like a big crate anchored a little distance out from the bank. It proved to be a fish-trap, and in it was a grinnel fully twenty inches in length. Dick swam out to the trap and took the fish in as spoils; he said it would soon have escaped anyhow.

Upon their return William ran across a huge water-moccasin, which was coiled behind a log over which he jumped. Upon catching sight of the ugly reptile he screeched, and "riz agin," as he told it, making a greater leap than he had ever taken before. Slowly uncoiling its rusty body, the snake started for the river, but Dick soon killed it. Then tying a strip of hickory bark around its neck, the boys dragged it with them to the ford. When they came in sight of her, Mrs. Flint beckoned them to hurry and they responded at top speed. She told them that something had been pulling at one of their fish-lines for half an hour, and upon hauling it in, they were aston-ished to find what looked like another snake dangling and squirming upon the hook. Dick informed them that it was an eel. It was the first they had ever seen, and quite as slip-pery as it is said to be.

In the cool of the evening they started for home, swelling with pride over their trophies, and full to the brim with con-tent in their day's sport. In later years they had many a fishing excursion, but never one which for pure fun and unmixed happiness quite equalled that with their mother down at Big Bend.

During the next few days the boys followed their own idle devices, and finally the time began to drag. On Saturday, how-ever, Muckemtady signaled them from the barn. He had the body of an old fiddle which he had picked up somewhere about town. It was the first instrument of the kind that the boys had ever handled, and consequently was as wonderful to them as a Barnum's talking machine. After long examination Nathan proposed to trade for it. Muckemtady had been waiting for this proposal; so Nathan gave his top, and William contrib-uted three glass marbles, and the fiddle changed hands.

Muckemtady told them they could make strings with pa-per-cord if they did n't stretch them too tight. This was im-mediately tried, and as they had no bow, the former owner showed them how to make one with a hazel switch and a wisp of hair from Daniel's tail. Rubbing this rude bow with rosin obtained from his mother's fruit-canning supplies, Nathan eagerly applied it to the fiddle-strings. Both he and William were electrified; there arose a sound much like the miaulings of some wandering midnight cat.

In truth, both the boys inherited a natural love for music from the Parson whose revival singing was one of his greatest successes. But other than in "spiritual hymns and songs" the musical art had never been extensively cultivated in the Apostle's family, and some forms of it were entirely forbidden.

So absorbed did the ravished boys become in their novel occupation that they failed to hear a creak of the lot-gate, and both were nearly struck silly when recalled to earth by a well-known voice, whose owner they supposed to be miles away. The tones were full of menace, and had a chilling rasp:

"Young man, where did ye git that thing?"

In his sudden terror Nathan made a foolish effort to conceal the "thing," but of course it was too late. Then the voice spoke again, and this time louder:

"Did ye *hear* me; where did ye *git* that thing?"

"From a boy," replied Nathan feebly.

"Well, do you see if ye can teck it back to the boy: and if I ever ketch ye with sich an article ag'in, I 'll warm the wax in yer ears."

The dream had faded. For the first time in the entire affair the boys really believed that they had been doing something wrong. They felt,

> "Like thief o'ertaken in his track,
> With stolen chattels on his back."

Nathan crawled weakly over the fence to hunt Muckemtady, and William, with fluttering heart and trembling legs, sneaked away to the house. Muckemtady would not trade back. Nathan used much persuasion and some threats, but to no purpose. Finally he laid the fiddle down by the roadside and went slowly home, occasionally looking back with great longing, and grinding his teeth with rage and shame.

The boys had acquired a perfectly natural habit of concealment; it had arisen from a long series of unpleasant experiences in honesty and the results of telling the truth. In those stern old Methodist days "fiddles" were regarded as "sinful instruments." The Parson verily believed them to possess a large measure of the Satanic influences supposed to belong to "the Father of Lies." Of course he never stopped to compare them with the more scriptural "harps" believed to fill heaven with glorious music.

But serious as was this fiddle episode, it was quickly forgotten in a very exciting revelation. The Parson's mysterious trip was at last explained; he had bought a farm. It was located a hundred miles away, and lay wholly in the woods. He had purchased the land from a railroad company, at a wonderful bargain, of which he boasted mightily It had left him money enough to build a good house, buy a few head of stock and some farming implements, so that they could start in well equipped. The Parson was full of genuine enthusiasm. Before he was called to preach he had been accounted a good farmer; and for these reasons the new step had stirred within him many pleasant memories.

He gave a glowing description of the land; how it lay; how rich and deep the soil was; how it was watered by a fine branch, and what quantities of cord-wood might be cut from its tall timber. The entire family listened with intense interest, the older members now and then asking various questions. When the story was finished the discontented girls grumbled something about "being buried in the woods for the balance of their lives," but Nathan and William began to dream of wonders

The wily Apostle so fascinatingly portrayed the raising of pigs, calves, corn, pumpkins, etc., that really the prospect seemed glowing, and appeared to point an ideal life. The boys had never been initiated into any of these sublime mysteries, so they were easily beguiled, and began to lay all sorts of extravagant plans.

Among other things the Apostle said that he had set men to work clearing off a field for cultivation; also arrangements had been made to have a house built as soon as possible, thus preparing for the family's coming The farm lay within four miles of Hightown, a railroad station, where the Parson said they could find ready market for all the produce they might raise.

It was then known that before making this trip he had consulted his "Presiding Elder," and arrangements had been made, so that at the close of his present year he should be appointed to the circuit upon which this prospective farm was situated He would then rent out the town parsonage and live on his own property

All these things grew more and more in the imagination

of the boys, and were full of vague, magnificent promise. They had never lived on any kind of a fa'rm, much less one in the woods, new and full of stumps. All their notions of rural life were based upon visits made with the Parson to his country parishioners. Here they had always been feasted upon the best to be had; notably poultry. For this diet they had inherited a natural taste; and in their inexperienced minds farm life was synonymous with a perpetual mess of chicken.

But there was great craft in this new enterprise of the Parson. He wished to remove these troublesome youngsters from "evil communications," and knew there was no surer way than to retire them to rural life. On this woods-farm they would be completely isolated. Besides, they would learn useful habits, and in time be able to add considerably to the family's scanty revenues.

"There are a good many wuss things than livin' on a farm," he rejoined in reply to the girls' grumbling.

As for his wife no one knew what she thought of it. She was submissive to any plan proposed by her imperious husband.

The six weeks before "Conference" and the end of the pastoral year passed quickly. A week after that assembly met the boys read among a long list of appointments printed in "The Methodist Christian Advocate" what all of the family had expected to see:

"Hightown Circuit...........Josiah Flint."

Three days later the Apostle returned. Then came the old excitement and hard work of moving, and the eager boys set their faces toward a new and unfamiliar life.

9

CHAPTER X.

NEW SCENES.

O F the Methodist itinerant it is strictly true that he "has here no abiding city, but seeks one to come." Yet this is not always such a calamity as it might seem. There is some compensation in every phase of existence, and there is a great deal to offset the apparent misfortunes of the wandering Methodist preacher's life.

As before stated, Parson Flint was a preacher of the pioneer pattern. In these latter days he could have succeeded but poorly. He was too domineering; too unskilled in the courtesies of life, and more than all, he sadly lacked what is called "book-learning." However, he had a strong and aggressive mind, being full of restless energy. Yet somehow he never remained more than two years on any charge, and when he moved he left behind a few staunch friends, but many bitter enemies.

This was perhaps the fault of a too puritanical, rigorous manner, but the Parson was hardly aware of it. In the midst of the storms his overbearing conduct raised he contented himself with a passage of Scripture, "I came not to send peace, but a sword." If this was a legitimate purpose, certainly Parson Flint was very successful.

In his earnest life religion meant everything, and he forced
the topic upon everyone's attention. His best friends, however, often thought him unfortunate in the kind of piety most .
valued by him, and were sure he was so in his way of presenting
it. But whatever Walnut Hill people might have thought or
felt about his departure, it was certain that the Parson himself
experienced only deep satisfaction. When the last load of
household goods started on its way he followed with a double
star of hope at the end of the journey—a new circuit and a new
farm.

Full of excitement and glowing speculation, the boys were .
to ride with one of the wagon-drivers; and with the exception
of "Tomp-tely-tomp-tily" and "Muckemtady" they looked the
last upon the village without a single regret.

Early in the afternoon of the third day the teams arrived
at Hightown. The journey had been uneventful. But a single
episode enlivened its progress. William grew sleepy with the
slow pace and fell from his seat, damaging his nose, with which
he tried to plow up dirt in the hard road.

The wagons drew up before a low, weather-beaten house
in a dingy, dismal yard. Most of this enclosure was knee deep
in dog-fennel and "jimpson" weeds. In front there was a rickety board fence, which was flanked by rotten rail wings that
extended back about two hundred feet, helping to make a barn-
lot; and in this was a mournful apology for a stable, near which
was a straw-covered cow-shed.

The driver told the boys that the shanty in the yard was the
parsonage. They instantly looked for a woodpile, and saw

only the former place of one outside the fence. It was marked by a rotting pile of chips, but not a stick of wood was in sight.

A more desolate, poverty-stricken kennel than the parsonage would be hard to picture. The boys made quick exploration of the entire premises and felt profoundly thankful that they were going to live on the farm; at least they thought so. But this consolation soon vanished; the Parson came up and began to help the drivers to unload the wagons. Then the boys learned that they should not go to the farm for several months, as the house was not yet even begun.

When they gazed upon the desolate premises the poor girls raved, and even the patient mother shed silent tears. But realizing that this was useless woe they soon regained their composure. As for the Parson he had long before "set his affections upon things above, and not upon things on the earth," so he was very little disturbed. Seeing their grief, he even tried to soothe the feelings of the girls with a Scriptural quotation about the "lust of the eye, and the pride of life," but Eunice replied savagely that some people took more pride in their disgusting poverty than others do in riches. This so snubbed the Parson that he made no further comments.

With their accustomed energy the family soon completely revolutionized this forbidding place. The Apostle mended the fences, mowed down the rank growth of weeds and repainted the house. By much scrubbing and cleaning the girls renovated

MOWED DOWN THE WEEDS.

the inside of the dwelling, and a month of toil rendered it a passably comfortable place to occupy.

It must be said that Hightown was an overgrown village and had a numerous Methodist fraternity. The town itself was what is known in Methodism as a "Station," and was not part of the Parson's circuit.

The local pulpit was filled by a very spruce-looking minister, who wore a long black coat, white tie and "stove-pipe" hat. He had a strong "Episcopal" flavor, with but little Methodist appearance. This gentleman's home was a model of elegance and comfort, making the Parson's mean abode more unsightly by contrast.

When the long siege of house-cleaning and remodeling was ended, life in the Apostle's household fell into its usual routine. Then the thoughts of all turned with real longings toward the farm. One of the Parson's appointments was situated within a mile or two of his new purchase; and when about three weeks after his arrival in Hightown business called him to this place, he made it an opportunity to pay a visit to the farm itself.

Of course, when the boys learned where he was going they were eager to accompany him; he readily consented to this, and soon they were on the way. Half an hour out of town they reached a dense forest Fall had well begun and already the coloring leaves indicated near approach of winter. After a tedious drive of two miles more, over a rough road, they came to a small post-oak flat, where the Parson looked carefully around and called out: "Whoa, Daniel!"

Then he pointed to a blazed tree near the road and told the wondering boys that it marked the eastern boundary of his land. The two green youths were astonished. William asked innocently where the farm was, and why there was no fence, to which the Apostle replied that the clearing was a quarter of a mile further on yet, but that they would soon reach it. In a little time they drove on and soon came to a three-acre clearing where a man was chopping, and all about him were piled long wind-rows of brush from the timber he had felled.

"Hello, Mr. Robinson! Anybody living hereabouts?" called the Parson.

"Not yet, Mr. Flint; leastways, nobody but me and my old womern," replied the wood-chopper.

At these words the boys began to scan the clearing for a

First View of the Farm.

house. At the far side they discovered a cabin which seemed to have been made from old logs, although it had a new clap-board roof. Afterwards they found that the logs had belonged to a farmer who lived upon the edge of the prairie near by, and the Parson had bought them. By winding about through the brush heaps, old Daniel finally reached this shack, in the door of which stood a fat, blowsy woman, chewing a snuff-stick. The Parson informed this female that he was the owner of the place, and she immediately set about making preparations for the meal that always followed the preacher's coming. When the Parson had unhooked and tethered Daniel he seized an ax, directed the boys to follow him and set off to help Mr. Robinson. In a little time he was dealing heavy blows upon the opposite side of the tree that man was cutting down, uttering loud grunts with every fall of the ax. Presently the giant oak came crashing down, and the Apostle said briskly:

"Here's work for you, boys; haul off yer coats, and as we trim off the brush you pile it up. Some night we'll have a big bonfire."

By this time the Parson was much flushed with his exertions, and the sweat running into his eyes had made them very red. He always did everything with a rush, and often tired himself out needlessly. He preached, chopped and threshed the boys with much the same gestures.

The boys set to work and kept at it manfully until a shout from the cabin announced noontime. Then they had their first meal on the farm. William was properly disgusted. There was no chicken upon the table; and indeed none about the premises. Keen hunger only could have made them relish the black coffee, cornbread and strips of bacon that formed the major part of the meal.

When they had eaten, the boys set out to explore this novel farm, while the Parson was preaching a sermonet to Mr. Robinson upon the sinfulness of tobacco using. That worthy was puffing at his pipe, assenting to all the Parson said, but bewailing the "holt" tobacco had got on his constitution.

Nathan and William marveled much to find what manner of farm this much-boasted place was. It had neither fences, barn, stock, nor fowls. "The fine branch" mentioned by the Parson was but a shallow affair, and at this season had no water save in a few holes, and these were a foot deep in mud at the bottom.

The Parson's shout soon recalled them to work, and he left to transact his pastoral business while they went to piling brush. About two hours before sundown he came back and they returned home, utterly disgusted with the farming prospect before them. But when they had described it all in detail to their mother, she put on a brave face and said confidently:

"Never mind, boys; we'll change all that fast enough when we move out there."

The following forenoon a huge load of cord-wood was delivered from the farm, and piled up outside the fence by the ancient chip-pile. There was no saw-buck upon the premises, so the Parson made one out of four stakes driven into the ground, and crossed over a small log. Then the boys were once more put to their old trade.

On Sunday morning early the Parson rode away to one of his appointments, five miles distant, and the family went to church in Hightown together for the first time. The unwonted splendor of the chapel quite fascinated the boys, and they were astonished at the display of rich dresses and milli-

" Tacky."

nery among the congregation. Never before did their own appearance seem so mean, or their clothes look so old-fashioned and rustic. And what made it more embarrasing to the girls was the way in which they were looked over by many of the silken clad ladies. These supercilious dames slightly elevated their noses and seemed to say as plainly as if they had spoken it aloud, "tacky!" Very few people spoke to them at the close of the services, and the mortified girls returned home full of loud, feminine wrath.

Late that night the Parson came back tired and out of spirits. The next morning he ordered the boys to prepare for school, and at eight o'clock marched them through a staring crowd of scholars to the school-house, where he said to the teacher, a very firm but kindly looking man:

"Here are my boys, Mr. Forbes. I want 'em to learn their lessons and behave theirselves. Jist report to me if they cut up any shines. And"—to the boys themselves who stood sheepishly by—"I want to tell ye that fer every whippin' ye git at school I'll give ye another and a good deal harder one when ye git home."

At these words Mr. Forbes looked somewhat amused; he shook hands with the boys, however, and said he never had much trouble with his scholars, very seldom using the rod either.

To this unorthodox remark the Parson responded with a Scriptural quotation about "foolishness" being the natural contents of a child's heart, and "the rod" being the best means of removing it.

Then followed six months of pleasant school days; and during this entire period the boys actually got along without the use of the rod, although the Parson made diligent inquiry as to their conduct, both from them and the teacher.

As Spring approached there was much renewed talk about the farm, which of course greatly interested the boys. One day, in the latter part of March, the Parson came home from a visit to his purchase and said that everything was ready for them; they would move out to the farm at once. The household goods were again packed up, and two high-piled wagons started with them for the new home.

On account of the rough forest road direct from town, the teamsters concluded to take a circuitous route, ten miles in length. Mrs. Flint and the girls stayed all night at a neighbor's, intending to drive out next morning; so that afternoon the Parson and boys walked to the farm that they might put the goods under cover in case of rain.

Upon their arrival the boys were astonished at the changes in the place since their first visit The clearing had grown to six acres, and was now under fence. A neat story-and-a-half house had been built, using the former cabin for a kitchen "L." Between the two buildings was a broad covered passage way, and running from it along the cabin a big, roomy porch had been constructed. The structures stood in a large, shady yard, enclosed by a substantial board fence in front, which was flanked by paling wings that ran far enough back to embrace a newly-ploughed garden. Compared with the squalid parsonage in town everything here looked so neat and clean that the boys were immensely delighted, and again began to dream wonderful things for the future of such a lovely home.

To the north of the house was a half-acre lot, in one corner of which was piled a lot of lumber, out of which the Parson informed them a barn was soon to be builded. At the present time the lot contained nothing else but saplings and a huge trough. This latter article had been hollowed out of a post-oak log; at one end it had two legs, but the other rested upon a queer, wart-like knot, that seemed to have grown upon the original tree most conveniently for the purpose.

Near one corner of the kitchen was a large cistern, walled to the top with stone; it was about two-thirds full of dark-looking water, which the Parson said had been slightly discolored by the nails in the new oak clap-boards on the roof. Upon exploring the larger house, the boys found that only its lower story had been completed; the upper story was as yet only a shell, and at the sides they could reach the shingles The whole interior smelled strongly of new pine

Towards evening the wagons arrived, and their contents were all piled off in the front yard Then the teamsters helped to carry in the stoves and heavier articles, after which they drove away. The Parson first set up the kitchen stove, in which the boys at once built a fire for its cheerful looks. Then they helped carry two beds and their furnishings up stairs to be ready for the night. After this was done a lunch their mother had provided comforted their hungry stomachs, and the Apostle said it was time to retire.

Grim shadows had already gathered over the clearing, and the forest around looked like some black, craggy-topped wall. With the falling dusk everything became so gloomy and solemn that an unutterable sensation of home-sickness fell upon the boys They climbed the narrow stairs after the silent Parson, looked apprehensively out of the uncurtained windows, and wondered if there might not be catamounts prowling about in the rustling gloom below. The solitary candle cast uncertain light around, and stealthy shadows flickered among the rafters and studding as if afraid. A soft wind was blowing, and when the Parson raised a sash for fresh air, out in the dim yard the tall, slim saplings bowed gently, sighing like skeleton ghosts

Now, the boys were superstitious by nature and education. Darkness was always a menace to them. They looked upon every cawing crow and wondered if it might not be one of the Scriptural, avenging ravens, come to pick out their mocking eyes When by themselves in the woods at dusk they thought about Elisha and his she-bears on general principles. A Nemesis seemed always at their guilty heels.

This night the Parson slept alone After divesting himself of his upper garments, he knelt by his bed, groaned forth his petitions, blew out the candle, and stretched his weary length upon the couch. He nearly always slept flat on his back, and, as for snoring, nothing could approach him. When in full swing, about every half-hour following a series of hisses, gurglings and groans, he would break out into a snort that sounded like the explosion of a big popgun. Then he would stir a trifle, rub his hands down his face to straighten out his nose and begin again in a different key.

A few minutes after retiring he began these noisy demonstrations, and while the racket kept the boys awake for a long time, it also kept them from being so horribly lonesome. In spite of the rasping sounds however, they finally began to doze, and drop off into the uncertain beginnings of dreams. Then suddenly they were brought wide awake by some outlandish noise that made them both start up in bed and put out their hands to feel if each other was there. Directly over the roof outside something was making sounds that to them were utterly weird, and ominous as death. It was a whirring growl, interspersed with queer clacks, that resembled the clapping of jaws.*

Both the boys imagined they could dimly discern all manner of hairy faces, terrible eyes and gleaming tusks in the gloom about them. The Apostle's throat was croaking and gurgling as if a pair of those clamping jaws were gripping it, and "goose-flesh" rose all over the boys until their skins felt prickly as cucumbers.

Their terror was so great that they were about to call aloud when the noise upon the roof abruptly ceased with a "chork" and some soft, heavy body seemed to have alighted

---

* Noise of the whippoorwill just before it sings

in place of the animal that made it. Then just as the Apostle exploded a terrific snort, a scream like the yell of a maniac slit the air. Instantly both boys were at the Parson's bedside, Nathan clutching him by the arm, and William clinging to his hair and beard He jumped up like a jack-in-the-box, and as he did so there came from the roof a loud, hoarse "Hoo, hoo hoo, hoo hooahh!" which died away in a growl.

"Oh, pa, it's a jagger!" chattered William, burying his tow head in the pillow

William did not know that jaguars did not inhabit Illinois; but he had read about them, and knew that they screamed.  This night monster had done so, and he felt sure that a jaguar, or one of Elisha's bears had suddenly come to make way with him

The now awakened Parson burst into a guffaw, and unhooking William's twitching fingers from his beard, said contemptuously:

"See if ye kin git back into bed; and do n't pull all the hair off 'n my head because a pore hoot-owl hollers!"

Weak from fright, and bathed in a clammy sweat, the boys tremblingly slunk back to bed, where they crept close to each other and pulled the covers up over their heads Every few minutes, as the absurdity of the thing struck him forcibly, the Apostle was heard to snort and chuckle; but the scare was too much for William's creeping nerves, and he began to snuffle

"Aahhh, my sons," the Parson said at last, feeling it the proper time to impress a pious lesson, "if a innocent hoot-owl kin scare ye half to death, what 'll ye do when the world 's on fire? It is always best to be ready, for no man knoweth the day nor the hour!"

Then, after a solemn pause, to let this sink into their minds, he repeated in a deep, chesty voice:

> "Dangers stand thick through all the ground
> To push us to the tomb;
> And fierce diseases wait around,
> To hurry mortals home!
>
> "May we this life improve,
> To mourn for errors past,
> And live each short revolving day
> As if it were our last!"

Then, with a lugubrious sigh, as if the picture was very real to him, he groaned, "The Lawwerrd have mercy upon us!"

The reaction from fright had one good result; it relieved the fearful strain upon the boys' nerves, and in a short time they slept soundly, forgetful of nightly terrors until aroused by the Apostle's joking call:

"It 's time ye was a-gittin' out of here, 'fore some kind of a jagger or night-bird gits holt of ye!" The sun was up.

Three hours later they were overjoyed to see old Daniel's long head come bobbing down the road by the field-fence; and their mother's dear face was a second sunrise, more welcome than the first.

Before night-fall the house began to look homelike, and in a week thereafter everything was in its place. There was abundant material at hand to give the premises a rustic loveli-

10

ness, and all worked hard to gather about their new dwelling as much beauty and comfort as they could.

Of course the Parson told the ridiculous story of their first night with him on the farm; and he would have poked fun at the boys for many a day, had not Mrs. Flint told an incident of his own life which was quite as funny. Thereafter, when the Apostle said "jagger," the boys never failed to come back at him with great satisfaction.

Spring advanced rapidly. The trees were growing green, and every morning the air fairly thrilled with bird songs, while at night owls and whippoorwills took up the refrain.

The boys' life on the farm had begun; we shall soon see how it fulfilled their expectations.

CHAPTER XI.

THE PARSON'S YARN.

SHORTLY after moving to the farm, the Parson went on business to Centerville, twenty-five miles away. Here resided one of his sisters who had married well, and was living in quite luxurious circumstances. Learning that the boys had begun life in the woods, their uncle rightly supposed that they should have a gun. His own son was very fond of hunting, and had several guns of various models, some of which were rusty and out of order from long disuse.

After exploring closets and garrets for half an hour, the uncle came back with what had been a fine English-twist, muzzle-loading double-barrel shotgun. One of its locks was out of order, but a gun-smith near by soon set that right. Accompanying the gun was a complete hunting outfit. A powder-flask, a shot pouch with different compartments for various sized shot, a game-bag, wad-cutter, and corkscrew fixtures for the end of the ramrod, so that unused loads could be extracted when the owner wished.

As the Parson inspected all these articles, visions of savory pigeon and squirrel pot-pie floated through his mind, and brought back many pleasant memories of his earlier days. In fact, the generous gift was as acceptable to him as he knew

"CAME BACK WITH A GUN."

it would be to the boys. It had the unusual effect of loosening his pocket-book, and before returning home he bought a bountiful supply of ammunition, among which were two boxes of caps. Upon these were printed the letters "G. D." And afterward the boys privately concluded that the initials stood for "gosh-dern," because the caps were not reliable, failing to burst at times, and thus losing them many a good shot.

When the Parson reached home with this unexpected treasure it fairly took away the boys' breath. To his astonishment Daniel was unharnessed without a single pass being made at his ribs. The excited urchins hurriedly turned him loose in the lot, and scampered back to investigate the tremendous wind-fall; "a real, sure 'nough gun, that shot twice at once," as William said.

After supper the Parson took the weapon apart, cleaned it thoroughly, and explained each detail of its construction to the boys. This was a cautionary measure, as he knew that if it were not done the youths would examine its internal mechanism for themselves. With great care the Apostle told them how to load; to pour in the powder first, and ram the wad down hard upon it; how much shot must be used for a squirrel, and how the wad must be pressed lightly upon it, or the gun would kick. Especially he exhorted them always to remember which barrel was loaded, lest they "git a double-charge in one and bust the thing, knockin' their heads off." Last he showed them how to hold the gun; to shut one eye while drawing a bead, and hold steady when pulling the trigger.

They listened and looked with absorbed interest, and

wished it was only day-light, so they could try the thing at once; and each felt certain that he could knock over a squirrel or 'possum, or even a "jagger" the first shot. In turn they tried on flask and shot-pouch, bracing the gun firmly to their shoulders and sighting carefully at imaginary game, which, of course, was supposed to fall with great certainty.

The gun was too heavy for William to hold steadily off-hand, so he rested it on a chair-back, squinting along the barrel and screwing his mouth around in the neighborhood of his left ear. When he had drawn a fine bead, he uttered a loud "Poom!" and straightened up with a hunter's fire flashing in his eyes. The Apostle was in one of his rare good-humors; he watched all these exercises with critical eye, corrected their blunders, and gave them many useful lessons.

"There, now," he said finally; "put the traps by, and I 'll tell ye how yer Uncle Jick, an' Uncle Clint, and another feller and me tuk a week's hunt once, down at Puncheon Camp."

THE PARSON'S YARN.

The boys were always eager for a story: they hastened to stand the gun in a corner and hang the accouterments up by it. The Parson drew his chair before the fire-place, for the evening was chilly, parted his coat-tails, straddled the chair and sat down with his face to the back.

"Before I begin," said he, "I must hev a mighty good drink of warter. William, you break fer the kitchen and git it, while Nathan throws another stick of wood on the fire."

William started on a run.

"Look out fer a jagger," called the Parson after him; and at the same time he uttered such a frightful caterwaul that William's skin crept and his teeth chattered.

He came back faster than he went, slopping water over the mouth of a big, crooked-handled gourd. Mrs. Flint made a protest against frightening the boys, but the Parson only chuckled, and drank three or four big gulps of water.

William hung the gourd over a chair-back by its handle, sat down on the floor in front of the Parson, took one of his great toes in each hand, and thus with open mouth and eager eyes made ready to listen to the story. He had heard it before, but there was something very fascinating, even in its repetition. The Apostle told it well, too, for it was part of his early experiences.

Nathan sat midway between the Parson and the new gun, toward which he cast occasional admiring glances. Mrs. Flint and the girls were knitting or piecing bed-quilts, and the scene looked very homelike and cozy.

"Once upon a time," began the Parson dramatically, " 'way long in the fall of the year when corn was gethered and everything made ready fer winter, Uncle Clint, Uncle Jick, Buck Poundstone and me all concluded we'd take a week's hunt down at Puncheon Camp. This was in Jefferson County, 'way over on Hoss Creek in the backwoods, more than ten miles from anybody's house. There was jist any amount of turkeys, deer, panthers, bears an' the like. Punch'eon Camp was a old log cabin that some of us had put up jist to sleep in when we went there to do any huntin'; fer of all the places fer game you ever see, that beats 'em. The cabin was made of logs notched in at the ends; but it had no chinkin' nor daubin', nor any winder, but jist a hole in the dirt roof to let out the smoke.

"It was right on the banks of the crick, where we could git plenty of warter, and when we wanted to could ketch plenty of redhoss an' pearch. The hull bottoms were kivered knee deep in grass, and had underbrush scattered through it. Back of the cabin was a long ridge, an' when ye'd gone about a mile through the woods that kivered it, ye come to what old settlers called the barrens: it was a clayey post-oak flat, where nobody lived, ur wanted to.

"Well, we wuz all ridin' along, tellin' tales of how we'd killed game, when we struck the bottoms. The wind was right in our faces, and all the hounds trottin' at our horses' heels. There was Sounder, an' Goodeye, an' Pluto, an' Little Britches, and Fludix, an' Spud. Goodeye hed one eye knocked out when he was a pup, and he always kept the other pintin' to the front; an' when old Sounder let loose on a deer's trail you'd a-thought that fourteen bulls was a-bellerin'! We was n't looking fer anything jist then, but all at once, a little to our left up jumps a deer and tuck a bee-line fer our rear, so's to git the wind of us Clint was always the quickest with a gun, so he turned in his saddle and whanged away, while the deer was up in the air jumpin' a log He tuck it right through the body; then the

hounds got a smell of blood and powder, an' of all the howlin',
yellin' and roarin' it was then. We broke after them, lickety
cut through the grass and brushes, the dogs bayin' like mad.

"Uncle Jick was a leetle ahead. Purty soon we could tell
by the noise that the dogs were close on it, an' when we got on
to a little rise of ground we looked over and saw 'em all around
it, barkin' an' snappin', while Leetle Britches was trying to
grab it by the jew-huff. It's hair was all stannin' up, an' it
looked fierce, I tell you!

"Uncle Jick had an old Yager that shot a bullet about
the size of a crab-apple; he got within fifty yards of the critter, an' tuck a bead on it jist back of the shoulders. Ye could
a-seen it fairly bounce off'n the ground when the ball hit it;
an' the hounds pitched onto it, an' Leetle Britches grabbed
holt of a leg an' shuk as if he 'd done it all.

"We hed venison steak that night, you 'd better believe:
fer when we 'd reached the cabin, hoppled our horses an' cut
grass fer beds, Buck Poundstone was app'inted cook the fust
turn. He got us up a supper that would jist a-made yer mouth
warter.

"After we 'd e't, we hung the rest of the deer up high, out
of reach of varmints, and purty soon we went to bed. Next
mornin' we divided up in couples, to hunt ag'n each other;
Uncle Jick an' me ag'n Buck Poundstone an' Uncle Clint. It
was an all day's tramp, but we did n't get anything except two
wild turkeys. That night the hounds left us an' went back
home, which was good fer us, I reckon. We got up before
daybreak next day, an' after talkin' it over concluded we'd

better go in opposite directions and hunt alone. I lit out jist before sun up, climbed the long ridge back of the cabin an' slipped along the top of it fer nearly a mile. All at once up jumps two deer right in front of me, and streaked it away down the ridge to'rds the bottoms. I lammed away at one, but the bullet struck it glancing' on the back, an' only skived off a patch of hair: it was bad luck!"

"I bet ye could a-peppered him if you'd had our gun!" put in William excitedly. "Oh, I wisht *I'd* a been there!"

The Parson dragged his chair a little back from the fire and went on. "I heard some shot away off to the right pretty soon, an' I know'd it was Uncle Jick's an' Clint's guns; they seemed to be havin' some luck, anyhow.

"I tramped around until about two hours by sun, and did n't see another blessed thing but a passel of juggen hens. It was disapp'intin' an' finally I tuck back to camp so as to git supper ready by the time the other fellers had come in. When I got there I tried to start a fire, but it burned slow, an' I blowed at it till the smoke got into my eyes, and nearly choked me.

"I stepped out doors to git a fresh breath of air, when I saw the hosses with their noses all p'intin' one way, lookin' at somethin' comin' down the ridge. I looked in that direction, an' lo, an' behold, what should there be but a big five-prong buck a-trottin' down to the crick fer a drink! I see she was goin' to cross the trail in the bottoms about fifty yards away; so I reached inside the door fer my gun an' run down to'rds him a little distance, where I got on a stump. When I looked ag'in the buck hed stopped, and wuz pintin' his nose right at me. I took a quick sight and tore loose. Then I heard somethin' drap.

"The smoke lifted, and there he lay kickin' like sixty, shot right through the skull. I jerked out my frog-sticker on the run and bled him. It made me proud, I tell ye! He wuz too big fer me to drag to camp, so I went back and got the fire to blazin', then cut some bacon an' mixed the meal fer our hoe-cakes.

"By this time Uncle Jick got in with a fine young doe, and he helped me drag my buck down to camp. Presently Clint and Poundstone come back, an' each had one apiece, so we was even that night; but yer daddy got the purtiest one of them all.

"Well, we tuk the insides out of 'em an' hung 'em all up in a row on a pole. We hed fine tender-line steak, cornbread and coffee, all sweetened nice with maple-sugar; and we wuz so hungry it tasted good. After that we wartered the horses, an' put the hopples on 'em so they could graze, an' then we all set down to talk over the day's hunt.

"Along about nine o'clock Uncle Jick, who was a-settin' near the door put up his hand and said, 'Hark!'

"We stopped talkin' to lissen! an' 'way up the crick some-where, so faint it sounded ten mile off, we heard somethin' go—

" 'Ow-o-o-o-o; oo-oo-oo!'

"Purty soon off in another direction somethin' else begin:

" 'Yoo-yoo-yoo; ooo-ooo-ooo-ooooo!'

"Then 'way round to the right of this another:

" 'Wow-wow-wow; woo-oo-ooo-ooo!' "

The Parson curved a hand at the side of his mouth, turning in the indicated directions and imitating these strange sounds so well that William's eyes bulged out and his breath came fast. After locating a number of the howlers, the narrator went on:

"We knowed in a minute it was wolves,—a hull drove of 'em. They smelled our fresh meat and would never stop 'til they got to us. Presently they all got together up the crick, howlin' an' barkin' an' screechin' until it seemed like there must be more 'n a hundred of 'em. We grabbed our guns an' went out doors a little way, where we all knelt down in a row to be ready for 'em.

"Here they come; Ringwell, Tingwell, Towser, the old slut and nine pups, screamin' an' yellin', jist a-meckin' things hark!

"When we thought they'd got about thirty yards from us we all whanged away at once't, an' set up a yell like forty Injins. With the noise of the guns they all turned tail and tuck back up the crick the way they'd come, an' we did n't see or hear any more of 'em."

"How many did ye kill?" asked William in a trembling voice.

While the Parson had so vividly imitated the advancing wolves, William had risen to his knees, and taken hold of both heels to steady his nerves. He had frequently asked the question of how many wolves were killed, but there was a great satisfaction in having the answer repeated.

"Aahh," said the Parson reminiscently, "we went out next mornin' to see, an' only found the scratches where they'd tore up the ground as they whirled to git away. We made their hair fly, though!"

"Yes," put in William, "but the meat flew with it."

Admitting this with a grin, the Parson continued: "I guess it wuz too dark an' we wuz too excited to take much aim. Anyways we never wuz bothered with the varmints any more.

"We stayed two d a y s longer an' by this time hed all the meat our horses could carry home; so on Friday we started back, an' about noon got to old Uncle Jacky John-son's place. He made us all stop fer dinner, an' while the hosses was bein' w a t e r e d Uncle Jacky said:

" 'Boys, thar 's a big buck uses down in my cornfield yander, next to the woods, an'

AT UNCLE JACKY JOHNSON'S.

I should n't be s'prised if one of ye might n't find him thar now. I seed him once't ur twic't, an' you better believe he 's a rouser. Suppose ye try fer him,' he said to me.

"So I tuk a long musket of Uncle Jacky's that was loaded with buck-shot an' set off. I wuz going' down one side of the fence when the corn over in the field begin to rustle, an' I come purty near whanging loose at Uncle Jacky, who 'd cut across an' overtook me. He p'inted out a big tree at the far side of the field, and said there was where the buck had found a low place in the fence to jump over. Then he said if I'd go there an' wait, he'd slip through the corn an' drive the game out fer me. I had n't more than got there when I heard Uncle Jacky hollerin' at the top of his voice:

"'Looooook out! Looooook out!'

"Sure enough here come the buck twenty feet at a jump. Jist as he riz over the fence I blazed away, an' the old musket come mighty near kickin' the side of my jaw off. It fairly keeled me over, an' when I got up there lay the buck on his side, winkin' his eyes and sorter twitchin', jist about to git up an' start off ag'in! I jumped on his horns and felt fer my knife, but found I'd left it among the traps on my hoss. Then I begin to yell fer Uncle Jacky, and here he come, chargin' through the corn, gittin' out his knife as he run. When he cut its throat, I tell ye I wuz glad; fer only two shots had struck it, one on the shoulder, an' the other jist under the ear; so it was only stunned a little.

"I do n't think I ever see a bigger buck in all my born days. It had lived in the cornfield until it wuz jist rollin fat; too heavy fer us to carry back to the house. So Uncle Jacky went and yoked up his oxen to a old truck-waggin an' come down after it. The waggin wheels was made by sawin' off about two inches from the butt of a big tree, an' borin' holes through 'em fer axles Here the old contraption come,—scree—scraw, scree—screak, scrawak,—an' Uncle Jacky hollerin' at his oxen till ye could ha' heard him a mile, easy. We h'isted the buck in an' went back The critter was so fat it jist shuk an' wobbled from side to side of the waggin-bed. When its hide wuz

Big Five-prong Buck.

dressed I sold it fer two dollars and fifty cents in silver, which was jist about twenty-cents a pound.

"Aunt Rhody, Uncle Jacky's old woman, soon got dinner ready. They hed a big double-log house with a wide entry way between where she set the table. She 'd baked a venison saddle with sweet pertaters; an' if ever ye saw anything good it was like that. When she brought out a big plateful of flaky white biscuits with honey, an' rich gravy from the roast, s-s-s-sp! teck keer, boys, or ye 'll swaller yer spoons!"

At this climax William rose to his feet. His arms hung limp, the water ran from his mouth, and in his eyes were unshed tears. In a ravished voice he asked gaspingly:

"Is that all?"

"Yes," said the Parson, "that 's all. It 's gittin' late; we 'll have prayers an' then go to bed."

Nathan read an easy Psalm. Then the Parson changed his look and tone to suit the occasion, and in a slow, solemn voice offered up the evening petitions.

When prayers were over the boys went to bed in a daze, and soon fell into a tangle of dreams that were full of five-pronged bucks, six-pronged wolves and seven-pronged sweet potatoes.

CHAPTER XII.

TWO KINDS OF GAME.

THERE was no need for the boys to be called next morning. They were up with the sun, excitedly planning a hunt which was to be as nearly as possible like the one related by the Parson.

Before leaving Hightown they had once visited a parishioner's with the Parson, and that good man made them a present of a pup. Any kind of a gift was eagerly received by the boys, but a dog delighted them beyond measure. They smuggled the animal under the buggy seat where she lay hidden until they had reached home.

When the Parson saw her he waxed wroth and threatened to kill her; but recollecting the then near by migration to a farm he finally listened to the boys' pleadings and spared the pup's life.

It was some time before the fond owners could decide upon a suitable name for her dogship, but finally it came about in this way.

Once, while "acting the fool," as the Parson expressed it, Muckemtady sang a song for the boys. It ran as follows:

"Somebody stole my old 'coon dog,
And I wisht they'd bring her back,
She'd chase the big pigs over the fence,
And the little ones through the crack."

.This had caught the boys' fancy; they now remembered it, and called their dog "Coon," a name she quickly learned to recognize.

Coon proved to be very smart. She quickly showed great intelligence, and developed many fine qualities. Not long after being taken to the farm she betrayed great excitement at sight of some chipmunks that were scurrying along the lot fence. This led the boys to hope that she would make a good hunting dog, which she finally did.

Very early in life she would plunge into a pool and swim about with much satisfaction, or bring out a stick that had been thrown in: of course it was then thought that she had spaniel blood in her: but then she learned to track a bird, and that indicated "pointer" qualities.

The Parson finally settled her pedigree. He said with a sniff of unmerited contempt that she was a "mongrel." The boys did not know what this meant, but they supplied a good meaning out of Coon's many excellent traits of character.

As breakfast was not ready when the Apostle got up, he loaded the gun for the boys, and told them to "slip around the field, and see if they could n't fetch in a squirrel, but to be careful and not blow their noggins off."

They at once started to "slip," and Coon wanted to go along; but when the Parson saw her motions he said sarcastically:

"Ye 'd better leave that critter here if ye want to git anything."

"No, we want to train her," replied Nathan earnestly

The Apostle grunted, but as he did not forbid her, Coon went. She trotted ahead of the boys about thirty yards, pausing every little while to listen, or peer out into the woods. This she did with one foot raised and her ears cocked in a very beautiful manner.

The hunters had not gone half way around the field before a sudden rustling was heard in the bushes, and Coon sprang out to see what caused it. Presently she began to bark and whine as if a catamount might be after her, and the boys ran to see what she had found.

When they reached the spot she was acting crazy, trying to climb a tree, and not succeeding beyond a very high jump up its side. Upon looking among the branches overhead, the boys caught sight of a fine fat squirrel. It ran out upon the end of a limb and from that sprang to another tree, the sight of it meanwhile tantalizing Coon so as to make her dance along on her hind legs, right under it.

A Frisky Thief.

Nathan got his gun ready to shoot as soon as the squirrel stopped running, but the nimble creature kept up its leaping until it reached a big, knotty oak, round the trunk of which it slid with a saucy chipper and disappeared. The boys searched to see where it had gone, and soon discovered about thirty feet from the ground a smooth, well-worn hole. The game had escaped them.

Their disappointment was very keen, and it grew more so as they neared the house without seeing anything more. However, Coon's very brilliant conduct was something to feel proud of; and the boys related it in such glowing terms that the Apostle said:

"She may be good fer somethin' else besides a meat trap."

When the boys had told how the squirrel got away from them, the Parson gave them a lesson in hunting-craft. "When ye see a squirrel start to run on the trees, he's meckin' fer his hole, an' ye'll hev to shoot him on the run if ye git him at all."

After breakfast the Parson called the boys and went to work. There was garden to make, grubbing to do, and an endless number of odd jobs which kept them very busy.

About noon old Uncle Bulger Baldwin came over from the edge of the prairie a mile distant, to rive clapboards for the new barn and a smoke-house the Parson intended building.

To the boys Uncle Bulger was a wonderful character. He was more than six feet in height, and was in the habit of saying that he had "been a mighty powerful man in his day." This was undoubtedly true, but the hand of Time had been laid heavily upon him, bending him somewhat about the shoulders and knees.

He was ugly as a mud fence. His eyes were red about the lids, having a bag under each that hung down and pulled away the lids, exposing the lower half of his eyeballs. As the upper lids were always raised in a questioning fashion, altogether he had a very unusual stare. He had high, prominent, cheek-bones, with a long, lean jaw. And as he plastered his hair down on each side of his face, "roaching" it straight up in front, it made his countenance decidedly striking. He wore no beard save where the neck and jaw came together, but here there was a grizzly necklace of bristles, stiff and standing out under his chin like a ruff.

As the Parson described it, Uncle Bulger "chawed to-backer," but he always raised his own supply, and went about with a twist in his pocket, and a quid stowed away in one cheek.

He wore a checkered shirt and blue-jeans pantaloons, the latter held up by a pair of knit yarn suspenders. His boots were number twelve, and sadly run down at the heels.

Not alone for these personal peculiarities, but for other reasons as well, Uncle Bulger was a great favorite with the boys. Having "emmygrated" in early days from Tennessee, he was full of pioneer memories, and ever ready to relate "a leetle sarkimstance," as he called the stories. His tales were always a little more marvelous than any one else ever heard or could tell

One day while working in the edge of the woods, a short distance from the house, he set up a loud yell to the Parson.

"Bring yer gun, and come here quick, Mr Flint; here's more 'n forty sque'lls up one tree!"

With a vision of savory stews in mind the Parson responded to his call in a tremendous hurry. When he reached the spot, Uncle Bulger was looking excitedly up a big hickory tree, but suddenly he remarked in a tone of great disappointment:

"Oh, shucks! Yer jist too late. The last one hez run inter thet hole up yander My, how full thet tree must feel!"

The Parson saw the hole, and likewise the point of Uncle Bulger's joke Turning on his heel with the dry remark, "Yes, I see, the tree seems to be swellin'" he went back to the house. In answer to Mrs. Flint's inquiry of what luck had resulted from his rush he made but one disgusted remark:

"That man's the beatin'est liar I ever see!"

As Uncle Bulger rived clap-boards, it was the boys' duty to pile them up and weight them down to keep the sun from warping them. This gave them many coveted opportunities to hear the wonderful yarns the old man told so well.

Upon the special occasion of which we write he had taken a fresh chew of tobacco, and entered upon the relation of a tragic tale of "p'isenous snake-bites."

"I know'd a leetle sarkimstance one time when four diffrunt men war killed by one pair o' boots. It was like this. The fust man was mowin' in a fence corner; when a big, six-foot rattler struck at him, an' bruk off its fangs in his boot-leg. He didn't notice this, but killed the reptyle, and went ahead with his work. Purty soon the teeth scratched the calf of his leg, and by night he hed swelled up and died, as pided as the snake itself. Nobuddy could imagine what ailed him; an' after he wuz dead, his wife guv the boots to the oldest boy. He got scratched the same way, and purty soon wuz dead; and it kept up till all four of 'em wuz laid out 'fore they found what was the matter"

The boys took all this in with open mouths, and marveled much. But soon they led the talk around to firearms, and told Uncle Bulger about their new gun.

"Thet reminds me uv a leetle sarkimstance," he said. "The antickest trick in the way of shootin' I ever seed was down in Bill Simpson's clearin', in old Tennysee;—"

Just at this interesting juncture, the Apostle, who saw how matters were drifting, called:

"Oh, Nathan! You and William see if ye can come here and help me set out these sweet-pertater plants. Meck haste about it, too!"

This work required them to stoop a great deal, and was very tiresome, but they were kept at it all afternoon, so that by nightfall even the Parson himself declared he "was clean beat out."

At dusk a slow drizzling rain set in. The wind sighed weepingly around the house, and a constant drip, drip, of rain made a doleful sound that was very depressing. After supper the Parson spent some time in setting up pieces of boards at various corners where the eave-troughs overflowed, to catch as much water as possible for washing purposes. He was by nature and training a most economical man, and did not like to see even water going to waste.

Having arranged sundry tubs, buckets, wash-boilers and pots to his satisfaction, he came stamping into the porch, shook the rain from his hat, and after putting on a dry coat went into the sitting-room. Here he assumed his usual position of rest, tipped back in a chair against the wall, with one foot on a rung, his legs crossed, and his arms folded across his chest. Thus lost in his own reflections he volunteered no remarks, replying to a few questions from his wife by a brief "Yes," or "I suppose so." She finally gave up all attempts to draw him out, and plied her knitting.

The boys had stretched themselves out upon the floor, where William was soon asleep, and Nathan very drowsy. Eunice and Louise were crocheting and talking some enigmatical lingo about their beaux and the neighbors. Suddenly without a word of warning the Apostle tipped his chair forward and said, while kneeling, "Let us join in prayer."

Nathan got up and sank on one hip near a chair, upon which he laid his sleepy head, while the rest of the family dropped into postures of devotion, all save William; he had not awakened; but still lay sprawled upon his back unconscious of what was going on.

Pausing in the first phrases of his petition, the Parson looked at him, and called in a sharp voice:

"William!" But William said never a word.

Then the Parson arose, stepped to him and turned him over with a big foot, administering a smart smack which at once brought the sleeper to a feeling sense of his duty. He reared into a sitting position, stared around in a dazed fashion, and then crawled over to his mother's chair, where he subsided upon his knees, while the Parson knelt again, and resumed his interrupted exercises.

He was unusually deliberate and solemn; for when the Apostle felt least like praying at length, he always denied himself and took up his cross in a very pious manner.

But it so happened that near the close of his prayer a great clamor arose from the poultry yard, accompanied by a terrified, metallic screech from a gander. Coon started from her box on the porch with a sharp yelp, and the Parson brought his words to an abrupt "Amen," exclaiming, as he arose from his knees, "Run, my sons; there's a varmint after the chickens!"

Nathan flew to the kitchen for an old tin-lantern, but found considerable difficulty in lighting it. William was so excited that he forgot all possible danger, and ran out to "sic" Coon, who was scratching frantically at the paling gate that opened into the lot. As soon as it was open she darted in, and William followed, being familiar with every inch of the way.

When he reached the shed where the fowls roosted, Coon was snuffing about near by, and he gave her constant encouragement Thus incited, she suddenly sprang forward, seized something that was passing between William and the gate, and began to shake it furiously.

The next second the air was fairly thick with the most horrible odor that ever assailed the nostrils of man! Coon held her breath and continued to do her duty; but William, gasping and retching, made a blind run for the house, only to stumble over the gander and fall right on the dog and her terrific adversary He scrambled up again and staggered away, clawing the air and working his mouth without being able to utter a word

By this time Nathan had lighted the lantern, and, preceded by the Apostle, appeared at the door of the porch, just as William tottered through the gate near by.

"Great Methus'leh! What on earth hev ye been doin'!" cried the Parson, catching a whiff of the air.

"Owww!" sputtered William, for all he could not speak. He thought his very soul would faint within him.

As soon as they caught a breath of the dreadful odor, the girls all stampeded upstairs, Louise calling as she flew·

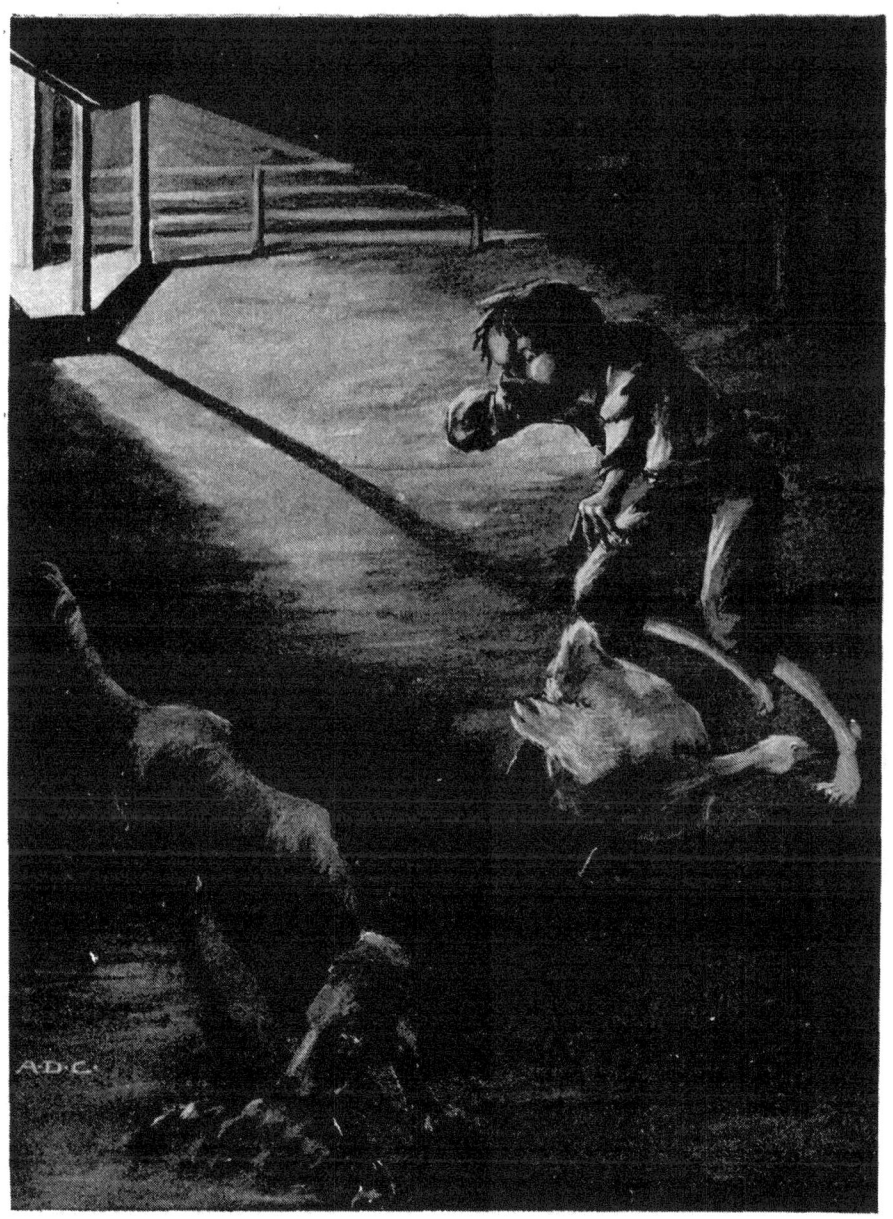

Stumbled over the Gander.

"For gracious sakes, do n't let him come in the house with that stench, or we won't be able to live in it!"

It seemed that poor William was about to be left in the cold world alone, but as usual his mother came to the rescue. She brought him a change of clothes, telling him to go out under a tree and make the shift. William did so, and the Parson asked between his snorts of laughter from the shelter of the porch:

"Did ye meet a jagger, my son; or was it some kind of a night bird tryin' to ketch ye?"

"Naww! I *did n't* meet no jagger," bawled William in a rage. "Why did n't ye tell me what the thing wuz, an' not let me go out there by myself?"

In a little time he appeared, while Coon came in from the opposite side of the porch, chewing a bunch of grass which she had torn up in her distress to take the taste out of her mouth. The look she cast around appealed for some word of praise, but meeting only the most clamorous rebuff, she slunk out into the yard, and wallowed in a puddle of water, the while groaning dolefully.

Having relieved himself of his malodorous clothes, William felt much better, although there was still a most persistent trace of the dreadful perfume about him. When he came in Nathan ran and poked his head out of the window, calling back over his shoulder:

"I ain't going to sleep with him *this* night."

William lost all patience at such an insulting suggestion, and roared at him in great dudgeon:

"I do n't want ye to sleep with me, ye big coward! Ye wuz afraid to go out there yerself!"

"I ain't very brave when jaggers is about," replied Nathan.

William was about to fume again, but the Apostle interfered:

"There now; that 'll do," he said in stern tones. "See if ye can both git to bed!"

William occupied a pallet by himself for the balance of the night, and sleep soon settled over the household. The rain continued; sometimes with a great downpour, and again with a gentle drip, drip, drop, and when the boys awakened they saw it promised to continue all day. This made them rejoice inwardly because they would not have to work. Nathan's antipathy toward William was quickly forgotten in a new interest. Breakfast was not ready, so they paid a visit to the scene of the night's encounter. Even the heavy rain had not washed away all the lingering odor, but the dead invader was there, drenched and harmless. They carried it on a pitchfork to a distance from the house, and Nathan exclaimed:

"My, ain't he a sounder!"

"You 'd a-thought so, and a smeller, too, if you 'd been out with me last night," replied William positively. "He 's more 'n I want to run across ag'in."

"But was n't Coon some punkins to jump on it? The blame thing might a-eat up the gander and a lot of chickens, too, if she had n't grabbed it in time."

"I wisht it had a-eat up the gander," rejoined William spitefully. "He 's always doin' somethin' he ain't got no business to. He tripped me up an' like to broke my neck, besides makin' me fall right on this nasty thing."

He emphasized these remarks by throwing a wet cob at the unlucky gander that had been trying several minutes to crawl through a two-inch crack in the lot fence.

Presently a voice called them to breakfast, and when the "blessing" had been asked, William remarked:

"Well, the thing is dead."

"Yes, I should judge so," replied the Parson. "From the smell last night I'd a-thought it had been dead a long time. Air ye goin' to skin it?"

The boys had not thought of such a thing, but of course they could sell the creature's hide. It was impossible to guess what a skunk-hide would bring, but they fancied it ought to command a good price, as few would care to skin such odorous game.

After breakfast, however, the Parson told them to soak the dead animal in the branch for a few days, as that would entirely deprive it of its offensive qualities; so they tied a stone about its neck and dropped it into the deepest hole they could find.

The rain had by this time grown fitful, coming in showers, and about ten o'clock the sun broke through the scattering clouds. Then the boys suggested that it was a good chance to go hunting, and the Parson gave hearty assent, saying that it was just the right time to find any amount of squirrels.

In a minute the boys had on all their accouterments and whistled for Coon. She rushed in and went nearly frantic at the prospect of a hunt. She crouched at the boys' feet, drew back her upper lip in a radiant smile, offered to shake hands, and finally relieved her feelings by knocking over a chair or two. Attracted by the racket Louise soon came down stairs and drove the devoted animal out of the house with a broom, the while holding her own nose.

Coon waited eagerly at the door until the boys appeared, and then set off ahead of them, looking back at every fork in the trail for directions. They crossed the branch and took a road leading toward the prairie, about a mile distant. Coon was eagerly watchful. Every few rods she would pause with lifted foot and "hark," as the boys called her listening. Presently with a bound and sharp yelp she sped out into the woods, the boys following at top speed, and coming up just in time to see her leap upward and snatch a fine, fat gray squirrel from the bole of a tree. This unexpected feat nearly paralyzed the spectators with admiration, and despite Coon's fearful odor, they hugged her on the spot. She seemed to be proud of herself. Her sparkling eyes and expressive antics were as nearly talk as any dog can approximate.

Stowing the squirrel in their game-bag, and giving Coon very minute instructions, the boys went on again until they reached a wood-pasture belonging to the nearest neighbor. Through this enclosure flowed a small branch, which had wide, grassy bottom lands along its course, scattered through which were several large elm trees.

In a trice Coon was over the fence, capering about on her hind legs under one of these elms, whining and barking, telling in the plainest dog-language that she had found more game.

The boys quickly followed her, and upon reaching the spot were instantly bedazzled!

It seemed as if the entire elm-top was blossoming with squirrels. There were at least two dozen, some lying close to the limbs; others looking for a way to escape, and a few that cocked their tails, peering down upon their unexpected enemies with saucy chattering.

The tree stood in an open glade, so that there was no chance for the victims to escape by leaping to other trees. In a huge fork of the elm was a hole, but one lucky fellow had taken possession of this retreat, and persistently drove out all intruders.

As soon as he could command his nerves Nathan leveled the gun, and with its crack down tumbled a big fox-squirrel, whose yellow belly presented a most inviting target. The second shot was equally as well aimed, but when he came to reload, to his intense chagrin, he found that the wadding had been left at home.

"Tear out some of yer coat-lining, and I'll hike back home fer some paper," shouted William.

He sped away, and Nathan extracted enough of the aforesaid lining to make one shot; but then he happened to think that such destruction of his clothes might bring unpleasant results, so concluded to wait and watch for William's return.

It so happened that the Parson himself had conceived the idea of following the boys, and at the time William started home was but a few hundred yards distant. William was overjoyed to meet him, and gave such marvelous accounts of

12

the condition of the elm as to fetch his father on the run. He had a "Christian Advocate" in his pocket, and under such extraordinary inducements sacrificed it at once.

"Hooray, me brave boys," he shouted encouragingly, as he beheld the squirrel-studded tree top. "Give 'em goss!"

Then with all a hunter's zest he took the gun and made quick exhibition of his skill as a marksman. When a dozen hapless squirrels had fallen, some of the remaining ones took fright in earnest, jumping from the tree to the ground and trying to flee their fate. But Coon was on the watch and caught one or two before they got a good start. When the last one disappeared sixteen victims lay about on the grass, a heavy load for William, who proudly wore the game-bag.

Upon the way home the boys told how Coon had actually scaled a tree and caught their first trophy; but the Parson was unbelieving and said dubiously: "Ump, ump; fall a snake, my sons." However, Coon settled the matter soon by repeating her performance only in a more brilliant manner   Then the Parson frankly admitted that she was a "mighty good hunter"

When the squirrels were dressed, the secret of so many in one tree was fully explained. Their paunches were chock full of elm-buds.

A delicious pot-pie gladdened the boys' stomachs that evening, and they still had half a dozen fine squirrels left over. Everything being too wet for outdoor work that afternoon, the Parson allowed the boys to drive their mother into Hightown, where they sold the remainder of their game for a dollar. This handy sum enabled them to buy a good supply of ammunition, and treat their mother to ice-cream.

The butcher who bought their squirrels also agreed to give them forty cents for the skunk-hide when they brought it in, and they returned home full of pride in their day's gain. It had been a time of unalloyed pleasure; a real rarity in their secluded lives.

CHAPTER XIII.

FARM LORE.

PERHAPS there is nothing that will so thoroughly develop a boy with active brain and average energy as to bury him two miles deep in the woods, on a grub-patch.

Does the doubtful reader ask how?

Well, he becomes a child of Nature, and is thrown wholly on his own resources. Then there is no danger of contamination from evil associates, nor indeed from anything else. The youth is left to the impulses of his own solitary genius.

But if anyone still remains dubious about the truth of this theory he is referred to Parson Flint's logic. He himself had been "born and raised in the back-woods," and was accustomed to regard himself as a fine example of its advantages.

Now, that his family was fully anchored on the farm, Parson Flint was happy.

There was no longer any danger of the boys "standing in the way of sinners, or sitting in the seat of the scornful." He could go away to an appointment and have no dread of finding the youths in a fight with some son of Belial upon his return; besides, an eternal task was possible, and so all chance for idle habits was averted.

Therefore, as we have said, the Parson was happy.

But lest the reader should fancy this repetition common-place, we must remind him that as the Apostle looked upon it, "happiness" was an entirely different article from the usual types of felicity. To him it was often a kind of congenial dismalness; a real relish of "hard trials and great tribulations," since he believed that these would work out for him a "far more exceeding and eternal weight of glory."

Even in rare fits of hilarity his face always kept an undersmear of the solemnity with which he looked upon life. If betrayed into extraordinary mirth he usually recovered quickly, and often relapsed into his usual sobriety with an inward groan;—a kind of secret plea for pardon upon such weakness.

Many among his parishioners failed to appreciate such strange enjoyment, and some of them thought him sour and morose. Only among those who had outlived all the sunshine of youth was the Parson's style of thought and conduct ,fully appreciated.

It was very seldom that he attracted children, and when obliged to respond to his advances, they usually got away from him at the first opportunity. He always asked so many embarrassing questions:

"Are you good? Do you behave yourselves? Do you ever forget to say your prayers? Do you ever tell lies or say bad words?"

During this catechism his grim face usually abashed the children very much, and by natural instinct they always gave the most favorable accounts of themselves

The Parson was a true type of old-time Methodist spirit

and energy. He utterly abjured everything that did not accord with his standards of piety and religious consistency. It was his own ambition to rear his sons after this inflexible pattern, and that too before their moral bones had hardened. Every immaturity of boyish thought or freak of juvenile mischief was regarded by the Parson as certain evidence of "original sin;" and he undertook by what seemed to him inspired means to reform and bring them up in the way they should go.

But even now that these wayward youths were secluded on a farm, the Parson had to be absent much of the time, for Hightown circuit was by no means a small charge. When, therefore, duty called the Apostle from home, the boys often followed the devices of their own imaginations.

Being deprived of companions of their own species, they sought others, which, if not so interesting, were at least tolerable substitutes. In their loneliness they studied the animals upon the farm, and conceived many queer ideas respecting them.

The place had sundry specimens of stock, such as an extra horse; a half-dozen sheep; two or three breeds of chickens; ten or a dozen hogs; a fine Durham calf; and what was more remarkable, a scrub donkey for which the boys had traded a couple of sheep to one of their prairie neighbors To the hungry minds of the youths all these animals became reasoning, thinking creatures, expressing something in every feature and motion

As Adam is said to have done, the boys named "all the beasts of the field," and very few of the names were entirely fanciful, generally being suggested by some peculiarity of the animal considered.

For instance, the extra horse, a tall, short, clumsy brute, was at first called "Bobtail." His caudal appendage was very short, having first been broken and then cut off by his former cruel owners, who tried to make him pull a load by it when he balked, a bad habit he had if put in a team.

The loss of his tail had rendered "Bobtail" moody and sullen, so that his owners sold him to the Parson for a song. He worked very well alone, but when hitched up with another horse would not budge an inch. The boys soon rechristened him "Pe-coob-coob," this was the sound of a "nicker" he always gave when anyone approached the lot to feed him.

"Pe-coob-coob" had a head as long as a water-cask, and looked as solemn as the white horse in Revelation. Like the Parson he "meditated" much, and while doing so always stood under a particular sapling which the boys called his "fig-tree;" here he would doze for hours, switching his stub tail up and down, and occasionally reaching around to brush a fly from his sides with his nose.

At such times his under-lip hung down an inch or more below the upper; and he had a habit of drawing it back and up at one corner, as if making a wry mouth at the remembrance of past sorrows. While trotting he had the motions of a stamp-mill, and this was a powerful inducement for the rider to let him walk, a gait which "Pe-coob-coob" much preferred. When driven to a bob-sled or plow, he would stop at intervals to rest, and at such times he would look back as if to explain the situation, while no amount of persuasion would induce him to move until he felt quite ready. By Nathan and William this habit was much appreciated, because they wanted to rest oftener than the horse did, especially when plowing among the grubs and roots.

The pet calf was called "De-big-head," owing to the extraordinary size of its cranium, which winged by its tobacco-leaf like ears, struck the boys as something excessively comical.

The donkey was called "Ump-ump," which is as nearly as his title can be spelled. The name arose from the following incident:

When brought to the farm and turned into the lot, the donkey created an extraordinary sensation in all its occupants, but especially in the mind of Daniel. Daniel's tail had never been tampered with, and so for a Parson's horse, he took quite a cheerful view of life. His curiosity was consuming. He looked upon the new arrival with amazement, and approached him gingerly, a few steps at a time, sending forth at intervals a loud snort of salutation.

Every few feet he would cautiously pause, and if the jack made a movement, would start back as if fearful the unheard of phenomenon might go off. When finally the donkey raised his thick head and wagged his ponderous ears back and forth in lazy majesty, the horse whirled and trotted away a few yards, only to begin his approach again with more ostentatious caution, approaching nearer the dread object of his wondering investigation.

At last, concluding that "Ump-ump" was not an infernal

machine, Daniel concentrated all his sociability. in a sudden mighty rush, and undertook to seize the donkey's neck with his teeth. But to his astonishment the victim turned tail, reefed his ears and fled around the lot, Daniel following in hot pursuit.

Presently the horse ran him into a corner from which there was no escape. He was about to reach out for a mouthful of back when there arose a long-drawn, terror-stricken "Haa-w-w-e-aw-e-aww" from the new arrival, who promptly presented his rear, and when his pursuer came within range, said vigorously, "Ump-ump! Ump-ump!" at the same time kicking so rapidly that Daniel was entirely held at bay.

The watching boys witnessed this remarkable encounter with yells of laughter, and ever afterwards called the donkey "Ump-ump."

There were belonging to the farm three principal hogs and several others of lesser importance. The first of the notable three was presented to Nathan by a Hightown physician. He was a sickly-looking brute, but owing to change of scenery and good care this animal grew into a long, slim, spike-nosed rooter of remarkable appetite. He was known as "Doctor," or "Lop-ear," according to the humor of his owner. Although nearly six feet in length, he was little more than a foot through. He had a tail-position, but no tail; and in fly time he constantly twitched the place where this missing member should have been. His ears were like cabbage-leaves, entirely concealing his small eyes, over which they hung, two vast, grisly concaves. So large were they, and so pendant that it was hard for the animal to hear; he was obliged to raise his head very high in order to tell when the hogs were called to feed.

"Lop-ear's" mouth extended far back toward his shoulders; and when corn was thrown to him, he always snatched three or four ears and ran off to enjoy them alone. But despite a ferocious appetite, he never acquired any fat, and this was a standing marvel until he was finally butchered; then the Parson said that "his lights had grown to his ribs."

The second of these notable porkers was a plump, pretty white Berkshire, to which dirt would hardly stick. A farmer's wife on the prairie had kindly presented this pig to Mrs. Flint, and the animal was named after her donor. Maggie was a very friendly, sociable hog, and generally got the best of everything, which made her very proud.

The third hog of the trio was Maggie's antithesis. She was a sharp-nosed, wicked-eyed, long-tailed vixen, with a pair of keen, curving tusks. A dog had bitten off one of her ears, and the other, a sharp, triangular appendage, stuck straight up from her head like a jackal's. She had a cruel voracity, and was the embodiment of all that was low and cunning.

The boys called her "Hation," a corruption of Hessian, which, in the Parson's estimation, stood for everything mean and base. "Hation" deserved her name. She was rapacious, thievish and without conscience. She was artful, hateful and low-bred; a very outlaw among decent swine.

During the summer "Hation" continually wallowed in the mire, and most of the time wore a ball of dried mud nearly the size of a quart cup on her tail, while her sides were plastered all over. If there happened to be a hole anywhere in the fence she could find it; and if there was not, she often managed to make one. When she got into the field to root up the corn, she entirely forgot the place of entrance; but once out again, she always knew where to crawl in. The Parson was greatly annoyed at her depredations; for a long time the place of her entry was unknown, and William said she must climb the fence.

At last her ravages of the corn-field became so persistent, that the boys determined to watch her: so one day after Coon had dogged her from the field, they piped her afar off, and witnessed the following astonishing exhibition of her cunning methods.

"Hation" went grumbling off down the road, stopping occasionally to look and listen. Not perceiving anyone in pursuit she worked her way around the field-fence, stopping finally at the branch. Here a rotten tree-trunk had fallen across a panel and mashed it down. One end of this log rested inside the field, and a long pole had been laid over the crushed rails, leaving a space of two feet between it and the log.

After meditating a few minutes, and glancing suspiciously all about, "Hation" mounted the rotten log, and deliberately walked along this bridge under the pole and entered the field. The boys were both astonished and overjoyed. They hastened back to the house and told the incident to the Parson, but he hooted at such an incredible story. Yet so positive were the boys in their details that finally he told them to drive "Hation" out again, and he himself would go to see if she could really do such a thing. The boys obeyed, and then with the Parson cut across the field to reach the spot before the marauder had time to get there.

Presently they heard the scolding growl of the old thief as she approached along the fence. The Parson got a stout hickory club, and telling the boys to get out of sight, hid himself in the weeds near Hation's bridge, and awaited her coming. She reached the log, stopped as usual and seemed to be thinking. Finally she mounted sullenly and began her old tactics. Upon reaching the fence she seemed to scent danger, halted, swung her mud-ball, wiggled her solitary ear and appeared to meditate a retreat. But love of mischief finally won the decision, and with a guttural grunt she stuck her head under the overlying pole to enter the field. This was the Parson's opportunity. He sprang up in wrath, and smote her a mighty blow along the earless side of her head, knocking her clear off the log into a big mudhole of the branch. As the blow took effect, she uttered a loud scream, and lunged about in the mire until she regained her feet, and having done so went barking off down the bed of the stream, never halting until she was out of sight.

The boys roared with laughter, but the Apostle remarked savagely as he hurled the club in Hation's wake:

"There, ye old torment! I reckon it's the last time ye'll be wantin' to try any more of sich shines. Mebbe ye'll want to dig a tunnel next."

He then proceeded to mend the broken fence-panel, quoting as a lesson for the boys, "A stitch in time saves nine" But

Hation was completely cured this time; she never got into the field again.

The most joyless hour of the old wretch was at feeding time. With her sharp tusks she would mercilessly rip up the sides of her companions, and if not prevented would drive them away from the food. However the boys knew her tricks, and had collected an arsenal of stones, cobs and clubs in one corner of the lot with which they kept Hation at bay while the other hogs ate. Many a crack did she get upon her ugly snout as she tried to spear her associates. After receiving one she would run barking off to a safe distance, and stand there sullenly working the button on her nose, saying "Roooh!" When the other pigs had eaten a fair share of the corn or slops, then the guard would retire, and Hation would sweep in like a besom of wrath, making everything fly before her, especially what corn might be left.

※ ※ ※

Special chickens had their titles. The big Cochin-China rooster was called "Co-hoke," from an ejaculation that always escaped him when surprised or excited.

A favorite hen was called "Ala" because she held her wings in such a queer fashion during hot weather. In their old blue-backed spelling-book, the boys found that the Latin "ala" meant wing, and immediately the old hen received that name. "Ala" was an exceedingly happy hen, and frequently sang a song of sweet content which sounded much as follows:

"Kwaw-aw-aw-awk; kwak kwak, kna-aw-a-ak-awk!"

She could cackle louder and longer than any other hen on the place, and when imposed upon could, and would fight to beat anything.

The big lone gander was named "Crank," from the note of his terrible din while attacking "Co-hoke." For the rooster considered the presence of this stranger in his harem an intrusion, and forever-tried to resent it. Invariably however, he got the worst of the battle. The powerful gander would seize a bunch of feathers upon Co-hoke's back, hang onto them and beat terrifically with his long wings until the plumage came out. Then Co-hoke would flee to the fence top, but the victor, shaking the feathers from his mouth would elevate his long neck and march about, screaming triumphantly at the routed enemy.

From its strident note of warning when anything strange happened about the place, the single Guinea-hen was called "Pot-rack!"

The old mother-cat, always with a brood of kittens at her heels was called "Hoo-woo," it being the sound she made when purring.

The Thomas-cat, ever wise-looking and sedate, was known as "Shikespoke," a beastly corruption of Shakespeare, who, the boys read in their school-reader, was the wisest man in history.

Shikespoke was the laziest cat in the world. He would lie under a hot stove, or in the chimney corner until the very hair was scorched from his back. When the heat finally became unbearable he would squirm, maow and wriggle until forced to vacate the place. Then he would slowly drag himself out, arch his spine and look the very picture of injury and discontent.

Thus through the entire domestic fraternity, down to the smallest animal that merited any special attention, the boys invented some sort of odd name for them all. Even the Apostle finally adopted many of these names, although at first he used them only in sarcastic contempt for their "foolishness." To the lonely urchins however, all these animals became pets and companions, furnishing numerous diversions for them as time went by.

Occasionally they may have been cruel to these dumb playmates, but never with real intention to be so. And if they briskly clubbed Hation, or punched Ump-Ump with a sharp stick, or threw clods at the chattering Guinea-fowl to the hurt of these creatures, it was soon forgotten by both persecutors and victims. Usually the punished animal got an extra feed, or some other mark of special attention to offset what scare or hurt had come to it.

CHAPTER XIV.

"THE ROD OF CORRECTION."

CORN-PLANTING had gone by. It was the first work of this kind the boys had ever done, and before the job was finished they were sick and tired of its monotony.

But one trifling incident had happened during the time, and this the boys had completely forgotten until it was called to their minds by the Parson and a five-foot hickory; then they had cause for remembering the matter very distinctly.

One day while dropping corn from a tin pail in which the supply was carried, Nathan was bare-footed, and happened to tread upon a hidden black-berry brier. He sprang into the air, and in the awkward lunge spilled nearly a quart of corn on the ground, at the same time managing to kick some dirt over it.

TRAMPED ON A BRIER.

Being hurt as well as strongly provoked, he did not stop to pick up what he had spilled, but covered it over with an inch of soil and left it to bear witness against him in the day of its resurrection. In three or four weeks from that time the fatal day dawned.

When the corn was up about hand high, Parson Flint harnessed Pe-coob-coob to a small plow and went out to cultivate the crop. He took the boys along with him and said:

"Now seize yer hoes and foller along behind me; un-

170

kiver all the stalks the plow throws dirt on, an' teck out all the weeds that I fail to reach."

The day was decidedly sultry, and Pe-coob-coob was full of the "meditating" spirit. He wanted to reflect upon his past life, and evidently thought this could be done best when he was sheltered under the shadow of his favorite sapling in the barn-lot.

But the Parson was full of energy, and had no patience with the old horse's obstinacy, especially as the sun grew hotter and the sweltering corn-field compared so exasperatingly with the shady side of the house, where he longed to be. Moreover the plowing had to be done in a spot off which forest growth had been newly cleared; and the plow point would catch in sundry grubs and roots which lay in ambush to wreck the Parson's morals. When the plow came in contact with one of these Satanic devices its handles would flop about astonishingly; and as the Apostle very often had to hold the plow with one hand in order to slap Pe-coob-coob's rascally old ribs with the lines, the perverse handles sometimes struck him amidships with terrible force, knocking quick ejaculations out of him unawares. Three or four hours of such tribulations had rendered the Parson like Nebuchadnezzar's fiery furnace, seven times hotter than he was wont to be heated, and caused him to project a sermon on the future condition of the lost.

SOMETIMES STRUCK HIM AMIDSHIPS.

13

While thus exasperated he reached the spot where Nathan's accident had formerly occurred; and lo, what at a distance he had supposed to be a thrifty grass-plot turned out to be a mass of cornstalks, all growing finely, and which seemed to be doing much better than the legitimate planting, despite their very crowded condition.

The Apostle understood the situation at once and looked up quickly to call the boys. But they had slipped off to the house for a drink, and having taken it had been attracted by their mother's presence in the cool sitting room, where they stretched themselves out upon the floor to take a rest.

Plowing angrily through the bunch of corn, the Parson reached the fence, and drove the horse into a corner, where the tired brute was glad to stand without hitching. Then jerking off a hickory sprout some five feet in length, that tapered beautifully to a hard bud on the end, the Apostle strode towards the house with retribution in his eye, and the fell instrument of execution in his hand.

William lay near the front door, and he caught sight of the avenger coming to overtake them; so just as the irate Parson stepped upon the back porch, the boys slid silently out of the front door and in a jiffy were back in the field, hard at work. Both the culprits supposed it was their desertion that had aroused the Nemesis of justice, yet they wondered at such extreme measures for so trifling an offense.

"Whacher reckon he's got that hick'ry fer?" asked William replanting a missing hill of corn from seed in his pocket.

"What 'se always got one fer?" replied Nathan disgustedly, emphasizing his reply by a tremendous thump of the hoe upon a hard clod. "He wuz a-goin' to larrup us for restin' when he wuz at work." Then at the thought he uttered a horrible objurgation: "I'll jist be diddle-de-diddle-de-daggon if I don't wish the dern corn wuz in Halifax and him with it!"

"Where's them triflin' boys?" asked the Parson sternly as he entered the house and did not see them.

Their mother had not at all understood the boys' sudden and silent exit until she heard the Parson's heavy step. Then perceiving the gad in his horny fist she sighed deeply and said:

"They were here, but they went back to their work awhile ago."

Dear old heart! From her non-committal tone one might have thought it had been an hour since the boys went back to the field.

The Apostle made no comment, but turning with a jerk he started again for the spot where the boys were now bestowing most laborious efforts upon the corn.

"He's a-comin'," said William in a low voice; and just then Nathan having finished his row straightened up and saw the stern-faced Parson striding towards them with "the rod of correction" gripped in his redoubtable fist. It happened that he reached William first, whom he asked with a sharp snap to his words:

"Young man, was it *you* that spilt a peck of corn over yander,"—pointing towards the place with his switch,—"and then kivered it up to go to waste?"

In a flash Nathan now understood everything, and from

his hard inflection he knew that the Parson meant business. The first second brought to his heart a kind of sickening dread; but the next, for the first time in his life, all fear of punishment left him.

As the Apostle spoke William looked up, and with his fear-haunted face all blossoming with relief answered what was rather a novelty for him;—the straight truth.

"No, sir; it *was n't* me."

"I done it," remarked Nathan in a tone of dogged unconcern. "I tramped on a thorn that made me jump, and when the corn was spilled there was so much dirt in it I did n't stop to pick it up."

"No, I *see* ye did n't," said the Parson with a metallic rasp in his tones. "Ye kivered it up to save a little work, and act a lie because ye thought it 'ud never be found out."

He paused to let these words sink deep in the culprit's mind, or, at least, to get a fair start before proceeding to drive them still further in with the gad. Nathan hoed along industriously, and made no reply. Somehow he felt strangely brave; —even a little defiant. And the contrast of this sensation with that other feeling, which can be described only as a cramping recoil of body and soul under the slow torture of the Parson's threats, quite astonished him and he grew almost reckless.

After an ominous interval in which William pulled up several stalks of corn instead of weeds, so nervous was he, the Apostle asked with that bitten-off inflection which meant an end of parley

"What did ye kiver up that corn fer, an' try to act a lie?"

" 'Cause I knowed you 'd lick the hide off uv me anyway, if ye found it out!" barked Nathan in a voice that fairly paralyzed William, and so took the Parson aback that his jaw dropped fully an inch, while the sprout hung limp in his relaxing hand.

But it was only for a moment. His jaw shut with a click, and his fingers tightened on the butt of the switch like a vise. With three long strides he reached the foolish youth, and seizing him by the arm rained a perfect tempest of blows over his shoulders and back. Nathan had on no coat, and the punishment hurt him like fire; but he clamped his teeth and held his breath until he was like to have burst.

"Ye 'll *sass* me, will ye?"—whack, swish, killip! "Ye 've come to a purty pass now, ain't ye?"—whack, swish, whack! "But I 'll learn ye a thing ur two yet if I 'm not mistaken," snapped out the chastiser between his vigorous blows.

"Beat! beat! lick! *Kill* me if ye want to," screamed Nathan in a perfect frenzy of rage and pain. "I want to die anyhow! Beat! beat! kill me an' be done with it!"

And the Parson freely accepted the invitation; he by no means spared either rod or child. Beginning afresh on the boy's shoulders, he worked carefully down; but the harder he lashed the louder Nathan screamed for him to lay it on.

By this time William had recovered his wandering wits, and he verily believed Nathan was being murdered. Bawling at the top of his voice he started for the house as fast as the stone-bruise on his heel would permit. His mother heard

him yelping, and came to meet him, knowing that trouble was
afloat, although the **full** import of it did not dawn upon her
until she caught sight of the fracas **in** the field . William came
up with long crow-hops, panting and calling:

"OH MA!   COME QUICK."

"Oh, ma, come quick!
Pa's a-killin' Nathan!"

But from the noise made
by the victim it was **evident**
that he lacked much of being
dead just at that moment, for
he could still b e h e a r d
screeching viciously:

"Kill me! beat, beat! kill
me!" and the Parson, nothing
loth, was heartily fulfilling
at least a part of his demand.

In his descent over the boy's body he reached the legs,
and Nathan's trousers being rolled up nearly to his knees, the
executioner's eyes caught sight of the naked calves; quick as
a flash the lithe hickory lapped around them, its hard bud
cutting the skin like a lash.   Just as Mrs. Flint reached the
spot the blood flowed.

"Oh, pa, look!   You're cutting the blood out of the boy,"
she cried in an agonized voice.   Then, seeing that the Parson
was too much absorbed in business to heed her words, she did
what she had never done before; interfering, she grasped the
brawny arm that was flaying her child and stopped the
blows.

This unheard of thing brought the Parson to his senses. He let go Nathan's arm, but from very force of habit began those inevitable questions that always followed such exercises:

"D 'ye think ye 'll ever be guilty of the like of this ag'in?" but the boy was sobbing in his mother's arms; the first sign of weakness he had shown during the entire affair.

"Yes, yes; he will be good, pa; you 've whipped him enough; he won't be bad any more," replied Mrs. Flint, raining tears all over Nathan's head, the while holding him to her heart as if she never intended letting him go again.

The Parson feeling it his duty to act as if nothing unusual had happened, stood with arms out and hands on his hips, addressing Nathan as if it had been *he* that had promised reformation:

"Well, this ain't a circumstance to what I 'll give ye if ye ever do the like ag'in! Now, see if ye kin git back to yer work, and never do you try to sass me any more!"

Then to avoid any attempt to enforce these commands he turned and walked away. Old Pe-coob-coob was dozing comfortably in the fence corner, and the Parson started him going again, wreaking upon his stubborn old hide all the self-loathing and reactionary disgust that began to fill his heart. William went blubbering to work, but Nathan, weak from the nervous strain was taken to the house by his mother, who put a soft bandage on his wounded leg, crying bitterly as she did so. When it was done up with infinite tenderness, she rolled the trousers down over it to hide the wound; then she kissed him and whispered in his ear, while straining him to her breast:

"Be a good boy for my sake, Nathan. I believe it would kill mother to have such a thing happen again."

After a brief rest Nathan went back to his work, feeling very bitter and subdued. The Parson never afterwards referred to this episode; and for a long time was not nearly so prone to fault-finding, and did not find half so many excuses for correction as usual. It is fair to remark, too, that his manner greatly softened toward the boys; and he always looked uncomfortable when he saw Nathan examining his wounded leg. True, he said never a word about it; but what do words signify if the heart be all right?

William, however, marveled greatly, being much bedazzled. It was all so novel and unexpected. He remembered the scene long afterward with a feeling of awe; and somehow the subject seemed to be too impressive for light discussion. He seldom referred to it, and when he did speak of it always indicated it as "that time."

He could not understand what had aroused Nathan to such incredible disregard of the Parson's direful wrath, something William fancied must be next to the vengeance of God.

With Nathan it was a kind of moral epoch; one of those sudden awakenings of the nature, that bring to life ideas and qualities that lie dormant in growing youth. The punishment had been severe, but not nearly so much as William in his terror had imagined; and such occasions had been too common in the boys' lives for them to dwell upon it.

Nathan himself seemed thereafter to have clearer ideas of justice in the matter of punishments; and although punished often at other times, he submitted with lack of protest that secretly astonished the Parson, stern as he always was.

In many things the youth was a better and more obedient boy; so the Apostle once said to his wife,—and the good man felt his remorse very much modified on account of these results. Besides, he reasoned that the course he had taken was the Scriptural way, consequently it could not be wrong.

But always down in his heart Nathan seemed to hear that distressed whisper of his patient mother:

"Be a good boy for my sake, Nathan; I believe it would kill mother if this should happen again!"

CHAPTER XV.

"SOME FOOLISHNESS."

THE Summer, so full of hot, uncomfortable days dragged slowly along, and the latter part of July blackberry season came on. Fence corners on the farm and great patches of ground on the prairie, a mile away, were dense with bushes, from which jetty festoons of delicious fruit hung ripening every day.

The Parson's family gathered and took great loads of them to town until they became a drug on the market, after which they proceeded to can, preserve and "jell" them for winter's use.

One sultry afternoon, after having cooked dinner and cleared away the dishes, Mrs. Flint looked with a sigh of weariness upon three brimming buckets of berries that stood waiting immediate attention.

The Parson was dozing on the shady side of the house, tipped back in a splint-bottomed chair as usual, and holding "The Life of Nathan Bangs" loosely in one hand. The girls, who had spent the entire morning at the berry-patches, had eaten dinner and retired to the cool sitting-room, where they were enjoying a restful nap.

Everywhere the atmosphere was dancing with

heat-waves. All the leaves hung listlessly from their stems, and not a breath of air was stirring. Down at the lower side of the field a noisy rain-crow could be heard screaming, and a few puffy white clouds, known to the boys as "thunder-heads," were slowly rising in the West, pearly pink with the fierce rays of the already stooping sun. It was hardly a day to beget energy or stimulate one to great action; but Mrs. Flint was not a woman who hesitated long before any task that fell to her lot, so stirring up the embers of the kitchen fire, she was soon sweltering in steam from the simmering fruit.

A large brass kettle of 'slops was boiling on the back of the stove, and finding that the room it occupied was needed, she went to the porch to call one of the boys. They were perched upon the lot fence in the shade of a hickory sapling, making goose-quill pop-guns from which to shoot potato stoppers.

"Nathan, son; come empty this slop to the pigs for mother," called Mrs. Flint. "Be quick about it; I want the kettle."

Nathan jumped from the fence and went to obey, tread-ing gingerly through the burning dust of the road, and keep-ing in the shade as much as possible to save his bare feet.

"Be careful it do n't slop over and scald you," warned his mother, handing him the kettle at the door. "The stuff is boiling hot."

At these last words a very wicked idea entered Nathan's head. He had noticed old Hation lying in a fence corner about thirty yards from the pig-trough; she generally deposited her-self there about feeding time in order to be first at the feast.

As he went by, Nathan coughed at William; that youth instantly suspended his work to see what would happen. The loud splatter of the slop when poured into the trough aroused Hation in a hurry. She came bolting around the corner, full of expectations of a solitary meal, for none of the other hogs were in sight. Upon seeing Nathan she halted abruptly at a respectful distance, signifying both her caution and discontent in a deep, growling grunt. Great was her astonishment, however, when the enemy retired quickly, and climbed upon the fence! This was her opportunity; she broke into a quick gallop for the trough and did not stand on ceremony, but plunged her slim snout into the slop nearly to her eyes.

"Weee! Wooh! Wooh! Wooh!" she exclaimed loudly.

Then elevating her stinging nose at an angle of thirty degrees, she went barking off in the direction from which she had come, stopping about five yards away to reflect.

Presently it was evident that greed was stronger than pain; she seemed not to comprehend that the trouble was with the slop, but evidently fancied some new kind of club had warmed her snout. So after a short time she began slowly to work her way back towards the trough, and when no objections were made to her approach, she made a second rush, this time plunging into the slop with both fore-feet, and fathoming it about six inches for what solids might be at the bottom.

"Weee! Wooh! Wooh! Wooh!"

"W-e-e-e-e! Booh! Boo, Boo-uh-wooh!" she screamed. .

Then bolting for the woods she did not stop before reaching a spot fifty yards away, under a big hickory tree.

The boys lay along the top of the fence, beating themselves, and nearly choking with wicked laughter. They could catch glimpses of the old vandal out in the brush, where with nose pointed at the ground, and the button on it working furiously, she would occasionally plow up the loam and dead leaves, saying "rooough!" which was doubtless some suicidal resolve, or swear-word in hog language.

When the slop had cooled so as to be eatable, the boys called the other hogs that were taking a siesta down at the branch; upon hearing the well-known signal they came up the fence in a long grunting file. In a short time Hation heard them eating and issued from her retirement, full of wrath, and was soon digging her companions in the ribs, fully revenging herself for the great disappointment.

After laughing until it didn't feel good any more, the boys called Coon and started on an aimless tramp towards the branch. When about half-way there, they saw the dog who as usual was trotting on ahead, suddenly jump a yard high, and upon coming down disappear like a black streak into the bushes. They found her by a huge rotten log, under which she was digging furiously. Such unusual actions led the boys to fancy that she must have chased some new kind of game, and they gave her every encouragement, even trying to overturn the log.

Presently Coon, who was already half buried in the hole she was digging uttered a smothered yelp, backed out with a hurried scramble and brought with her a big, pied chicken-snake, fully six feet long. As it came free of the log Coon gave it a flirt, and when it struck the ground she sprang after it, snapped gingerly a few times, finally snatching it by the middle and shaking it so fast it cracked like a whip. So rapidly did her head jerk that the excited boys could hardly see it, and they whooped with all their lungs in hearty applause.

When Coon dropped the reptile, there was no deader snake imaginable, and her proud owners added another lustrous item to the already long list of her virtues.

Tying a piece of stout string about the snake's neck, they took it back to the house to show their mother, and give her a glowing account of Coon's prowess in capturing it. Mrs. Flint told them what kind of a serpent it was, relating at the same time an experience of her own with a similar reptile. Then she told them to carry it away, and throw it upon some brush-heap, so that they would never by any chance get its bones or teeth in their bare feet.

They sauntered out to the barn lot, and happened to meet Shikespoke on the way. He had been on a foraging expedition at the stable. When he saw the snake his hair rose, and with a spit he scaled the fence, going in long leaps to the kitchen. The boys laughed at his antics, and then sat down on a big stump to give the snake a more thorough examination. Upon pulling its mouth open with sticks they were greatly surprised not to find any dangerous teeth. It had been their belief that all serpents had fangs, and the absence of these weapons in the present specimen was very puzzling. William finally suggested that Coon must have shaken them out. In a short time he asked Nathan:

"Whacher reckon made Shike act so when he seen it?"

While attending school in Hightown William had begun the study of English grammar; but up to this time he had no idea that it should affect his talk on a wood's farm. He thought the study specially designed to embellish Sunday-school speeches and catechisms.

"He wuz skeered, I guess," replied Nathan briefly.

"My! Whacher suppose he *would* do if it was tied to him?" asked William, as he dangled the snake by its string.

No sooner was this outlandish suggestion conceived than it was tried. Nathan went promptly to the kitchen, and found Shikespoke curled snugly in a basket of carpet-rags in a corner. Picking him up, and covering his eyes with one hand, he went back to the lot. Then, while William held Shike's head under his arm, Nathan made a slip-noose in the end of the string, put the animal's tail more than halfway through it and drew the loop tight. Shike winced and uttered a smothered "maow" as the cord pinched him, and then William let him go. He sneezed, winked his eyes lazily, and started for the house again.

When the string pulled taut, he looked around and suddenly saw the strange appendage to his tail within two feet of him, and on the move. In a second his eyes became big as half-dollars; every hair of his body stood on end, and he fairly swelled with excitement and terror.

"K-h-h-h-h! Woww!" he exclaimed with a spit and howl, springing forward as if shot from a gun.

But this abrupt motion jerked the snake all over him,  and turned him silly in a trice. He sprang five feet into the air and looked down in time to see the snake rising after him, at which he yowled in frenzy, spitting so hard it seemed that he might loosen his lungs. Coming down squarely on the snake, he next described a fine curve some ten

"K-H-H-H! Weow!"

feet in length, and went raving insane to find the serpent hanging over his back as he struck the ground.

Then he tried to flee away and leave the enemy. Skipping over the rail-fence into the corn-field, he started up between two rows at railroad speed. With every jump he made the snake lapped around a cornstalk, or jerked forward, piling all over him in a life-like fashion that kept him going and spitting like a steam engine. Reaching the further side of the field, he mounted the fence to rest; but turning around to see how far he had got, he perceived the horrible burden of his tail about two-thirds of the way up, and right under him, swinging back and forth as if seeking a place to crawl along side him.

Suddenly Shikespoke felt completely rested; the place was in the hot sun, anyway, and there came to his mind a good cool place under the house. He started to pre-empt it, going about

fifteen feet the first jump. Just as he struck the ground he
was rendered explosive by the snake's winding around his neck,
and sliding off right in front of him. He struck at it with
one paw, peeling a flake of skin from its now bruised body;
then springing clear over it, panting and dizzy, he started
anew for the house. What he was going after had entirely been
forgotten, but there was no stopping for that reason; he was
consumed with a raging desire to go somewhere.

Swish, slap, snap, crack, went the snake among the cornstalks, and the watching boys were apprised that Shike was
coming home. On he came, clambered up a fence-stake,
jumped into the garden, staggered through the paling gate into
the yard and disappeared around the corner of the house.

Suddenly the wicked boys were almost paralyzed by a series of shouts and snorts from the Apostle.

"Yah-h-here! Yow! 'Scat! Git out! Good fathers above!
What on earth!!!"

The boys ran to the front yard, and around the corner of
the house appeared Shike, eyes green, and panting mouth wide
open. Running for a tree near the gate, the poor creature struggled up it as long as he could wiggle a paw, reached a fork
twelve feet from the ground and threw himself into it, as nearly
exhausted as a cat ever was.

The Parson had been meditating in the shade after his
usual fashion; but at last becoming unusually drowsy, he had
grown tired of holding his book; so laying his chair forward
for a head rest, he had stretched himself out upon the grass,
bracing his feet against a small tree that grew against the gar-

den-fence. In this prone situation he completely blocked Shike's passage, and the cat, now hardly able to keep its feet, jumped feebly over him and dragged the snake across his hands which were folded upon his stomach.

Thus rudely awakened, he sprang to his feet with a yell. Perhaps a suspicion flashed across his mind that the arch enemy of mankind had once more appeared in original form. But a second or two sufficed to inform him what was the matter, and he strode indignantly around to the front yard. Here he found the boys, now very remorseful at Shike's predicament, standing at the foot of the tree, trying to coax the poor cat down; but the victim stared at them with wide eyes and pulsating sides, too much scared and worn out to move.

The Parson said with a steely rasp:

"Why ain't ye always a-tormentin' something! Ye act as if Satan himself possessed ye! I'm a notion to frail ye till ye hides wo n't hold shucks!"

Then as this awful threat died away on the hot air, he added, "You pore triflin' creatures! If you do n't sup sorrow before you die, I miss my guess!"

The situation was dreadfully strained and embarrassing; but as the threatener did not at once proceed to carry out his "notion" about "frailing" them, Nathan took out his knife and began to shin up the tree to cut the string and free poor Shike from his dread pursuer. He had just time to sever the cord when the cat, imagining that his enemy had revived, scrambled to the very top of the tree, where he remained in security until nightfall.

The boys did not feel at all easy under the Parson's lurid eyes, and would at once have sneaked away had he not halted them with the words, still raspy and rebuking:

"See if ye can go an' ask yer mother fer some grease; then git and grease the buggy, and do you let that be the very last!"

The boys hurried away, breathing easier.

Now that all danger was past and Shikespoke once more safe, they began to remember the funny parts of the episode, and occasionally gave vent to bursts of smothered laughter. Hunting up the wrench and a piece of board to hold the axle while the wheel was removed, they rolled the buggy from its shed and set about business.

Pe-coob-coob was standing under his favorite sapling, looking as solemn as possible, and occasionally rubbing flies off his front legs with his long jaw. Ump-Ump was lying in a corner of the lot dreaming, with his nose almost on the ground. But at the noise of the falling shafts, as the boys rolled the buggy out, the sleeper awoke Slowly getting up he twisted his tail round and humped his spine in a yawn, shaking first his immense ears until they flapped, and then extending the exercise to his dusty body. Sauntering indolently toward the boys, he stopped about ten feet off to inspect their labors. Here he cast his long ears forward to shade his eyes, and appeared to wonder in a lazy sort of fashion what they were doing.

By this time Nathan had taken off a hind wheel, which he stood holding while William applied grease to the axle. Noticing the donkey looking on so near by, Nathan clucked to his brother, and then with a quick jerk rolled the wheel at the wondering animal. As he saw the odd-looking thing approaching, Ump-Ump gave a start of surprise; then whirling suddenly, he spread his ear-canvas to the breeze and sailed· mincingly away, looking from side to side over his shoulders as he went.

By some strange chance the wheel followed directly in his wake; he took fright and broke into a gallop down the lot, but when very near him the wheel grazed a tree, and after wobbling a few yards further fell round and round, like a copper flipped upon a table. This strange phenomenon completely overthrew Ump-Ump's presence of mind; he flew toward the gate, and finding it shut, jumped at a wide crack between the top fence-rail and the rider, piling over in the road outside in a confused heap.

Jumping up, covered head and ears with dust, he stuck his tail straight out behind and started for the woods, screaming at the top of his voice:

"Yaww-w-ee-aw-ee-aww-ee,"—just as the Parson on his way to the lot appeared at the front gate.

The comical sight was too much even for his stoicism; he snorted with half-suppressed laughter. The boys saw it and yelled aloud, slapping their sides in convulsions of mirth. Even old Pe-coob-coob seemed to smile as he raised his long head and twitched the corner of his lip.

As usual the Parson's mirth was short-lived; and in atonement for it he remarked with grim severity:

"At it ag'in, air ye!"

But he was at a disadvantage this time. He had already

laughed, and William made him grin besides, by sticking his arm straight out behind for a tail, and racing across the lot with a bawl, like the fleeing donkey.

The buggy being greased, Daniel was hitched to it, and the Parson prepared to go away to a distant appointment. That the boys might be prevented from any further outrages he said to them with a warning note in his voice:

· "I want ye to git yer hoes and go to diggin' them pota-ters,"—pointing to a patch near the lot. "They're to be tuck to market next week. As fast as ye git 'em dug, pile 'em under that tree in the yard, where the sun won't burn 'em; I want to find 'em all there when I git back. Ye'd better remember like-wise that if I hear of any more of yer shines, the way I'll warm yer back 'll be some!"

With this comforting assurance he went into the house, got his saddle-bags, and without a further word to anyone—not even to his faithful wife, who was suffocating over the hot stove—drove away.

WENT HUNTING.

CHAPTER XVI.

MORE FOOLISHNESS.

AFTER their numerous escapades the Parson often told the boys that their "hearts were as prone to evil as the sparks are to fly upwards;" not being very skillful theologians, and nearly always having guilty consciences, they supposed this diagnosis must be true.

The fact is, they often seemed to find even in the most innocent appearing things unheard of suggestions of mischief, which were always followed out with calamitous results. But when the fruits of their evil doings and thoughtless pranks became apparent, the culprits were always surprised, and would protest the most utter innocence of intention if called to account. Yet, alas! When the Pastor had "settled" with them for one misdemeanor, it was their misfortune the next hour to get into some other scrape, worse if possible than the former. The persistent bent to "evil" much vexed the Parson, and caused him to groan in spirit.

When he drove away to a two-days' meeting, and disappeared down the winding forest road, it lacked about three hours until sunset; so the boys took their gun, with which Nathan had become quite expert, and set off on a hunting expedition.

Roasting ears had long been tempting the squirrels, and these frisky thieves were already making great havoc in the rows of corn next to the field fence. It was not long before the hunters returned with a half-dozen fine fat specimens, and secured their mother's promise to make them a pot-pie next day. Then being too tired to dig any potatoes that evening they strolled out to the barn-lot and caught horse-flies off Pecoob-coob, tying feathers to them with a fine thread, in order to trace the flight of the insects when they were turned loose.

While thus experimenting they saw "Crank" and "Cohoke" come together in one of their ferocious encounters, and for the space of a minute the feathers flew. Then, as usual, the gander came off victorious, with a mouth full of plumes. He flapped his broad wings and stalked screaming about, while "Co-hoke" flew upon the fence and began to crow lustily, like some coward that seeks safety before he boasts His disgraceful conduct quite disgusted the boys, and they forthwith planned to teach him a good lesson.

That night when all the fowls were quietly roosting, the conspirators went out to the poultry yard and caught the gander. He was squatting on the ground as near as possible to the spot where the rooster would fly down from his perch next morning. The snickering boys placed him on a broad shelf close beside his enemy, and tied the two gladiators together by their legs with a stout piece of cord. This began to seem so funny that they added two or three old fighters among the hens to the group, and then sneaked away to bed, indulging in subdued laughter and sundry speculations as to what would happen on the morrow.

About daybreak Co-hoke's loud crowing awakened them and they crept to a window to see what might come to pass. As it grew lighter they heard the rooster's usual note of surprise

"Co-hoke-co-hoke, co-hoky!"

In a minute or two more he uttered a loud squawk and flew down off the perch, jerking three much astonished hens with him. Their combined weight dislodged the gander, and he followed them, hitting the ground with a thump. Crank was bewildered; but presently recovering his wits he pitched into Co-hoke with a screech of rage. After two or three feints at fighting, the rooster wanted to go away; but he had not gone three feet before he brought up at the end of his tether, and Crank went at him again.

Then the old hens wanted to go to breakfast, probably to hunt an early worm; but they too had limits. For the next few minutes there was a perfect tempest of wings, legs, necks, feathers, squawks and screams that probably had not been heard since the time of Noah's ark.

Prominent in the entire fray was the gander, plucking feathers first from the rooster, and then from a hen, each time spitting out the mouthful he had got and going after more, while his powerful wings kept flapping and knocking his victims in every direction.

At last Co-hoke gave up in despair, and lay upon his side while Crank walked up and down his anatomy screaming victoriously. The defeated rooster croaked a dismal minor, while the scandalized hens lay scattered about as audience.

At this interesting juncture the snorting boys saw their mother issue from the porch side-door and hurry to the rescue. They slipped back to bed, but when called to breakfast, Mrs. Flint soon made them ashamed of their transparent attempts to play innocent. She administered a severe rebuke which actually hurt them more than the Parson's thrashings usually did.

Breakfast finished, they went to digging potatoes. It was not the most delightful work imaginable; for on account of wet weather some of the tubers had begun to rot, and while grabbling in the dirt the boys were frequently exasperated by clawing into one that was far gone in the last stages of decay.

William had just unearthed one of the largest of these, and was gazing at it with nose puckered at its unsavory odor, when he spied Shikespoke sitting demurely in the shade on the further side of the fence. Shike had recovered from his violent exercise of the previous day, and was lazily making his morning toilet. With closed eyes he combed himself deliberately, all unconscious of danger.

Just as he raised his head to begin dressing a new spot, William launched the rotten potato at him, ten feet away; the mushy thing struck him fairly on the forehead, bursting all over him.

Shike jumped a yard high and spit, certain another serpent must be after him, and not being at all reassured as he fled by a loud "ha! ha!" from the wicked boys. Making a bee-line for the barn, his usual place of refuge, the cat climbed into the hay-mow, and spent the next hour cleaning his coat, and wiping the potato from his face with a handy paw.

The boys resumed work and kept steadily at it until noon. Then while making heroic attacks upon the delicious pot-pie their mother had ready for them, they hear a well-known voice at the front gate: "Yaawww-ee-yaww-ee-yaww-ee-awww!"

It was the wanderer returned, seeming to have forgotten the scare that made him flee. Old Pe-coob-coob looked from the barn door and welcomed the arrival with an affectionate "nicker," as the boys turned him into the lot.

Steady work during the afternoon nearly completed the job of potato digging, and about an hour before sundown the boys were delighted beyond measure to see Uncle Clint of hunting fame drive up, on his way home from Centerville, where he had been visiting. With him were Wesley and Ames, his two sons, youths about the age of the Parson's boys, and the first young person to visit the farm since the family had moved out there

Uncle Clint greeted them with great affection, and in answer to their eager inquiries as to how long he could stay, said that he must start for home bright and early Monday morning.

The boys knew that unless they sneaked off alone no playing would be permitted on Sunday; so as soon as the team was taken care of they began to put in the time most diligently. With their cousins they raced all over the farm, showing them everything that was interesting and a great deal that was not. The gun was examined, Coon's marvelous qualities praised, and their many adventures related. When the moon rose all four of them began to play "hi-spy," choosing the one who should act as hunter by repeating the old doggerel stanza:

UNCLE CLINT.

"Eery ory, ickery Ann,
　　Fillison fallison, Ni'klas John;
Queevy quavy, English navy,
　　Stinklum stanklum *buck!*"

With each word the reciter would point his finger at one of the four players, himself included; the one reached when the word "buck" came round was proclaimed "Hi-spier."

It was ten o'clock before the voice of Uncle Clinton called them in from their boisterous sport for family prayers. William was very greatly interested in his uncle's manner. It was such a strange contrast to the Parson's funereal methods; so simple; so direct and tender. He did not speak in a depressing orotund, but talked as if addressing someone whom he loved and in whom he exercised perfect trust.

When the family circle knelt, William had first squatted. on his feet, but becoming a little cramped by this position about the time Uncle Clint was closing his petition, he dropped over on one thigh and laid his head upon his arms which were resting upon the chair before him.

Now, it so happened that an ireful, crippled wasp was lying on its back near where he had kneeled, and for some time had been feebly reaching about in space for a foot-hold. As William subsided on his thigh, a rent in his trousers' leg exactly included the struggling insect, which promptly harpooned him to what he thought must be an inch or more in depth. He forgot where he was and what was going on, putting up a yell that chilled the blood of the entire kneeling family. The prayer came to an abrupt close and everyone asked at the same time what on earth had happened.

"Sump'ns bit me!" bawled William loudly.

Hasty search quickly discovered the wasp, and the sting which had been left in the wound was extracted, after which an application of soda to the swelling relieved the pain.

When the boys awakened next morning it was broad day, and Uncle Clinton had done the feeding At breakfast he had a droll story to tell about "the father of all rabbits" which he had seen in the lot The narrative had proceeded some time before William suddenly saw the joke and exclaimed laughingly:

"Why, that's our jassack, Uncle!"

There were no Sunday services at the church, a mile distant on the edge of the prairie, and consequently there was nothing to do but wear out the long day. The boys went up stairs and talked over everything they could think of. Uncle Clinton sat by the front door reading the Bible for a long time, after which he solaced himself with a copy of "The Christian Advocate." When this was exhausted he entertained the family with many stories of his early, pioneer days; notably of the glorious camp-meetings they used to have. At break of day next morning he drove away, taking with him most of the sunshine the boys had enjoyed for six months.

They returned to the potato digging and finished the job before eleven o'clock. Up to that time the Parson had not returned. About three in the afternoon while poking around the barn-lot, they noticed that Pe-coob-coob was very dirty, having been trying to rid himself of the tormenting flies by rolling in the dust. Nathan fetched the curry-comb and began to restore him to his usual condition. The old horse seemed to like it very well until his legs were attacked, and then he showed a decided preference for his dirt.

Nathan finally rose up from scraping one of his hocks, and got a thump across the nose from Pe-coob-coob's stub tail. Greatly exasperated the urchin grasped the offending member, elevated it and clapped the curry-comb under it teeth out, letting the obstinate stump squarely down upon it.

With the first nip it gave him Pe-coob-coob clamped his stump hard, perhaps on the theory that some people take hold

of a thistle; but the reputed effects in this case did not follow.
The harder that gripping stub pressed, the deeper the curry-
comb bit. Then the victim tried to kick it out, and evidently
thought the higher he elevated his heels, the brighter prospect
there was of succeeding.

Never since the days of his sanguine youth had Pe-coob-
coob shown so much agility. He stood on his forefeet and
delivered passes at the saplings. He kicked high and low,
long and short, round and round, but the bite on his tail was
vicious and immovable.

In a pause for breath, he strove to pick out the irritating
thing with his teeth, curling round like a hoop; but he was
too short by a foot, and failed to reach it. Then he returned
to his kicking, and being impressed that he had not reached
high enough, tip-toed and stretched himself to the utmost limit.

Attracted by the noise Ump-Ump came from behind the
barn, gazed upon the performance with admiration, applaud-
ing it with a long melodious bray. But Pe-coob-coob was
busy, and had no time to listen to sounds of adulation. He
thought upon his latter end; yet his combined mental and bod-
ily exertions failed somehow to rid him of the gnawing curry-
comb.

In his wondrous gyrations he approached the barn, and
a new idea seemed to strike him; he would back up and rub
the cause of his torment out of existence. No sooner thought
than done; and he put his whole weight on it at once.

Worse and worse! The thing took a fresh hold, and
Pe-coob-coob launched out a kick with both hind-feet that hit the
barn broadside with a noise like thunder. It loosened his tail-

Pe-Coob-Coob's Dilemma.

grip, however, and the nipping curry-comb flew out. He trotted off to a far corner of the lot, whirled round and snorted forth his indignation, while the conscienceless boys were beating themselves and squealing with heartless laughter. It had been a circus all by itself.

At last Nathan picked up the curry-comb and with William sauntered around the corner of the barn. Then they felt that a special providence had interfered in their behalf; for just turning the last bend of the road that brought it into view came the old family chaise, and the sound of the Apostle's cluck was heard in the air. Hastily putting away Pe-coob-coob's toilet articles the startled urchins composed their flushed faces and welcomed the grim Parson with every imaginable appearance of innocence and joy.

Without saying a word he drove up, looked to see if the potatoes had all been dug, and leaving the boys to care for Daniel, went wearily into the house. As he led the horse into the barn, William said to Nathan with a caper, "Was n't that lucky?"

To which Nathan replied earnestly, "You jist *bet* it was!"

The Apostle was very tired and depressed from his two days' labor. Doubtless it was a fortunate thing that he had not arrived three minutes earlier than he did, or the last state of those boys might have been worse than the first!

"WAS N'T THAT LUCKY?"

CHAPTER XVII.

PE-COOB-COOB BEATS HIS RECORD.

FOR two days following his return home, the Apostle did not exhibit much energy. In preaching he always labored so hard that his spirits were depressed and his frame greatly relaxed. He was too sluggish to set the boys at anything but trifling jobs, and they dawdled along, taking their own time.

On Thursday, however, the Parson was quite recovered. That morning he put Daniel in the spring-wagon and went to Hightown with a load of potatoes.

At the time of such trips Mrs. Flint was in the habit of making out a bill of goods needed in the household. While the Parson was writing it down in his note-book Nathan came in and asked him to get some squirrel-shot, as all the last supply was exhausted. With his usual economy the Parson objected. He told the boy that the shot must have been wasted by loading too heavy; one shot would kill a squirrel if it hit him right. Then setting the youngsters to task he drove away.

However, when his other purchases had been made he recalled Nathan's request. Not finding the usual sized squirrel-shot in market, he purchased a pound of duck-shot. The boys' hunting saved his family much expense for meat.

It was late in the evening when he reached home; and as the marketing was inspected he handed the shot to Nathan, at the same time measuring out a proper load, which was nearly a teaspoonful.

Among other articles which had been purchased were about two pounds of honey in the comb; it was for cough-medicine, being too costly for table use. This was placed on the kitchen table over night, and the next morning Mrs. Flint found quite a colony of bees busy transferring it to their own stores. She had lived in the woods before, and noticing what kind of insects they were, called the Parson, who immediately pronounced them *wild* bees, and said there was doubtless a bee-tree near by.

After breakfast he took some of the honey, called the boys and went out into the field to try an experiment. Down at Puncheon Camp he had been an expert in finding bee-trees, and the renewed occupation reminded him pleasantly of those halcyon days.

The boys were deeply interested. The chance of getting a bountiful supply of honey which they might eat on mother's biscuits without its being mixed with hoar-hound and elecampane was quite sufficient to enlist them very zealously.

The Parson carried his bait on a chip which he laid on top of a large stump; then tying a bit of pink cotton to a fine silk thread,

BAITING THE BEES.

they all sat down to wait events. Presently a wandering bee lit upon the honey; soon another followed, and then another. This the Parson explained, saying the bee tree must be close by He then deliberately picked up one of the busy insects, and greatly to the admiration of the boys, did not wince when it prodded him with ready sting. With the noose in the free end of the thread he attached the cotton float to the prisoner's body, and let it go, sucking his finger, which was very hot despite his apparent stoicism.

The released bee crawled slowly about in a sickly manner, braided its legs, and after a few trial vibrations of its wings took flight. It circled round and round, the red banner floating behind After rising about forty feet in the air it darted like a bullet over the field toward the branch, while the Parson watched it out of sight.

Then not relishing the pain in his fore-finger, he plucked a plantain leaf, and when he saw a bee ready for flight, he hit it a slight tap, so entangling its legs in the sticky fluid as to delay its journey. Directing Nathan to watch it, he quickly prepared another bit of cotton which by adroit handling he tied to the struggling insect without getting stung a second time

The bee cleaned the honey from its legs, rose and disappeared in the same direction as the former one. This satisfied the Parson of the general locality of the bees' home; he directed the boys to prepare a piece of ground for turnips and set out on his hunt It was nearly noon when he got back, and his pleased expression told that he had been entirely successful.

The bees, he said, occupied an oak tree nearly a mile distant; there was a great swarm, and he expected to secure a large amount of honey. After dinner he took two buckets, some rags for a smudge, told William to bring along the ax and Nathan the gun, and they all set off to capture the prize.

In a short time the three reached the scene of operations. The bees had taken possession of a great oak-tree. About fifty feet up the side it had a crevice that evidently led to a hollow core. Out of the dark opening a never-ending procession of bees entered or emerged, all unconscious of danger below.

The Parson set his pails in a safe place, stripped off his coat and began to chop down the tree. The job took fully an hour, and toward the last the jarring blows raised a great commotion with the swarming inhabitants; they grew excited and flew in every direction except that of the enemy.

Finally, with a warning crack and a loud crash, down came the tree, its hollow top bursting open in the fall, exposing a long, smooth-worn interior filled with brown honeycomb. Most of the bees were stunned by the fall of their home, and the incomers flew wildly about in the air, bewildered at not finding their accustomed entrance.

The Parson set fire to his bunch of rags, and in the protection of its smoke, began transferring the honey to his pails. When both were full there yet remained much that was unfit to eat, being mixed with dirt and trash from the crushed tree-trunk.

Having collected all that was fit to use the party started back. William and Nathan walked ahead, on the lookout for game. About half way home they were surprised by the soberly plodding old Pe-coob-coob who, with Ump-Ump in his wake, had somehow escaped from the lot, and was taking a journey of which he alone knew the object.

The horse stopped, and gazed with wondering solemnity at the returning bee-hunters. Nathan gave William the gun and caught the old rascal by the fore-top to lead him home. But Pe-coob-coob would never lead willingly in this fashion; so the boy finally mounted upon his back, being accustomed to riding so, and guiding the bridleless horse by an occasional box on the jaw.

When Nathan had mounted, William handed him the ax, and set off ahead of the Parson, feeling very proud of being entrusted with the gun. Pe-coob-coob and his long-eared follower brought up in the rear of the procession, halting from time to time as the Apostle paused to rest.

"Keep yer eye skinned, my son," said the Parson to William; "and keep the pint of yer gun up, or fust ye know ye 'll be blowing the top of somebody's head off."

"I 'd like to see a buck or a jagger," remarked William with grim earnestness as he elevated the muzzle of the weapon.

"Yes, or a hoot-owl," chuckled the Parson, "I reckon ye 'd just teck and tear the gable end off'n it!"

He felt unusually facetious, and was inclined to joke William about his scare during the first night on the farm. But his load of honey became tiresome, and presently he paused for a breathing spell while William marched on by himself. He had gone perhaps two hundred yards ahead when suddenly

jerking the gun from his shoulder he began to prance wildly
about and yell for the Parson to come. It was evident that he
had found something of a promising nature, so the Apostle
picked up his burden and responded to the call very promptly.

The boy had treed a fox-squirrel; a veteran, as wary as
he was nimble. For some time nobody could get sight of it,
but William insisted that it was in the tree somewhere, for
he had "seen it jist a rackin' up the side."

At last, far up in the main fork of the tree the fur on
the tip of the creature's tail was discernible; it had flattened
out its body on a huge limb, and lay perfectly quiet. The Parson walked all about the tree to find an open
place in the undergrowth from which to take a
shot; but as he moved the watchful squirrel slid
from one side of the fork to the other, always
keeping out of sight.

There was but
one spot from which
the fork was plainly
visible; it was on the
side of the tree op-
posite the road.
Here about half the
squirrel's body was
visible, and the Par-
son called for
the gun. Wil-
liam took it to

ON THE WAY HOME.

him, but made so much noise in pushing through the bushes that the wily victim again hid itself, showing but a mere fringe of hair on the root of its tail.

"Ye remind me of a bull in a chiny shop," said the irritated Parson. "Why do n't ye make noise enough to wake the dead! Gimme the gun, an' see if ye kin stand still a minit!"

"O pa!" pleaded William; "lemme shoot this one! I treed him, and I never shot one yet!"

"Humph!" said the Parson irresolutely. "Ye 'd likely blow the top of yer head off. I do n't think ye could hit the side of a barn; an' besides ye can't hold the gun off-hand."

"Yes I could hit the side of a barn too!" exclaimed William indignantly. "I never git a chanst to hit anything; an' how 'll I ever learn if I do n't try? I 'll rest the gun ag'in the side of a saplin'; Nathan does that sometimes."

The Parson always had a myriad of excuses when he wished to prevent the boys from doing anything; but this grieved protest from William rather touched his heart.

"Well, we 'll see now," he said. "Come here and lemme show you where the animile is hid."

As William eagerly approached, the Apostle sighted along the side of a small hickory sapling, and found that if it were on their side the limb, the squirrel would be in plain sight.

"D 'ye see that big fork up there?" he asked.

"Uh huh," responded William, gazing

"Well, d 'ye see down nearly to the crotch, what looks like a little smiggin of moss?"

"Uh huh," rejoined William again, squinting prodigiously, his mouth wide open.

"That's where the critter's lyin'; now ye want to squirt-a-shooel, d'ye think ye kin hit him that far off?"

"I'll jist bet a *hoss* I kin," said William excitedly.

"How? How? How is it?" asked the Parson,-pausing long and looking daggers of rebuke between the questions. "Ye'd mebby better put up some of yer small stock fust. What's the matter with yer hands?"

"I got the buck-ager," said William falteringly; "but I'll jist rest the gun on this piece of limb,"—pointing to a rotten snag on one side of the sapling,—"an' then I kin hold it stiddy."

Saying this he laid the gun-barrel upon the support and found to his great satisfaction that he could get an excellent bead on the spot where the crouching squirrel lay.

"I can't shoot it through that limb," he remarked, taking a trial squint along the sights. "You ride up a little furder, Nathan, and skeer him over this way."

Astride of Pe-coob-coob, Nathan had himself been trying to locate the squirrel. When William called to him, he urged the horse forward a few paces, and stopped in the road. Here he was hidden from his brother behind the tree, but Pe-coob-coob's head and rear were in plain view. Reaching up to an over-hanging bough, Nathan shook it and shouted; the victim crept quickly over the limb until most of its body was visible to William.

Just here Ump-Ump, who had been standing about ten yards behind the old horse, wondering at the strange move-

ments around him, began to feel very funny. Giving his tail
two or three coquettish twists, he threw back his ears and
minced up to Pe-coob-coob, where he stopped to nip the old
fellow's tail that, as usual, was waving listlessly up and down.
The sedate animal laid back his ears and raised one foot as
if to kick the frivolous donkey, but at that moment the Parson called aloud to Nathan:

"Hold; he's fur enough this way now."

Attracted by his voice the jack suspended his amusement
and gazed indolently at William.   That over-strung youth
tightened all his muscles, took a long sight, held his breath,
closed his eyes and exclaimed:

"Look out! I'm a-goin' to shoot!"

The next second a variety of startling things happened.
In the first place William's muscular contraction added to the
weight of the gun was more than the rotten snag could stand,
and just as the urchin's finger was about to press the trigger,
the support snapped off, letting the gun-barrel drop.   It fell
in a direct line with Pe-coob-coob's tail and the donkey's head,
exploding with a loud bang.

As it did so William slightly relaxed his grip, and the
weapon kicked viciously. The poor boy staggered back, thinking one whole side of his head had been crushed in   He dropped
the fire-arm, clapped both hands to his aching jaw and roared
with pain. But the next second he had reason to forget his
own condition; for, as the explosion occurred, Pe-coob-coob
uttered a loud grunt and angry snort. Immediately followed
frightened shouts from Nathan

"Whoa! Whoa! Whoa there, you old fool! Whoa there!"

Through the thinning smoke could be caught a glimpse of the old horse, flying at top speed among the trees, while Nathan, with fingers woven into his mane was ducking and dodging to avoid limbs and saplings that threatened every moment to knock out his brains.

At the gun-shot Ump-Ump dropped like a beef under the butcher's ax: but he had not more than reached the ground before he sprang up, looked wildly about, and catching sight of his foster-father's hind quarters flying in the distance, he leapt out in pursuit, uttering as he flew a loud, prolonged and squealing

"Yaaww-eee-aww-ee-awwe-aw-eawww!"

"Oh, pa!" screamed William in a frenzy of fear, as he saw the speeding animals and heard Nathan's terrified shouts dying away, "I 've killed 'em! I 've killed 'em!"

"Good fathers above!" exclaimed the Parson in a state of utter exasperation and disgust. "I jist lay you 've ruined the old hoss, and put out the jackass's eyes. I never did see your beat in my born days! Teck yerself out of here and see if ye kin meck fer home; and do n't you ever lay hands on another gun as long as you live!"

William was nearly distracted: he had a double load to bear His own bruised jaw ached as if every bone in it were mashed, and his mind was racked with a sickish fear that he had mortally wounded, not only old Pe-coob-coob and the jack, but his only brother as well. He took his throbbing face in both hands and ran down the road, adding to his anguish by trying to kick up a small grub in the path with one of his big toes. It was enough to make him wish he were dead.

In reality his unfortunate accident had only peppered old Pe-coob-coob's stub tail and spattered the donkey's head with duck-shot; but had it been at close quarters, perhaps the result might have been more serious than that of merely frightening the unsuspecting brutes out of their wits. Neither of them liked the sound of a gun; and when this frightening noise was accompanied by burning pangs in head and tail, they at once felt an uncontrollable desire to get away from the dangerous spot, and hunt a place of safety.

None of the shot had touched Nathan, as he was sheltered behind the tree; but to be run away with through the woods was not a very desirable adventure; and it frightened the clawing rider quite as much as the gun-shot had the bolting animals.

When the episode occurred, they were not far from the branch, and Pe-coob-coob soon emerged from the trees into an open glade on the bank of the stream. He did not stop, but rose at it like a hunter, clearing its eight feet at a bound. But he had not a steeple-chaser for a rider, and his awkward jump unseated Nathan, who alighted flat on his back, in about four inches of water and a foot of mire.

When the gasping boy got his breath he struggled to dry ground,

"ROSE AT IT LIKE A HUNTER."

looking as ludicrous as Hation after the Parson's club had knocked her into a like mud-hole.

Nathan's face was the only white feature about him, his hair and back being a mass of blue slime. Panting and gulping he started for the road, reaching it a few yards in advance of William, who called out in frantic distress and apprehension:

"Are ye killed, Nathan? Are ye shot much?"

When he found out that his shot had done Nathan no damage, William joined woeful figure with his brother, and the twain hastened home. Nathan took a bath and donned another suit of clothes. William bathed his swollen jaw in hot water and bound it up with bruised purslane.

Presently the Parson arrived, too glum and disgusted for comment, but he looked all his tongue refused to speak.

After carrying the pails of honey into the kitchen he followed the boys out to see what damage had been done to the old horse and his long-eared retainer.

A few shot had entered the skin of Pe-coob-coob's hock, and his sub-tail felt quite lumpy; but beyond this he was not hurt.

Ump-Ump had received the worse injury. The shot had barely missed his eyes, but it had paralyzed one of his eye-lids, and cut the tendon that held up his right ear. Ever afterwards he went about with his ear hanging straight out from his head; and he looked out of his right eye as if trying to wink.

16

CHAPTER XVIII.

WINTER INCIDENTS.

SUMMER with its varied experiences dragged away, and the fruits of its wearisome toil began to appear.

An orchard had been set out, and owing to the rich new soil was already in flourishing condition, some of the larger trees showing evidences of coming fruit. The clearing had been extended, and though thickly hampered with stumps, it was also full of splendid rows of corn. Great golden pumpkins nestled in the bottom land through which the branch flowed and squashes of immense size kept them company.

The Parson prepared half a dozen "sass-holes" about the garden, in which were stored plentiful supplies of cabbage, beets, turnips, potatoes and other vegetables. Besides this, much of the crop was hauled to town and traded for groceries needful for family use.

All these unusual stores gave great delight to the boys, and many were their speculations about the number of hogs they would be able to fatten; and how Pe-coob-coob, Daniel, Ump-Ump and other faithful servants of the place would smile and "nicker" when cold winter days came, and big ears of corn should gladden the hungry animals.

214

Coon had become indispensable; and when one morning she was missing, the boys became greatly concerned. Search was at once begun, and soon she was discovered under the crib, the proud mother of six whining puppies.

The boys hailed these new arrivals with immense delight. They would have kept the whole litter to form a hunting pack, but the Parson would not listen to such a thing. Several neighbors had heard of Coon's wonderful prowess, and had expressed wishes to possess a dog in all respects like her; so the boys quickly made bargains for the disposal of the pups as soon as they were weaned. Five of them brought a half-dollar each, and the sixth, a very lively, spotted fellow, the boys kept because they felt sure it would break Coon's heart to be deprived of all her family.

The pup Coon was allowed to keep was named "Purty-eyes," because of his queer visual organs, which were of different color, and one a trifle larger than the other. As he grew up the animal was brimful of fun, and always in search of mischief. This reckless spirit of his finally brought him to his death. One day when he was about five months old, he set out to tantalize old Pied, the cow. She lowered her head and gave chase. Purty-eyes galloped toward the yard, barking and looking back over his shoulder in great glee. By a sudden spurt the cow was almost upon him before he was aware of his danger. The low paling gate was at hand, and the now frightened pup made a spring to clear it, but was too far away One of his hind legs caught between two slats and was broken. Then the Parson said he must be killed; and though the boys begged hard for his life, it was no use. The Parson took him out to the edge of the woods and shot him.

The grief of the boys was loud and deep. They placed the poor pup in a box and buried him underneath a large tree, nailing over his grave a head-board with the following epitaph:

"PURTY-EYES FLINT,
Son of Coon Flint.
He was an orfand on his father's side,
And died from a cow, with a broken leg."

"PURTY-EYES."

＊　＊　＊

The school-house nearest the farm was about two miles distant, on the edge of the prairie. As time for the winter session approached, the Parson hastened his fall work so as to spare the boys. Next to religion he prized education; the more so, perhaps, because his own needs had taught him its value.

The road to the school-house lay mostly through the woods, and just before emerging upon the prairie, it was crossed by a small creek. In case of prolonged rains, this insignificant stream was sometimes much swollen, and rather dangerous to ford. But when it was higher than usual, Pe-coob-coob was brought into use to assist the boys and girls in crossing. At such times he was mounted by Louise, Ruth and William, the latter riding astride the horse's neck, just in front of his withers. Nathan would walk to the creek, and when the mounted trio had ridden safely over, William rode back, and carried Nathan to dry ground on the further side.

On the first day the two boys went to the school alone.

When they arrived the morning session had already begun, so the newcomers waited outside until recess before presenting themselves.

In a little time an urchin about Nathan's size came out of the school-house, and spying the boys sitting on a log shook his fist at them. They were by no means frightened at this demonstration, for their own fighting qualities had not been forgotten.

The neighboring prairie had been settled by five brothers, who owned the country for several miles around. They had grown quite wealthy, and were inclined to regard with clannish dislike any new comers among them. Each had a large family, and some of their children were married, possessing homes of their own; thus the entire district might have been called a settlement of relatives.

Tobe Corbin, one of these country aristocrats, after showing off as we have already described, came out to where the boys were seated and asked in his insolent manner:

"What's yer name?"

Now William's soul already loathed the swaggering fellow; so he stood up and aggravatingly replied:

"Puddin' tame."

"I do n't 'low no clod-hoppers to talk to me that-away," rejoined the bully threateningly.

"Well, what 'r ye goin' to do about it?"

"WHAT'S YER NAME?"

"See here, you dern stick-in-the-mud, you do n't want to gimme none of yer lip, ur I'll bust yer crust!"

"Oh, now," said William mockingly; "you would n't hurt a pore little boy, would ye, sis? I ain't afeard of no lummix like you. I come frŭm town."

"Well, if ye did come frum town, that won't keep me from moppin' the ground with ye if ye ain't keerful. You act too dern'd stuck up."

"All we got to say is ye'd better try it once," Nathan broke in. "You won't mop us as anybody knows of. We'll pound the soap-suds out of ye, if ye bother us anymore."

Just at this threatening crisis recess occurred. The scholars poured forth from the school-house in a noisy, yelling crowd, and without further remarks Tobe Corbin ran away to join them.

Followed by many stares and curious glances the boys then went into the house and were assigned seats. The teacher asked them about the Parson; where they had last lived, and how far they had gone in their studies, all of which the boys answered very promptly. Finally left to themselves they strolled out to the playgrounds, and as no one invited them to join the games, they watched the others play. It was not long, however, before the teacher came to the door and beat upon the side of the house with a stick, yelling loudly:

"Books! Books!"

Away went the scholars pell mell, crowding, jostling, and nearly wedging fast in the narrow entrance. All this seemed very strange to the Parson's boys; for they had last gone to school in town, where affairs were conducted in a more orderly manner.

In a short time the youths made acquaintances among the scholars, and had some fast friends. They did not come to an open rupture with Tobe Corbin until a month later; then it happened all at once.

There were two little Quaker girls attending the school. They lived in the direction of the farm, and traveled the same road as the boys for a mile on their way home. The smaller of these lassies was a doll-like midget with a perfect thicket of brown curls and two big gray eyes that were soft as a dove's. Her name was Hester Leffingwell, but among the scholars she was called "Sis."

These sisters "thee'd and thou'd" each other and the scholars, much to the general amusement at first. One evening after school, Tobe Corbin became offended at something Sis had said, and followed down the road to slap her. William happened to be near, and although Tobe was quite a head taller than he, it was impossible for him to witness the cowardly attack without some very withering remarks about "A great, strappin' two-fisted hulk a-slappin' a pore little girl." For these sarcastic remarks Tobe promptly turned and slapped William.

In the combat that followed instantly William would likely have been worsted if Nathan had not run up and pulled the enemy off him. Then while Nathan pummeled on top, William put in sundry kicks at the exposed portions of the bully's person, which soon made him call for quarter, and wish he had let out that job to someone else.

Up to this time the little Quakers had been very shy; but this brave championship on the part of the boys quite won their hearts. William walked with Sis that evening to the forks of the road, and among other tender things asked her if she could sing:

"How tejis an' tas'eless the hours."

Not being a Methodist, she had to deny that accomplishment, but said she should like to hear it, and William gallantly promised to sing it for her next day.

When the four had separated at the road leading to the little Quakers' home, William solemnly informed Nathan that he loved Sis Leffingwell "with a holy, tender love," and avowed that he intended presenting her with a pair of squirrel-skin shoe-strings the following day. Nathan returned this sacred confidence by telling William that his own bosom had long been unutterably full of affection for a certain Amanda Pugh, whom he avowed he should marry when he had sold "Lop-ear."

By the time the boys reached home a heavy rain set in, and continued with great down-pour most of that night. The next morning Louise and Ruth mounted Pe-coob-coob and piloted by the boys started for school. Upon reaching the creek they found it thirty feet wide, and over a foot deep, running very swiftly. Nathan lifted William by one foot, and placed him astride the horse's neck, and the animal stepped into the water to wade across. About the middle of the stream Pe-coob-coob suddenly felt thirsty, and stopped to take a drink.

William was entirely unprepared for this movement, and

"*Asked her if she could sing*
'*How te'jis an' tas'eless the hours?*'"

as the horse abruptly lowered his head, the boy pitched forward. However, he managed to clasp his arms about the horse's neck, and held on for dear life; Louise, who sat just behind him on the Parson's saddle, seized one of the feet that William waved frantically in the air, and tried to urge the scoundrelly Pe-coob-coob to move on; but not a peg would he go until he had secured a drink. William's position was becoming desperate; he snatched one of the horse's ears between his teeth, and bit like a rat. Under this new mode of persuasion Pe-coob-coob jerked up his head, and William tried to crawl back; but no sooner had he got into place than the old rascal stooped again for his coveted drink.

This time William shot right down over the horse's ears, and when he was about half-way over, the animal again jerked up his head. Having now neither hold nor support William lost his balance, and the next second alighted smack on his back in the muddy creek.

Snorting and bawling he scrambled to the bank, where he stood as if each of his arms weighed a hundred pounds, and he were trying to present them to somebody.

Seeing him safe, the girls burst into peals of laughter; but there was no mirth in William's heart. He stood storming on the bank, in a puddle of water that drained from his clothing. Pe-coob-coob got his drink, and unconcernedly waded out of the stream; but as he passed by, Wil-

WILLIAM SCRAMBLED TO THE BANK.

liam seized a stick and brought it down viciously on the hinder part of the old reprobate's anatomy. The whack was severe, and Pe-coob-coob promptly launched a kick at the tree-tops, when in a flash Ruth found herself in the middle of the road, with her arms nearly to the elbows in mire. Her laugh suddenly ceased, and William's tow head got several muddy cuffs as soon as she could get up.

Louise rode across the stream again and brought Nathan over. Then William returned home with the horse, and the others went on to school.

But insignificant stream as it was, Otter Creek was destined to be the scene of a tragedy more serious than anyone had thought

By special request of Louise, some of the larger boys of the school one day went down to the creek and felled a long, slim sycamore-tree across it for a foot bridge. The bridge was too narrow for safe passage, and to remedy this they made a hand-rail, by driving a fork in the ground at either end of the log, and laying a pole in the crotches This support stood about two feet higher than the foot log, and under all ordinary circumstances made it safe to cross.

But one day in February a deep snow fell. It was sport for the boys to wade through this, but the girls were not so fond of the fun, and so remained at home for a week. Four days after the snow-fall the sun came out warm and full of spring promise By half-past one o'clock in the afternoon most of the snow had melted, the weather turned cloudy, and a smart rain fell

When on their way home the boys and their little Quaker companions reached the foot-bridge at the creek, they were astonished to find the water within a few inches of the log, and booming along with terrible swiftness and force.

The two girls were frightened, and would not venture over until Nathan and William had crossed. Then the older of the sisters crept slowly after them, trembling as she went. It was now the turn of Sis; and already more than ever frightened at being separated from her companions, she made the effort to cross also. But the log was icy from sleet, and when she had gone about two-thirds of the way over, Sis slipped. She threw her weight upon the hand-rail; but the damp ground around the stake that held it gave way. She toppled for a moment, and then with a shrill cry plunged into the seething water. It poured an icy flood all over her, and quickly whirled her down stream.

Screams of terror arose from the bank as she disappeared; then both boys with frantic sister rushed after her. Once more she came up with face towards them, and her terror-widened eyes looked despair at the pursuers.

About forty yards below the ford was a sharp bend in the stream, and on the bank at this point grew an old oak that had been partly undermined by various overflows of the stream. A snarl of roots stuck out into the water, and the swift current boiled into the curve, carrying with it the helpless body of the child.

Upon reaching this spot, the boys saw a bit of dress fluttering in an eddy under the tree. Holding to some roots that were not submerged, Nathan reached down and caught the child's clothing, just as the rushing flood was about to tear her away. It took all the strength of both himself and William to drag the body out, and when she finally lay on the bank, to all appearance she was dead.

William and the sister stayed with her, while Nathan ran for help. He met the girl's father about half way to the forks of the road where the children turned off, the old Quaker often coming to meet them when the weather was bad. Upon hearing Nathan's tale, the terrified father dashed away and found Sis insensible and frozen at the ford. Wrapping his great coat about her, he ran the horse home hoping that quick warmth and restoratives would save her life. But the little Quaker never went to school again. The shock and exposure brought on lung-fever, which quickly choked the life out of her fragile form. The next bridge she crossed was a golden one, and tender hands must have led her safely over.

School was dismissed for the funeral, and the shadow of this sudden tragedy fell upon the scholars with a great awe.

For a long time William was inconsolable. He read and wept over a poem in his reader:

"The bark that held the prince went down"

In imitation of the bereaved father in that touching story, he felt that he should never smile again. But as time wore on other things occurred to divert the boy's thoughts from this sorrow.

Of these matters we shall hear in the next chapter.

CHAPTER XIX.

NO ABIDING CITY.

ANOTHER summer passed, and as fall drew on strange things began to disturb the Parson's mind. He often talked about them with his wife; and occasionally with parishioners who visited the farm; these exciting topics absorbed most of the conversation.

The boys continually heard such odd phrases as "Rebeldom," "Secession," "Coercion," "The curse of slavery," and others. By degrees it dawned upon their minds that there was a very large outside world, where a disturbed Nation was anticipating a dire civil war.

As we have before stated, the Apostle was a strong abolitionist; he had been born of radical parents, and was in everything radically bred. As political questions of the time began to foment in the public mind he partook of the excitement, growing hotter and hotter.

One day believing that it might be a religious duty, he even undertook to explain the subject of slavery to the boys. They listened in astonishment, conceiving the wildest kind of ideas, and learning to think and speak of the institution as the very keystone of all wickedness.

True, they were sadly puzzled to read in the Bible that

the Israelites practiced this heinous sin. William in particular was greatly confused by this fact. He asked the Parson one day if all "nigger masters bored holes in their slaves' ears with an awl, as the men spoken of in Deuteronomy were said to have done."

The Apostle was disgusted with such foolish questions; for whether it existed in fact or not, he found no difficulty in creating a broad distinction between Hebrew servitude and modern slave-holding.

As the days went by the boys heard the names "Secesh" and "Abe Lincoln" very often; and at the approach of the national election day, Parson Flint grew more and more excited When finally that great event arrived, he went to town early without even assigning the boys a task, and he did not return until late the following afternoon.

When he got back the boys were out hunting, but something so elated his mind that he forgot to chide them. During the course of the evening he told the family that he believed Lincoln was elected President of the United States, and so mightily did the Parson laud him, that Nathan and William learned to revere this great chief above all other persons.

At that time there were not so many abolitionists as might have been found a few months after the war broke out It was yet too early for the final test of men's opinion and sentiment. But what in bitter scorn the Parson called "Southern sympathizers" were quite numerous on his circuit, and the presence of these "rebels" only increased the fever of his intense indignation He began to thunder from the pulpit. He thundered

A REBEL.

(As the boys fancied him.)

in the market-places; in the very homes of these southern people. He thundered everywhere, at all times and in all places;
and when news of the secession of the Southern States spread
like a panic over the country, he thundered louder than ever.

The boys heard it all, moved by vague excitement. Its
full meaning, of course, they did not grasp, but the Parson's
vigorous talks always held attention and created strong impres-
sions. From time to time he read out of the daily papers much
about "The Disruption of the Union;" "The Imbecility of
Buchanan," and the certainty of a great war. Finally he read
with fervor a long article about the "Inauguration of Lincoln," and William eagerly asked what kind of an "auger" was
used in the process, in answer to which the Parson looked at him
in great contempt and said, "teck yerself away from here."

During all this excitement the Apostle's noise raised opposition echoes; he truly went forth, "not to bring peace, but
a sword," and the weapon he brought was double-edged.
Loudly did he fume and scold about "actual rebels" among
the parishioners; and so withering and scornful were his tirades
about them that the boys fancied they must have horns and
hoofs, greatly desiring to behold one.

Winter passed and spring came on; then one day when
the peach-trees were all in bloom, and the woods growing dense
with increasing green, the Apostle came home greatly depressed, and read in a fine rage about "The Fall of Fort
Sumter" After that he went to town regularly for news, and
at night pored over the situation until long past bed-time As
he read, he talked and stormed until the boys verily believed

that with a sufficient number of hickory sprouts, he would be able to "clean out the whole Southern Conthieveracy," as he satirically called the secession government.

In this furious state of mind he was not calculated to reap the fruits of peace upon his circuit. From remarks the boys overheard they learned that his salary was seriously curtailed on account of the defiant spirit he manifested toward sundry wealthy parishioners. But besides this disturbing news, they had a hint of something else that secretly gave them great joy. When the conference year closed, it was highly probable that the Parson would have to go to a new charge.

Conference came early, the latter part of April. And one day after the Parson had been absent a week, their mother told the boys that "pa had been appointed to Bluff City, a town a hundred miles distant on the Mississippi River."

They would have received this news with a double sommersault and shouts of joy, had not their mother been crying bitterly as she told them about it. All their anxious questions could not elicit the cause of her grief, so at last they wandered out to the barn-lot in a very subdued state of mind, wondering "what ailed ma."

Shortly after this the Parson returned home. He said he had tried hard to secure an appointment near the farm, but for some unknown reason

THE REBEL.
As he really was.

had signally failed; they must get ready to move at once, and everything was prepared for another migration.

It was a busy, pathetic time. All the property, association and sense of ownership that had endeared the place to them for so long had to be given up. And now that they had to leave it all, the boys found that the woods farm had far more charm than they had before discovered. They wandered through all the bypaths, down the branch, and up toward the prairie, where they had met with such wonderful luck in their first hunt. They went all about the field, and looked into every nook and cranny of the barn, chicken-house and other buildings, saying a sad goodbye to every place and thing they saw.

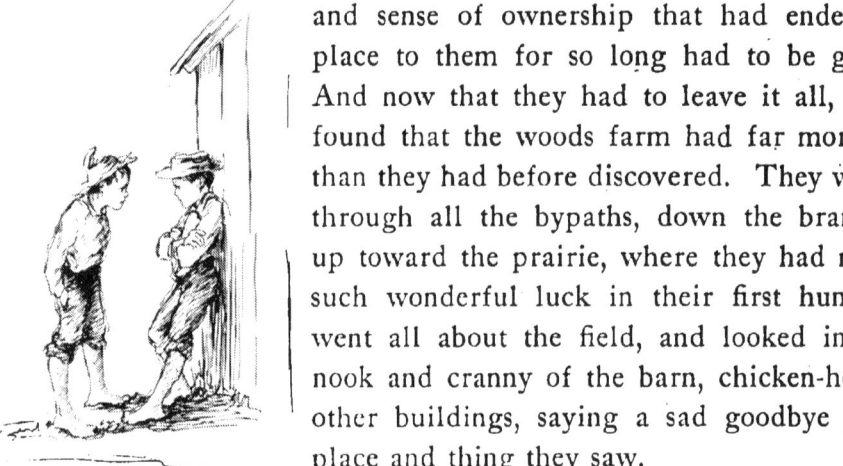

Wondered What Ailed Ma.

The Parson had secured a good tenant for the farm, who would move in as soon as the family left. To him all the stock was sold, and by this time it formed quite an item. William had more than fifty hens; and Nathan owned a dozen fine pigs, while the jack was joint property. But the Parson sold everything, even to the pretty white Berkshire that belonged to his wife. Daniel was the only animal not put into the sale, and Ump-Ump would not bring anything, so was turned out to fare for himself. The Parson hurried matters along, disposed of everything quickly, and without a word of explanation pocketed every cent of the cash.

It quite broke the boys' hearts, and they bawled for hours over the disappointment. But finally their grief was somewhat diverted by the news that they were to ride most of the way to their new home on the cars. This would be their first railroad trip, and the grief they felt was soon submerged in exciting anticipations of a novel experience.

On Sunday morning the Parson went to a distant appointment for his closing service on the circuit, and the family spent their last sad day on the farm. Save barely enough to cook with and sleep on, all their household goods had been packed. The floors were uncarpeted, the walls looked bare and lonesome, and the last dying embers of moving time smoked feebly.

Late at night the Parson returned, and next morning all the family drove into Hightown to take the train. They had an hour to wait for it at the depot; and during this interval the boys were devoured with curiosity at the numerous strange things they saw. They were absorbed in gazing through a window at the telegrapher and his clicking instruments, when suddenly the shrill screech of a whistle sounded.

The Parson seized William with one hand, some small baggage with the other, and followed by the rest of the family hurried out to secure seats in the train. As the great locomotive, snorting, hissing and roaring drew right up before him, William shrank back, and clung to the Parson's hand with a death grip. But the Apostle whisked him and Nathan into a car, and bestowed them compactly into a seat, at the same time giving them a hasty word of admonition:

"Now try an' behave yerselves an' keep yer seats. If ye go to pokin' yer heads out of the winder, ye 'll likely git yer brains knocked out; so set still an' look through the glass."

The Parson himself had arranged to drive to the new circuit as guide for the teamsters who hauled the household goods. So, when the whistle sounded a warning, he cast one comprehensive glance at his family and hurried away.

The train was soon roaring onward, making the boys fairly hold their breath with the unusual speed and motion. When they reached their destination it had grown quite dark, and they were truly strangers in a strange land. The station where the family alighted was about eight miles from Bluff City, and so they had to await the arrival of the Parson before finally reaching their home.

By this time the boys were tired, homesick and of course ravenously hungry. A long walk to the house of the Methodist preacher of the little town did not refresh them to any extent. They found his family packing for their own journey, and but little was left in the larder. After eating a cold lunch the boys at once went to sleep on a pallet spread for them on the floor, and this was their bed for the next night also. During the daytime they saw great crowds of soldiers marching somewhere, and nothing seemed to be talked of but the war.

When, on the morning of the second day, the Parson arrived, he found one of his new parishioners in town, with a two-seated spring wagon. This brother took the girls, and the boys rode with their mother and the Apostle in the family buggy. Bluff City was reached a little before noon; and as they descended the last long hill overlooking the town, for the first time in their lives the boys caught sight of the mighty Mississippi. Much the same sensations overwhelmed them that must have rewarded Balboa when he discovered the Pacific Ocean. They gazed in delight and awe; and as a big steamboat drew up to the wharf right below them, they nearly fell out of the buggy in a stupor of admiration and amaze.

The new parsonage was another delight. It was much larger, and almost as elegant as the preacher's at Hightown. It had eight rooms, and was situated in a beautiful yard. The stable was quite as good a building as the Hightown parsonage for the circuit preacher, in which the family had lived for six months. The barn-lot was roomy, and everything looked so prosperous and inviting that great joy fell upon the Parson's family.

Bluff City was nestled among hills, which next to the river descended in steep limestone bluffs, but on the side adjacent to the parsonage were covered with a tangle of forest, vines and every sort of flowering verdure. Within fifty paces of the parsonage gate was a small, noisy, but crystal-clear stream that came from a large spring near by, from which a third of the town got their drinking water. So rarely beautiful was the village, and so entrancing was the spot in which it was situated that the place looked to the boys like some wonderful fairy land.

Having seen them arrive, Brother Dickinson, a parishioner and near neighbor, came over and invited them to dinner. To the boys, the comparative splendor of his home was quite overpowering. He had no children save one puny little girl, and she was too cross or timid to make friends with anybody, so the boys sat uncomfortably upon the edges of their chairs, listening to talk about the war. This was a topic upon which the Parson and his new parishioner seemed to agree perfectly.

When dinner was announced there was not room at the first table for Nathan and William; so while the grown people were eating they went eagerly out into the yard and tried to get another view of the river. From that locality only faint glimpses of it could be seen, and William finally suggested that they climb a tree; this was quickly done, and then like Zaccheus of old they saw clearly.

The meal to which they were presently called was another bewilderment. There was a great profusion of silver on the table, and so many new things to eat that the boys scarcely knew how to begin. Some cups of *blanc mange* puzzled them

CLIMBED A TREE.

greatly; but William finally discovered the empty cups out of which the others had eaten, and so arrived at a proper conclusion respecting the strange edible.

In the afternoon the household goods arrived, and the next few days were spent in fixing up the parsonage. When it was all done, the girls were delighted, and felt the greatest satisfaction. It was much superior to anything the family had ever known before.

On Saturday Mrs. Flint took the boys down town and bought each of them a brand-new suit of clothes; and upon their return home the Parson told them that these articles had been purchased out of the money for which he had sold their stock.

He seemed to think that this fact ought to make a deep impression upon them, but somehow they did not act as wildly grateful as might have been expected.

The following morning the Parson preached in town, and the boys wore their new suits to church. They sat near a window, and lost much of the discourse in trying to divide attention between it and the river, a stretch of which lay in plain view.

On Monday Brother Slaten, a parishioner from one of the country appointments, came in to see the new preacher, and brought him a load of supplies. Brother Slaten was a jolly, round-faced man, who could laugh louder than anybody the boys had ever heard. He was full of funny stories, and no one could be more entertaining. Before leaving he invited the boys to come out and spend a week with him at the farm, which they promised to do when the Parson would let them.

To their unspeakable joy, that evening the Parson allowed the boys to go with him to the river, where numerous inhabitants of the little village went to meet the St. Louis boats, and get the daily papers.

In their tremendous excitement the urchins could scarcely contain themselves. When they arrived, a score of people were already there, and as the boys stood upon the old flat-boat that had been decked over for a landing-wharf, they gazed upon the mighty stream already dim with shadows, listening to its murmur against the sides of the barge, and felt very much awed, talking in low voices about the wonders that must be hidden in the depths of that mysterious channel.

Presently they were aroused by some one calling loudly:
"Here she comes!"

The words created a sudden stir in the waiting group.
And looking down the river the boys saw what seemed to be
a dim cloud that ever and anon shot forth numberless rockets,
Roman candles, red, blue, green and yellow, dancing and disappearing over the water.

"Here She Comes!"

Then came the hoarse "chow! chow!" of the pipes, from
which boiled dense clouds of smoke. Soon the melodious
chime of whistles floated far and wide; and when the gorgeous
spectacle drew right up before them, Nathan quite lost his
head. Seizing the Parson by one hand, he cried aloud in a
trance of amazement:

"Oh, pa, le's board her! le's board her!"

A post-boy came out with a bundle of dailies and was fairly
buried in the pushing crowd that surged to meet him. When

the Parson had secured his paper, and the loading and unloading had been done the great boat swept out into mid-stream again, her tremendous paddle wheels churning the water into huge billows all about her.

That night the boys did not sleep for several hours. They were wrought up with intense excitement, and talked long about the wonders of creation from which for two years they had been buried miles deep in the woods.

CHAPTER XX.

BLUFF CITY PEOPLE.

O N Wednesday night after the Sunday services spoken of in our last chapter, the boys, together with the Parson and Mrs. Flint all went to weekly prayer-meeting. Here they came into closer contact and acquaintance with the true children of Israel.

In the mixed congregation that came out to hear the new preacher on Sunday, the boys, who sat well up in front, could not detect sinner from saint. True, if they could have inspected the audience during prayer-time they might have been able to separate the sheep from the goats; for in those days all good Methodists knelt during invocation.

As by reason of parentage the boys were good Methodists, they knelt with the others, and of course this gave them no opportunity to look around, which they very much desired to do.

But prayer-meeting afforded them a better chance. They could be very sure that all who regularly attended this service were staunch pillars in Zion. In this assurance they looked the people over.

There were several more women than men, and both sexes were old-looking, or at least of mature years. All sat in the "amen corners" or well up to the front of the house, and there was an atmosphere of sedate piety in the entire group.

238

BROTHER DARN BECKWITH.

There was Brother Darn Beckwith. On the big church-book his name was spelled "Darnton," but for short, and when not addressed officially it was Darn. In private the boys some-times changed this singular title to "Dern" and "Dang."

Brother Darn was a long, lean, skinny man, with an im-mense Adam's apple that sloped away from his stringy neck like the corner of a cigar box. His jaws were very long and concave, except in one particular spot on the right side of his face; here he always kept stored away a good-sized quid of "old Virginny twist" tobacco. While talking he held in his bony chin, and puckered his mouth until it resembled that of a buffalo fish. There was not a surplus fibre of flesh about him; and the Parson accounted for this spare condition by saying that "the man spit hisself all away chawin' tobacker."

The good brother's eyes were very much sunken; he looked solemn; he felt solemn, prayed solemnly, and "chawed" as one who must give an account. His throaty voice sounded as if it had to tip-toe upon the prominent Adam's apple to get over his front teeth.

In class and prayer meetings, Brother Darn ever talked about the "weakness of the flesh, and the willingness of the sperit;" but the sarcastic Parson said it was no wonder he had weakness of the flesh, because "he chawed without ceasing." Be that as it may, Brother Darn did seem to have not only a great "weakness of the flesh" for the weed, but a very marked "willingness of the sperit" for it also.

When he talked about weakness or strength, or anything else, he stood with his hands lying one in the other under his coat-tails, which like everything else about him, were likewise long and solemn. But despite any shortcomings he might have had, Brother Darn was genuinely religious and deeply sincere.

On this first prayer-meeting occasion the Parson in due course of time called on Brother Darn to lead in prayer.

The brother duly responded. He began in a very slow, solemn voice, standing up perfectly straight upon his knees, and rapidly pinching together his already closed eyelids. As his prayer progressed he grew more and more inspired, until finally he reached a thrilling climax, and besought the Lord to give them all "faith to stand on Pisgah's top, and like Moses of old, view the promised land."

Just here the tobacco in his mouth created an overflow, and the brother had to pause to relieve himself. It was a tremendous mouthful, and sounded as if it had fallen clear from the top of Pisgah to the valley of Jehoshaphat when it struck the floor.

But that was not all: The listening Parson had ascended on the wings of Brother Darn's prayer. He had become greatly exhilarated, responding to the petition with many fervent ejaculations. Occasionally when the sentiments uttered struck his full approval, he spouted forth a perfect geyser of "Amens!"

It was a glowing climax that preceded the good brother's expectoration, and no sooner was it reached than it was followed like an exclamation point by the spat of the saliva on the floor. Fairly electrified by the climax, the Parson shouted a loud "Amen!" but he was just one awful second later than the splash!

Upon realizing this mortifying fact, his ecstacy suddenly died out, and his faith fell sheer into the valley before he could recover hold upon it. To climb up again was impossible; he fell a-groaning, and when Brother Darn's prayer closed, the Parson's final amen was quite subdued and feeble indeed

The boys happened to be kneeling in such a position that they could see Brother Darn, and had become deeply interested in his queer manner. They were peeping at him over their arms, that were folded upon the seat at which they knelt. When the brother stopped and spat so suddenly "it struck their funny-spots," as William said, and they giggled right out in meeting

The Parson opened his eyes wide, and shot a threatening glance at them which they did not fail to catch; for no sooner had the snicker escaped them than they looked at their father, out of simple apprehensive habit.

To their great surprise, however, the disgusted Parson did not refer to this breach of pious behavior after returning home. The incident that caused their mirth overshadowed everything else; and the Apostle indignantly declared that "any man who would do the like of that in the house of God, ought to be druv out of decent society."

But Brother Darn was not the only interesting personage at the prayer-meeting. There was Brother Lewis Somers, the shouting blacksmith. He sat three or four seats in front of the boys, and prayed aloud continually, no matter who was leading In the course of the services it came his time to lead.

He began in a low moderate voice, but in a most determined manner. As his prayer progressed he became greatly excited, speaking louder and louder. Then he began to sway back and forth, drawing in his breath like Shikespoke when the snake was after him. Pretty soon he pulled out every stop, put on the knee-swell and filled his bellows to bursting. After that he could have been heard for half-a-mile as he shouted vo-ciferously:

"Aouuuooo Lawerrrrd!"

He roared right at the ceiling, as if the celestial court could not hear him unless he called as Elijah exhorted the prophets of Baal to do. After getting as loud as he could, he supple-mented his voice by pounding on the bench with both fists, and accompanying the blows by rising slightly on his toes and stamping the floor with his knees. At every blow the bench groaned and jumped, as if resenting such rough treatment, but Brother Somers went right along.

Before this vocal cyclone the Parson's amens were like chaff, and after a few vain attempts to gauge his responses to the brother's voice he gave it up and relieved his feelings by sundry feeble means and tweaks at his heavy beard.

Brother Somers kept up his bellowing tornado for eight or ten minutes, and then suddenly descended to his natural voice in five words, the last of which was a whispered "amen."

The Parson did not slight the female portion of the congre-gation, which, it will be remembered, formed the larger part of the gathering. He called on a few of them to lead in prayer, and they responded according to their several abili-

18

ties. The last of these was a very fat sister, with a sharp. high-pitched voice.

She began in a thin, high tone, and ascended therefrom in regular gyrations. Her words were all of two or more syllables. She called hope "ho-wup," thee "the-yuh," praise "pra-yez," and now "now-uh." Well along in her petition she grew very tearful, and at last her voice became so fine that it completely vanished before the amen.

For some moments the kneeling company did not know that she was done; but the Parson finally perceived the fact and arose from his knees beginning a hymn as a signal for the others to arise.

There was another member of the circle, who lived within two blocks of the parsonage, and whom the boys had seen several times since they had come to Bluff City. He was the only young man in the company, and it was not many months until the boys had cause to remember him all their lives.

During a short "experience" interval, which the Parson threw in as variety to the regular service, this young man got up and spoke. He said that for a long time the call to preach the gospel had been sounding in his ears; that he had been resisting the summons, but felt sure he would never have any peace of mind until he harkened, took up his cross and obeyed the Master's voice. From the talk it seemed that he was terribly beset by Satan, and had a continual struggle to walk in the strait and narrow path that leads to glory.

He was a porky-looking fellow with pendant jaws and a chronic case of inflamed eyes But despite all his pious and

JORDAN BLAKE.

pathetic talk there was a vicious look about him that even the boys could detect. The skin on his face looked as if a gill of grease might have been scraped off it, and his hair was glistening with the same substance.

Now it so happened that the Parson had heard much about this young man. Brother Somers, in whose "class" the corpulent child of trial had been placed, told the Apostle with an apology for "evil-speaking" that "Jordan Blake was the laziest hulk in America;" so lazy, in fact, that had it not been for a brother he would have starved to death. He further stated that this idler of twenty-eight summers had been in the same religious tussle for the past five years, and the conflict seemed to absorb all his energy, leaving him indisposed for anything else that had a smack of honest work in it. He had a widowed mother and two sisters, besides the brother who did odd jobs about the river And Brother Somers also told the Parson the entire family were violent rebels, besides which they had a bad reputation in general, especially Jordan, who was thought to be a sneak thief or worse. The whole family lived on what they could pick up, aided by the one son's occasional earnings; but in summer he said they nearly starved, and in winter almost froze In further history of the interesting young man, he said that for three years the fellow had tried to obtain a license as an exhorter, but the quarterly conferences had persistently refused it because of Blake's "bone-laziness"

Now the Apostle was never backward in rebuking those whom he considered in need of it; so in his closing address he made some scathing remarks about the sin of idleness, and recommended labor as an appointed means of grace. Also in accordance with his usual habit, he held up to detestation and scorn "the traitors who were trying to tear down the country's flag and enslave their fellow-men."

This denunciation of Southern principles had a rather unexpected result. Jordan Blake could listen meekly to censures for his indolence, but at the Parson's bitter allusions to his Southern sympathies he got up and stalked indignantly from the room, and the boys never saw him at prayer-meeting again.

When, after a few weeks, Blake vanished from town, the event was commented upon as "good riddance of bad rubbish," and no one ever cared to ask where he had gone. The fact is that he had crossed the river into Missouri, and later we shall hear what his business was.

One morning of his second week in Bluff City, Nathan awoke with a raging toothache. The troublesome member was a molar in his upper jaw, and it seemed to have a red-hot pulse that jarred his whole head. The pain was so severe that he roared until the Parson threatened to "frail" him if he didn't stop; then feeling a little mean, the Apostle tried to be facetious. He told Nathan that an infallible cure for the toothache was to fill his mouth with cold water, "and set on the stove until it b'iled."

But Nathan was in no mood to feel funny; he groaned, stormed and howled, saying that his head was coming off. Finally he tried the first part of the Parson's recipe; filled his mouth with ice-cold spring-water To his astonishment he found that so long as the water remained cold it seemed to benumb the pain. He would take a large mouthful and when it became lukewarm, the supply was renewed.

During the day he used something less than a gallon of water in this manner, and by night his toothache seemed to be effectually frozen out. He slept well, but alas! when he arose next morning his jaw was swollen until it resembled Jordan Blake's, and the affected tooth seemed to be very much longer than any of the rest, besides being so sore he hardly dared to close his mouth.

During the next few days while the swelling subsided he nearly starved, and could scarcely endure it; then a bite of pickle suddenly awakened the tooth again, and it began trying to jump out. For two hours he made the parsonage noisy with his wailings and then the annoyed Parson ordered him to go over to Dr. Parker's office and have the acher pulled.

The boys had often seen Dr. Parker riding by on professional calls. He had a clay-bank mare, so swaybacked that when he sat astride her, the rider looked as if he might be mounted on a two-humped dromedary. When Nathan reached his office the Doctor was not in, so the visitor sat down to await his return. The place was quite a museum; shelves of bottles, pieces of skeleton, strange odors and numberless odds and ends very suggestive and gruesome in appearance.

In the presence of so many novelties Nathan's tooth suddenly stopped aching and he gazed about him in amazement. Presently the Doctor came in, and when he looked at his patient the boy entirely forgot what he had come for.

The Doctor was cross-eyed; extremely so. In fact, this affliction was so terrible that some untruthful people said he had to turn around twice, and then stand with his back to anything in order to keep his eyes on it. The look he fixed upon Nathan actually made the goose-flesh come out on his body.

Performing the feats necessary to see, and appearing to fix his optics upon the root of his tongue, the Doctor asked Nathan in a kindly tone what he could do for him.

This inquiry presently brought a recollection of his errand to Nathan's bewildered mind, and he said he had been having an aching tooth, and the Parson had told him to come over to have it pulled; but he added that he guessed it was all right now; it did n't ache any more.

The Doctor was familiar with such sudden cures, however, and insisted upon seeing the tooth, "just to make sure." So Nathan got into a big chair with fear and trembling. Pulling down the boy's lower jaw, Doctor Parker hooked a finger that tasted awfully bitter from quinine into the corner of Nathan's mouth and looked in; how he managed it the youth could never imagine.

But somehow for the life of him Nathan could no longer tell which tooth had been aching. There were several sore ones, and he responded with a wince and very much disguised "ouch" when they were tested. It proved to be a case in which the Doctor himself had to determine which was the aching member. At last finding a decayed molar he pitched upon it as the right one; and before Nathan suspected his design he felt a sensation as if the roof had fallen on his skull and the floor seemed to jump up and hit his lower jaw; there was an agonized,

"Owwwooo!"—but too late.

The Doctor held the tooth between the nibs of a pair of hawkbilled forceps, and blood streamed from its former socket.

"There," he said coolly; "it won't bother you any more," and he laid it in a box that contained many others.

The Doctor began mixing up some pills, and Nathan sat for five minutes, clearing his mouth of blood, and feeling the hole in his gum with his tongue; the place seemed astonishingly large. Then telling the Doctor that the Parson would settle the bill he went home. Some two hours later he discovered that the cross-eyed Doctor had pulled the wrong tooth; he was apprised of this by the right one's waking up and beginning to jump.

Out of fear alone he endured this as long as he could, but it was too much for him, and at last he began to roar. When the Parson found out the facts, he took matters into his own hands. Dragging the sufferer back to the doctor's office, he stood by while the affected tooth was tracked out with a steel gouge. Then while the Parson sat on Nathan's legs and held his hands, the Doctor wound one arm about the victim's neck,

"WRENCHED THE PESKY ACHER OUT."

and wrenched the pesky acher out. This ended the toothache, but Nathan said he "felt as if his head had fallen in."

Next day, although it lacked less than a month before the summer vacation, the boys were sent to school. The school-building stood about three hundred yards from the parsonage, across a stretch of beautiful common, which formed a spacious play-ground for the scholars. There were three teachers, in as many different rooms. Mr. Leckrone was the principal, and Nathan entered his room, while William, not being so far advanced, was placed in the room below.

Mr. Leckrone was a large, weak man, with a violent temper. Like the Parson, he believed in frequent use of the rod as the true method of reforming wayward youth; but in his own room there were several large, very mean boys, and for caution-ary reasons Mr. Leckrone was inclined to overlook much of their misconduct; but all the vexation these unruly larger scholars caused him was visited freely on the small fry.

The stern Parson had given Nathan and William his customary caution when they entered upon their studies; but the boys seemed to understand the art of behaving, and quite astonished the watchful Apostle by their good conduct.

They got along well for a fortnight, when an unfortunate thing happened; and as usual the victim of it was poor William.

Some of the big boys already mentioned were in the habit of playing "whip-cracker." Once, during recess, they formed a long line for the sport, and just as it started, the end man, who was nearly twice as big as William, seized him by the wrist in passing, and when the final sweeping crack came, let him go.

After flying through the air, William alighted upon his stomach, scooted about fifteen feet and finally brought up against the sharp corner of a fence-post. While skimming along he had kept up his head like a turtle, and unfortunately struck the post with his eyebrow, or more exactly speaking, where his eyebrow ought to have been. The contact was hard, and the sharp wood cut open the flesh, denting in the skull like the letter V.

William was of course knocked senseless, and most of the scholars thought he had been killed. One big, kind-hearted fellow picked him up and started for the parsonage, blood from the wound flowing down William's face in a stream.

It scared Mrs. Flint into a faint, and made the Parson so furious, that he went over to the school-house and raised a storm. Of course William recovered, but the boy that did the mischief was expelled from school. After that the others were very cautious about playing whip-cracker, and for the rest of the session none of them dared to nag and abuse the smaller boys

CHAPTER XXI.

THE PARSON'S TEMPER.

THE dark cloud of war which was threatening the country, had by this time filled all the southern skies. Everything else became of small importance before this one great theme; and as call after call came for volunteers to fight the battles of the North, a growing dread of the terrible struggle filled all hearts.

As the certainty of prolonged strife and peril became more apparent, no one was more profoundly affected by it than Parson Flint. Rabidly loyal to the North, and northern ideas, he felt deeply depressed and brooded over the threatened disruption of the Union day and night. At the same time he seemed to be torn by some internal struggle, which cast over his thought and features a deeper gloom even than was natural to them.

Mrs. Flint and the older girls watched him with anxious hearts and secret fears. They well knew his stern sense of duty, and believed that if he thought himself called, he would enlist among the volunteers without a moment's hesitancy.

But if the conflict going on within him was because of this matter he kept it wholly to himself. Not even to his devoted wife did he open his mouth, and she was too well acquainted with his disposition to question him about it. Yet the burden she bore during these gloomy days none but herself ever knew. The boys often saw her weeping, and at all times there was the shadow of a great fear in her eyes.

Day by day the Parson grew more moody and depressed. He became restless and irritable, always going early to the incoming boats to secure the latest papers. Then, during the long evenings, he would sit and pore over them, sometimes reading aloud, while Mrs. Flint and the girls were knitting socks, picking lint or preparing rolls of bandages to send to the hospitals, where sick and wounded soldiers tossed and struggled in fever and agony.

At times the boys would help in the lint-making, the while listening with vague terror to the description of bloody battles in far distant places, and watching the gloomy Parson as he read. But oftener, mesmerized by his resonant voice they would go to sleep stretched out upon the floor, and awaken only when it came time for family prayers. Then they would go to bed and dream all sorts of terrible things suggested by the Parson's reading.

Weighed down by his growing distress, the Apostle became more and more disturbed, retiring often to his place of secret prayer upon the leafy hillside back of the house. Loss of sleep rendered him nervous, and a fever of foreboding seemed to darken all his days.

This unhealthy condition did not improve his naturally stern temper. Generally austere, he now became harsh and impatient. The boys were the first to feel the weight of his moods, and he brought them up with many a hard jolt as often as any spirit of mischief or disobedience led them astray. They quickly learned the necessity of keeping out of his way as much as possible, and when guilty consciences led them to fear his vengeance, they dodged about like frightened rabbits.

But this bitterness of spirit on the Parson's part soon bore worse fruit. It overshadowed the family in general, and here it sometimes met with determined opposition. Not merely was the Parson cross, but he was sometimes unusually exacting and overbearing, so that even Mrs. Flint often had to endure trials and harshness she did not deserve.

Finally this brooding unpleasantness reached a climax; and the memory of it was like a plague-spot in the hearts of the unhappy household for many a long day afterwards.

One morning the Parson turned his aroused spleen upon Ruth, who was nearly seventeen years old, and who fancied she was a young lady, removed by her age beyond any practical visitation of the Apostle's wrath. When he spoke harshly to her she "sassed back." Instantly the outraged Parson drew his heavy hand across her face in a sounding slap.

With flaming cheeks and streaming eyes, Ruth poured out upon the Parson a storm of reproach and anger which had all the biting temper and fearless scorn that burned in his own bosom. She told him that he was brutal, or crazy; that just because he had the strength of some big animal, he need n't think he could scare everybody, and trample the feelings of others under his feet.

For a few moments the amazed Parson stood in open-mouthed astonishment; but he never could brook rebellion in his own family, so twisting round on his heel, he strode out of the house, only to return with a formidable "hickory" in his fist.

Ruth divined the purpose of his sudden exit, but instead of growing frightened, she worked herself up into a very frenzy of rage and defiance. At the time Mrs. Flint happened to be up stairs, but she heard the slap and Ruth's wild tirade. Trembling and sick with fear she hurried down, for she knew only too well the inflexible nature of the Parson's anger, and how he allowed nothing to stand in his way.

She threw her arms about the raging girl and forced her into a bedroom off the kitchen, shutting the door. Then with white face she met the Parson as he strode into the house with gad in hand.

"Pa," said Mrs. Flint in a pleading voice, "think of what you are doing. Ruth is too old to be treated like a child!"

"She is, is she?" grated the Parson between his clenched teeth; "well, I'd whip her, if she was as old as Methuselah, and as big as the side of the house! She shan't sass me!"

"No! No! Pa; for my sake, don't," cried Mrs. Flint, laying a restraining hand upon the Parson's arm.

But the Parson's anger had gone beyond his own "sake," let alone that of his wife. He had a religious duty to perform; and Solomon's method with a rebellious child was not only especially congenial to him just then, but it was the only system of reformation which he regarded as Scriptural and right.

Overhearing his determined words, Ruth slipped quietly

"The Boys Grabbed Each Other"

from the bedroom into the kitchen, intending to escape from the house and take refuge at a neighbor's until the storm had spent itself. But the irate Parson happened to be standing near the kitchen door and caught sight of her. Shaking off the clinging hand of his wife, he strode up to Ruth and seized her by the arm.

But alas! the Parson was dealing with his own courageous flesh and blood. The instant that Ruth saw escape was impossible she faced the executioner with blazing eyes, and cheeks of stormy streaked white and red. When the rod fell she uttered one scream like a wounded wildcat, and then stared into the Parson's angry eyes with the look of a fearless tiger. Her lips lifted in a snarl, while her clenched teeth ground together.

By this time the two older girls had hurried into the room. and the boys were beginning to yell in very terror. But when the hickory fell upon poor Ruth, as by one accord, Mrs. Flint, the two girls and the boys flung themselves upon the infuriated Parson in a body. The boys grabbed each a sturdy leg; Louise and Mrs. Flint his arms; Eunice seized upon his wrist, and with a mighty jerk wrenched the rod from his hand.

This sudden attack stupefied the Parson; he stood with dropped jaw, scarcely realizing what had happened to him. Eunice threw away the switch, and standing in front of her father, laid both hands upon his shoulders and bored her big gray eyes resistlessly into the Parson's wide ones.

"You shall kill us all before we let this go on," she said in a strong, vibrant voice. "You don't know what you are doing; can't you see that poor Ruth is nearly beside herself?"

19

Something in her firm tone, and the steady, unfaltering gaze recalled the Parson to his senses. He groaned, shook himself free from the detaining hands, turned and strode through the open door, making for his place of prayer on the hillside.

During this interval, briefer than it takes time to relate, Ruth had not moved, nor said a word. When the Parson disappeared, Mrs. Flint rushed to her and gathered the rigid form of the victim to her mother's heart. Then, and not until then, did the girl's consuming fury give way, and with a pitiful whimper she turned faint and weak in the moment of rescue.

Supporting her into the bedroom, Mrs. Flint called Eunice to her aid, and closed the door. Overcome by what to them was so awful a tragedy, the boys went snuffling and sobbing out to the lot, and not knowing what else to do, began to chop wood as a relief to their sorrows. They pegged away for half an hour, and the Parson had not returned. Finally they began to wonder if Ruth was still alive, and the fear for her became so great that they crept into the house to see. The bedroom door was ajar, and through its crack they saw Ruth sitting upon the bedside, while Mrs. Flint was brushing her long, dark hair.

"This has nearly killed mother," Mrs. Flint was saying to Ruth. "For my sake won't you go to pa and ask him to forgive you?"

"Never! Not as long as I live," was the bitter reply. "If I could die myself, I'd like to do it."

This declaration was so terrible that William broke out

crying, and rushing into the room both of the boys flung their arms about Ruth, sobbing wildly, calling her "honey," and

EUNICE.

patting her face until the poor, overwrought girl began to tremble; then with one choking cry she threw herself into her mother's arms, finding relief from the misery of her heart in a flood of tears.

Mrs. Flint strained the shaken girl to her bosom, soothed : her gently, and finally by a nod, motioned to the boys to go away. They arose to leave the room, and in a last effort at consolation William snuffled out to his unhappy sister:

"Do n't you cry, Ruth. We're *so* sorry for you, and if pa ever tries to larrup you ag'in, we won't let him. You 've told on us lots of times and got us whipped; but we do n't care; you kin do it ag'in any time you 're a mind to."

"I never will again," sobbed Ruth convulsively; "never again; not if I was to die for it."

The boys wandered disconsolately about the yard for awhile, and were finally joined by Jerry Ward, one of their schoolmates Fearing the Parson's return the three climbed into the haymow, where Jerry soon heard the whole tale of woe He had no such feeling about it as afflicted Nathan and William, but he sympathized with them in a fashion not at all good for the Parson's sons. The main idea he advanced was that of a deep and terrible revenge:

"I bet he would n't lick me mor 'n once't or twice't 'til I fixed him," Jerry remarked boastingly. "I 'd take the old skeezix out and drownd him in the river, or I 'd smother him in bed some night!"

But the hopelessness of all this dawned upon William. "We can't do them kind of things," he said despondently. "Ye see pa 's a good deal bigger 'n we are, an' he 'd take an' lick the hide off 'n us."

"Well," said Jerry, seeing the force of this statement; "then I'd get some powder an' blow him up when he wuz n't lookin': he would'n't have time to git you if you done that."

It must be confessed that because they felt so badly about Ruth, the boys lent willing ears to these horrible schemes of Jerry; and for several days many dark thoughts fermented in their minds. During this evil period William one day found the Parson's book-case unlocked, and managed to secure a full tablespoonful of powder from the bottle which the Parson always kept under lock and key. With fell and gloomy plots in mind he smuggled this out and hid it away. Then he hunted up the biggest cob he could find and made a most formidable cannon, which was loaded to the muzzle with buckshot. Not knowing just how to make an attack, however, he trained the weapon upon the lot-gate while his father was down town, and then covered it up with a big chip. It was his intention when the right moment came, to blow the Parson out of the water, or out of his boots, which, did n't matter.

There is no guessing what might have happened had not old Sally, the cow, put her big foot on William's ordnance and crushed it into several pieces. By this accident alone was the Parson saved from being horribly mangled, or William prevented from blowing his own head off.

After being interfered with in Ruth's punishment the Parson left the house as we have described, and he did not return until nearly dusk. He ate

TRAINED THE WEAPON ON THE LOT-GATE.

no supper, but all the long dismal evening sat with elbows upon his knees, and face buried in his hands. Perhaps the tooth of remorse gnawed him sharply, for his misery seemed very great, and during a week following he hardly spoke a word.

The sorrowful family sat silently about, waiting for the Parson to have evening prayers, but he gave no sign; and about ten o'clock they retired, leaving the brooding man alone.

Never before in all the recollection of the boys had family prayers been thus omitted, and the circumstance only emphasized the dreadful impression the event left upon their minds.

CHAPTER XXII.

THE DAWN OF GRIEF.

LISTENING TO THE
CANNON.

TROUBLES never come singly, but "like birds of a feather" seem to follow one another and fly in flocks. Day by day the rising red tide of war crept slowly toward the North, until at last it seemed to threaten the very seat of government. Numerous victories of the southern arms sent yet greater waves of fear and doubt through the Union; and as fell slaughter marched clamoring through the land, a sable pall of grief fell upon thousands of homes.

One misty morning nearly all of Bluff City was gathered at the river, or had mounted the hilltops about the little village. War had broken out in Missouri, and the dull steady throb of cannon pulsed through the foggy air. For several hours this frightening, fevered throb of carnage beat fast, and the listening people held their breath at times in nerve-racking suspense. When finally the far away booming had died down, everybody gathered at the wharf to meet the evening boat which brought St. Louis papers with news of the battle. Then it was learned that the Union forces had gained a hard-fought field which cost them all too dear.

Following this excitement came rumors of guerrilla raiding across the river, and wild tales were afloat as to the merciless butchery and inhuman cruelty of these "bushwhackers." The worst of it was that many of these fearful stories were true. Bands of lawless, irresponsible men, who assumed war as an excuse for their conduct, often played the part of mere robbers and cut-throats, wreaking vengeance on their personal enemies, or else torturing and outraging utterly harmless and innocent people.

One day rumor had it that several of these wolves of war had crossed the river a few miles above Bluff City, burned the house of an unprotected farmer and horribly maltreated his family. And when this story was confirmed the whole country-side was aroused to indignation and thoughts of vengeance before unknown.

Every able-bodied boy and man in the town joined the home-guards, being constantly drilled by their chosen officers. It was not known how soon the villagers might be called upon to defend their own homes from daring bands of depredators.

Foremost among the sympathizers and organizers of this home militia was Parson Flint. He turned his congregation into a church-militant, and preached such bitter, scathing sermons upon rebellion and rebels that the fame of him went abroad, awakening not only the muttered protest of sundry parishioners who had Southern prejudices, but drawing upon the orator the more dangerous notice of the guerrillas as well.

These latter favored him with several anonymous letters, full of threat and promise of dire chastisement if he continued to heap abuse upon them and the cause which they disgraced. But if they thought to scare the sturdy Parson they did not know his mettle. He read their letters aloud from the pulpit and in the market-places, with running comments of sarcasm and defiance; and when some of his more cautious friends warned him to be careful, he replied that he could thresh all such cowards as these anonymous letter-writers with only half a show and a couple of cornstalks.

But though the Parson himself was fearless and rash, these sinister warnings sent him planted yet deeper dread in the heart of his wife and the minds of the two older girls. They pleaded with him not to be so headstrong, but after his usual manner he laughed at their fears, and refused utterly to carry anything in the way of arms.

In his burning zeal perhaps the Parson somewhat enjoyed the notoriety his conduct gave him; but however dauntless and courageous he was, no one doubted the sincerity of his rabid politics. Yet the danger gathering about him was much greater than he knew, and it was to follow him with such a sinister front that even he, iron-hearted as he was, might well have halted and blenched before its blighting aspect.

The foreboding distress of Bluff City reached a climax when, in response to an importunate call, a hundred of the home militia finally went to join the Union force under Grant, down the Mississippi. They were the crack members of the home-guard, and when on the appointed day they marched from the public square down to the transport waiting to convey them to battle, one of the school-boys walked proudly at the front, beating his drum to time their steps.

With the great throng went the Parson, Nathan and William to see the last of them; and woeful to relate, it was the last of full half their number. Tears and wailings followed them. When the men had swarmed upon the great boat at the wharf, there were cries and sobs from terror-stricken wives and children, mingled with clinging farewells that in so many instances meant forever.

The scene became so harrowing as almost to unman some of the departing regiment; and to divert the overwhelming grief, several of the men called upon the Parson, whose tall form marked him among the crowd, requesting him to make them a goodbye speech. But his own heart was full; and when a cry for silence caused a hush to fall upon the crowd, the Parson mounted a pile of lumber on the deck; then instead of pouring out one of his fiery speeches, he dropped upon his knees, raised his great hands aloft and began to pray.

When he mounted to the top of the lumber-heap every eye in the murmuring crowd was turned upon him, and the breath was subdued to hear what he might say. Nathan and William had followed him closely, and stood just below him on his elevation. When suddenly he knelt, out of sheer force of habit they also dropped upon their knees. Then his first words had scarcely been uttered when it was as if some great

He Began to Pray.

hand of awe had been laid upon the throng about him. With one accord they got down upon their knees. Strong men clasping wives and sobbing children in brave arms; lovers hand in hand, shaken with the grief of parting,—all bowed down in tearful silence as the Parson's mighty voice rose and boomed upon the air.

For a brief spell the boat's crew hung in the wind, and then they too knelt, awed by the solemnity of the occasion. And when the gruff captain, whose heart had been hardened by many such scenes, and whose eyes had looked upon numerous battle-fields until they had almost forgotten how to weep, came out upon the bridge and gazed down upon the kneeling throng below him, he too took off his cap, and dropped his grizzly old head upon his breast with a sigh.

As the prayer proceeded, up from the kneeling throng upon the deck arose the response of murmured petitions, choking sobs and the whimpering of frightened children. The Parson's soul was shaken within him, and the fountains of his own sorrows were broken up; yet strong above all other sounds his great, deep voice rose and soared, like some dominant call of faith saying to the storm, "Peace, be still!" With a quiver and thrill that vibrated through every heart within sound of his words the Parson closed his pleadings:

"Oh, Heavenly Father, pour the comfort of Thy love and tenderness upon these sorrowing hearts. Be with these, our neighbors and brothers, who go from us to fight the battles of their country; guard them in the hour of danger; into Thy hands we commit them and the grief-stricken wives and children they leave behind. If it be Thy will, unite their hearts again in the love of home and fireside when this cruel war is over. This we ask in the name of Him who said, 'Let not your hearts be troubled; ye believe in God, believe also in Me.' Amen!"

And up from the weeping daughters, mothers and sons, as well as from the departing soldiers and even the gray old captain there swelled in heart-felt unison a great, responsive "Amen!"

When the clanging bell and the captain's roaring cry had sent the reluctant, lingering crowd ashore, the ladened boat pushed off and turned its prow down stream. So long as it was in sight there was waving of caps from its decks, answered by fluttering handkerchiefs from the wharf, until finally the mists of tears and distance hid the departing home-guards from sight. The forlorn ones then slowly dispersed, going back to lonely homes praying in their hearts that the ruthless dragon of war might spare their offered treasures.

When the boys got home from school next day, they found their mother in great distress, making hurried preparations to go away. One of her sisters, who lived a hundred miles up the river was dangerously ill and had sent for her. How long she would have to be away was uncertain, and to the boys her going was almost as grievous as death.

That evening they went with her and the Parson to the boat, and after numberless hugs and kisses and goodbyes, they saw her borne away in the dusk, watching her dear face as long as it was in sight. The next day was Saturday, and never did

the parsonage seem so lonesome and desolate. When breakfast was over and the Parson had gone down town the boys
wandered aimlessly through the house, finally going up to
their mother's room. All about were the articles she was in
the habit of wearing. Her work-basket was on a stand, and
a half-finished sock she had been knitting lay folded around the
needles on top. Finally they peeped into the closet, and in a
burst of grief William hugged one of her old dresses hanging there, burying his tearful face in its folds. Then he
wept over a pair of her shoes, sitting down on the floor
and hugging them tightly to his heaving breast. How many
steps they had taken for him, and now the owner had gone
far away!

After a time he and Nathan went out into the lot, and lay
down in the shade of the barn, afflicted with a spell of silence,
and thinking only of her. Presently William rolled over on
his stomach and with elbows on the ground, supported his chin
in his hands. Nathan said musingly, "I wonder where she is
now?" Then William's heart almost choked him; burying
his working face in his arms, he let out one piteous howl of
grief:

"Oh, I do *wisht* she wuz here!"

Nathan made no reply, but his own heart echoed that cry
of love and loneliness. He had been playing soldier, however,
and so made a great effort to hold back the hot tears which
made his eyes sting and wink so fast. He gulped a time or two,
poked a straw into a worm-hole in the ground and said never
a word.

In a little while some schoolmates of about their own ages came by and called to them to come and play soldier. It was well that something should happen to make them forget their sorrows.

In days gone by the Parson had been a member of the home militia where he lived, and during this time had bought him a sword. One day the boys had found this old weapon among some lumber in the smoke-house and confiscated it with great joy. It was a very long blade, and William could not wear it at all. This fact caused them to make a fair division of the spoils, Nathan having the sword, and his brother carrying the scabbard. Among their soldier-playing schoolmates the possession of a real sword gave them great prestige; and by lending it to the older boys occasionally, both William and Nathan were greatly promoted in the various drills of the scholars

Besides this, in some of his good-humored moments the Parson had condescended to recall certain of his old military tactics, and he gave the boys a few lessons which they quickly learned and proudly used in many mimic battles.

Called by their eager companions, the boys ventured out upon the commons, and for half an hour engaged in play. But all the while they kept a sharp lookout for the Parson's return; and when at last the dread lest they should be caught out of bounds became too great, they suddenly broke off playing and returned to the parsonage premises, assuring their clamorous companions that "pa was going away soon, and then they could all have a good time."

About half-past nine o'clock the Parson came back, and to the surprise and delight of the boys, he had a letter from Mrs. Flint. This had been written upon the boat, about twenty miles from Bluff City. A neighbor of her sister's had met Mrs. Flint and given her a full account of the serious sickness that had called her away. She said that from reports the sick woman was quite dangerously ill, which might detain Mrs. Flint for two weeks or more. The letter was brought back by a passing boat, and she had written them the first news.

All the wife's and mother's heart was in the quaintly scribbled pages, and when the Parson had read it, he tossed the missive to the boys. They seized upon it as upon some great treasure, taking it away to read. At the last of it there was a message for them alone, which they read with glowing hearts:

"I wonder what you've been doing since I left," she said; "you are both in my thoughts all the time; and I pray the good Lord to keep you safely day and night; so farewell, my own precious boys."

How many times they read her words and hugged the letter to their hearts it would be hard to say; it was a bit of comfort they had not dreamed of getting so soon after she had gone away.

A little after ten o'clock the Parson prepared to drive to one of his country appointments, expecting to be gone over the Sabbath. The place was about seven miles from Bluff City, and when he had got Daniel hitched to the buggy, suddenly he ordered William to get ready to go with him. Mrs. Flint was away from home, and the Apostle had no desire to leave

20

the boys together for two long days, fearing they might hatch up mischief.

Eunice dressed William in his best clothes and furnished him up for the trip, at the same time giving him sundry admonitions as to good manners and proper behavior. Then the Parson laid out some wood for Nathan to chop, enough to occupy him for the balance of the lonely day, and with William, looking very woe-begone, drove away.

CHAPTER XXIII.

WILLIAM TREADS IN THORNY WAYS.

NEVER for very long at a time was Parson Flint either jolly or sociable, especially with members of his own family. To-day he seemed to be more silent and taciturn than usual. Occasionally sundry ejaculations of a prayerful nature would escape his lips, or else he would groan dismally, as if his thinking machinery needed some of the oil of gladness to keep it from creaking.

So as William and he drove along the country lanes or through the leafy woods the trip was not at all enlivening. Once only did anything occur to break its monotony: a huge mottled snake that seemed recently to have shed its skin crossed the road in front of Daniel, making the old horse snort and shy. The Parson quickly halted him, sprang out and killed the ugly reptile, tossing its body far out into the brush. Then re-entering the carriage, he directed William to drive on slowly, while he himself took out his Bible and sought to fix his mind upon the coming Sunday sermon.

273

It was nearly twelve o'clock when they reached Brother Slaten's, where the Parson expected to stay during the next two days. William opened the big gate and the Parson drove into the barnyard. Then giving the lines into the boy's hands, he went to the farm-house, a hundred yards distant, to see if anyone was at home.

As he strode away three or four awakened dogs began to bark, and their clamor brought Sister Slaten to the back porch. She was a very fat woman with red hair, and a most jolly, beaming face. Hurling a stick of stove wood at them, she scattered the yelping dogs and hailed the Parson with whole-souled heartiness.

"Jist put yer brute in the barn, Brother Flint," she said; "and then come right into the house. Slaten is plowin' over yander,"—and pointing to a quarter of a mile distant,—"but it's nigh time fer dinner, an' I'll call him in."

Saying this she waddled into the kitchen, soon re-appearing with a big conch shell which she put to her lips and sounded a long note or two to summon Brother Slaten.

William helped the Parson to unhitch Daniel and then led him into one of the numerous stalls of the barn. When the horse was secured and fed, he followed the Parson to the house, and Sister Slaten ushered them into the cool sitting-room After shaking hands with the Parson and rolling up a big horse-hair chair for him, she turned with a motherly smile to William·

"So ye brought the boy along," she said cheerily. "I'm mighty glad he come How are ye, my son; and how's your ma?"

"Ma's gone off, and won't be back fer I dunno how long," William replied; and his tone and look were so forlorn that the good woman took him in her arms, giving him a smothering hug to her broad fat bosom.

"Bless the child!" she exclaimed pityingly. "I jist know he's been so lonesome he did n't know what to do. But then your ma will come back soon, I guess; and won't you be glad to see her!"

"I jist do n't believe I kin wait till she gits home," burst out William with a snivel. "She writ a letter and said she did n't know when she'd come back."

Mrs. Slaten gave him another squeeze and tender kiss, saying with a suspicion of moisture in her eyes: "Me and Slaten love boys. We have n't got any now. Jimmy went away to jine the army six months ago. But now you jist have a good time, my son, and I'll hurry and git dinner on the table."

It was not long before Brother Slaten came in from the field, riding one lusty mule and leading another that kept pulling back. The chain tugs, looped in its back-band constantly slapped him under the belly as he minced along, causing the animal to hump himself up, and look very much as if he would like to use his heels.

The Parson and William went out to greet the farmer, and his hearty grip fairly made the boy's fingers numb Turning the mules over to a hired man that came up presently, he himself went with the visitors back to the house. By the time Brother Slaten had washed up, his wife announced that dinner was ready. When William sat down to the table, his spirits were mightily uplifted by the sight of a great platter of luscious browned chicken, and a huge bowl of cream gravy.

The Parson asked the usual blessing, and then Sister Slaten seemed to resolve that William should be kept busy. She fairly loaded his plate with drum-sticks, gizzards and other tidbits of which he was very fond; and in the onslaught that followed her liberality the boy once more thought it good to be alive. The ride had made him ravenous.

The Parson himself was by no means idle, but he and the farmer managed to talk between bites. William regarded this as a waste of precious time, and employed his jaws to better purpose. Near the close of dinner a great squawking and outcry arose from the fowls in the back yard off the kitchen. Mrs Slaten got up, and as fast as her great weight would allow, hurried to the door, William at her heels. Presently she called urgently to her husband:

"Sam, bring yer gun quick; it's that pesky hawk after the chickens ag'in, and he's lit on the big tree out here."

Brother Slaten stepped quickly to a rack at the end of the dining-room and took down his rifle, throwing back the hammer as he started for the yard to see if the cap was in place. The Parson then got up from the table and said with considerable confidence:

"Let me try him, Brother Slaten; I used to be a pretty good hand with a gun, once upon a time."

"And welcome," replied the farmer. "I've banged away at the critter twice before, and never stirred a feather."

Taking the rifle, and hefting it in his hand, the Parson stepped out upon the back porch He caught sight of the hawk perching impudently upon the top of a tree near at hand, and raised the weapon to his shoulder. Standing steady as a rock, he glanced along the sights, while William clapped his hands over his ears, waiting for the shot, with eyes fixed upon the poised bird.

"STANDING STEADY AS A ROCK."

The keen, whip-like crack of the rifle rang out, the great hawk started, tottered, and finally pitched forward over the limb, where for a few moments it clung by one foot. Presently it let go, and with a swirl and tumble fell to the ground, driving the alarmed chickens and other fowls nearly frantic with its sudden advent among them. One old warrior among the ganders sailed at the carcass with a loud scream, but by some instinct seemed to find out quickly that the enemy was dead, and then stalked solemnly away, sounding his note of assurance to the other fowls.

"Thank goodness, Brother Flint hez killed the nasty thing," exclaimed Mrs. Slaten fervently. "It's been around here for two months and has e't up half-a-dozen of my best Bramah chicks."

William raced away and picked up the dead hawk, bringing it to the porch where the Parson stood, holding back the rifle-hammer with one toe, and blowing the smoke from its barrel.

"Why, Parson, ye knocked the daylights plumb out uv it," exclaimed Brother Slaten admiringly. "I did n't suppose ye were that handy with a weepun. What if a Johnny Reb had been off that distance and ye lookin' along the sights at him; it 'ud 'a' spiled his pussonal features fer him, I reckon."

"They used to call me a purty good shot," remarked the Parson complacently. "I could take the head off 'n a guinny hen at forty yards; and you know the critters dodge like lightnin'."

"Great Scott," said Brother Slaten, chuckling heartily. "You 'd ought to hev been a soldier."

"I 've sometimes thought so myself," returned the Parson sadly.

When he said this William laid the dead hawk upon the porch and stared at his father with a great jump of fear in his heart. It was the first time that the idea of the Parson's being a soldier had ever entered his mind, and the bare thought of it scared him.

Without pursuing the subject further, the Parson stepped forward and examined the hawk in absent minded sort of fashion. It was a large specimen of its kind, with cruel, hooked beak and long curving claws. The rifle bullet had gone through its body, breaking one of its broad wings in the passage. Presently the Parson took out his knife and cut off one of its legs at the thigh joint, skinning back the flesh and leaving an inch or so of the tendons on both sides exposed. Then he showed William how the bird worked its talons as it seized upon prey. By pulling the tendons on the front, the great foot spread wide, as when the bird is about to alight. Then by drawing upon the leader at the back, the toes shut up, clasping the keen claws like the fingers of one's hand.

To William this was something very novel, and he was as much interested as a boy could be. When the Parson and his parishioner had gone into the house again, the youth borrowed a knife from Mrs. Slaten, and cut off the other leg as he had seen the Parson do. The two made a treasure that would cause other boys to open their eyes when he got back to Bluff City.

Brother Slaten did not return to the field that afternoon, and when the hired man with his team had done so, Parson Flint and the farmer sat in the cool sitting-room, entering upon a long discussion of the never failing topic of war.

In the meantime William took a seat upon the back-stoop, and set about several experiments with a hawk's foot. He tried it on a chip, a bone and broom-handle, testing its powerful gripping qualities thoroughly. After awhile a lubberly, half-grown pup came mooning around the corner of the kitchen, carrying an old shoe in its mouth. Upon seeing William he dropped the shoe, and crawling apologetically up the steps, lay down near by and began to wallow about on his back.

The opportunity was too good to be resisted; William reached out with his hawk's foot and gently took the pup by one ear. With a whoop and start the animal tried to scramble up, but fell off the edge of the porch, went thumping down the steps and ran as if calamity were hot on his heels. William laughed softly at his antics, but felt sorry for the brute, so coaxed him back and soon soothed all his alarms, and made great friends with him.

While he was petting the animal Mrs. Slaten came to the door of the kitchen and said:

"Why do n't ye look around, my son? There 's lots of things to see, and mebbe ye might find some eggs for me in the barn "

This promised well. What healthy, normal boy does n't feel at home in a barn? Followed by the now reassured pup, William set off on a tour of exploration.

Farmer Slaten was very well-to-do, and in his sheds were many pieces of machinery that greatly interested William. His attention was presently attracted to an old-fashioned fanning-mill, used to separate chaff from wheat. He looked it over, and concluded to see if he could turn the fan; but at the first revolution an old setting hen flew out with a shriek and clatter, and William thought it best to abandon his efforts

Next he went into the barn, wandering in and out of the empty stalls When he reached the one next to which Daniel was quartered, he found a plank off the partition through which the old horse could be seen, sagged down on three legs, the hoof of his fourth barely touching the ground, taking an after dinner nap His flank was within a foot of the opening, and William reached in to wake him up with a hawk's foot. The experiment was instantly successful. Upon feeling the claws nip him, Daniel became very much awake, promptly launching out with both hind feet, and hitting the partition with a bang that sounded like thunder. William's tow hair stirred; he fancied the noise could be heard half-way to Bluff City, and was sure the Parson must have been aroused by it. Tip-toeing to the barn-door he peeped out to see, but no one appearing, he gave a long sigh of relief and went back to reassure the indignant horse.

But Daniel, suspicious by nature, had become more so through experience, and was not easily mollified. He stood back at the end of his halter, blowing out his nostrils and watching the persuasive William with most knowing eyes, as if sure he had some new instrument of torture to use. Not until the boy got him an extra ear of corn and went away did Daniel finally resume his usual state of nerves.

William now climbed into the haymow and looked about; but the place was so dark and spooky that he did n't remain long. Returning to the lower floor, he set out to examine every nook and cranny of the place; but until he reached the corncrib there was nothing particularly interesting to be seen. In the corn-bin, however, he came upon an unexpected treasure. Hanging to a nail by a length of chain was an old steel-trap. In his variegated career William had seen one or two of these hard-biting machines, and he uttered a grunt of satisfaction at having found one he could examine at his leisure. He carried it to the barn door and sat down on a little pile of hay to look the thing over. Its spring was not very strong, so that he found no trouble in setting the trap. He tried it many times, springing the catch with a stick, and starting slightly every time it snapped. Once it nipped his fingers, but upon pressing down the spring with his foot, he found that little damage had been done them.

Meantime the pup had been tagging at his heels; and when William sat down to play with the steel-trap, the contented animal stretched himself out near by and began again his favorite pastime of wriggling about on his back. The exercise seemed very comforting, and in his contortions he worked his way up close to William, and squirmed about as if a score of lusty fleas were nibbling his hide.

Never in all his life afterwards could William tell what made him so careless, but he laid the steel-trap down by his side, and watched the kicking pup with a half-drowsy feeling, in which he began to wonder what Nathan was doing, and when his mother would get home.

As in a dream he saw the flea-bitten pup squirm about slapping his tail here and there, utterly unconscious of danger. But presently the day-dreaming youth came out of his trance with a sick start of terror. The wriggling animal had managed to drop his threshing tail right into the jaws of the open trap, and they closed upon the member like the mandibles of a turtle!

The instant this awful catastrophe happened William foresaw the consequences, and made a frantic grab for the trap, but he was one second too late. With a screech and whirl the pup was on his feet, scared silly, and wild with the sudden torment at his tail. He dived through the open door and started for the house, making the air shiver with shrill yelpings that woke up the entire neighborhood.

"Wahee! Wahee!" went the Pup.

As the fleeing pup swept like a vocal cyclone up the home-stretch everything scattered before him; the hens squawked, the geese screamed and an old turkey-cock began to gobble frantically. Then three other dogs that had been sleeping somewhere rushed out barking, and all took after their screaming companion as he strove to flee from the wrath to come.

"Wahhh-ee, wahhh-ee, wahhh-ee!" shrieked the distracted victim, not knowing exactly where he aimed to go, but seeking only to put distance between himself and the nipping jaws that held him fast!

No sooner had the terrible din been heard than of course the Parson, Brother Slaten and his wife ran out to see what on earth had happened. By this time the crazy pup was racing round and round the house, while all the other dogs were hot after him, adding to his frightful clamor by their own excited barks and howls.

But the Parson, wise from long experience, instantly saw what had occurred; and as the flying pup swept by him, he snatched at the animal, missing him as William had, and then bracing himself up for the next heat.

In his unspeakable frenzy, the frightened animal had be-thought himself of a hole under the house where he was accustomed to crawl away out of the heat to sleep. As he came round again and made a dive for this place of refuge, the Parson succeeded in heading him off, caught him by the scruff of the neck and quickly removed the trap from his tail. Then the relieved brute plunged into the hole and disappeared for the rest of the evening, while the other dogs slunk away as if ashamed of their unseemly behavior.

By this time the surprise of the incident had gone, and the funny side of it struck Brother Slaven; he threw back his shaggy head and roared with laughter, while his wife's fat sides were shaking. But there was no glimmer of mirth on the Parson's outraged face. He laid the trap down, strode to a small apple-tree and jerked off a long, keen switch. Stripping the leaves from it through his hand, he called in a savagely menacing voice:

"William, come here!"

Utterly overcome by the swift tragedy of the affair, William was fairly shaking with grief and shame, being far more frightened than the loud-voiced pup had been. When this terrible summons to judgment fell upon his burning ears, all his heart seemed to break at once. He dragged his feet slowly forward until near the vengeful Parson, and then halting in a very climax of despair, he broke out into a wail of grief, calling aloud in some strange impulse:

"Oh, mother, *mother!* where are you? I did n't go to hurt the dog; I would n't a-done it for anything, if I'd a-knowed it!"

And so bitter and beseeching was his sorrowful wail that the laugh suddenly drained out of Sister Slaten's face, while the hot tears stung her kindly eyes. She hurried up to William, threw her apron over his head and squeezed him tight, while he clung to her desperately, burrowing his tow head into her fat, motherly stomach.

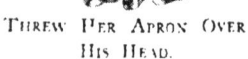

THREW HER APRON OVER HIS HEAD.

"I would n't whip the boy, Parson," exclaimed Brother Slaten at this. "He did n't mean any harm. Boys do n't think like grown up folks, and besides the onery pup is a nuisance. It 'll do him good to git a scare and take some exercise. He 's no good on earth." And again he burst into a fit of laughter as the vision of the circus came back to him afresh.

Thus adjured the Parson hesitated for a few moments; and then with a look of great disgust at William threw away the switch and said:

"He ought to know better, Brother Slaten, for I 've tried to raise him decently. 'Foolishness is bound in the heart of a child, but the rod of correction shall drive it far from him.' I ain't sure that I 'm doin' my duty by lettin' him off without a good larrupin'."

With this apology to his own conscience he went back into the house, followed by Brother Slaten. But the good wife took William with her around to the kitchen, where with many remorseful sobs he told her the story of the pup, and she talked soothingly, comforting him until his grief somewhat subsided. Then the two took a long walk about the place together, and in every way possible Mrs. Slaten tried to make him forget his bitter humiliation.

In spite of all she could do, however, there still lurked in William's soul a dread anticipation of the judgment to come. He knew the Parson well, and felt sure the matter would come up against him later. What the end would be he did not know.

That night, long after the Parson was sound asleep, Wil-

21

liam lay awake, so restless and homesick that it gave him the heart-burn. He snuffled to himself and watered his couch with his tears. Finally crawling quietly out of his cot, he felt about in the darkness for his clothing. Then after much fumbling through the pockets of his round-about, he seemed to find what he wanted, and crept back to bed, falling asleep at last with the object of his search hugged close to his heart. It was a long gray stocking, with a tiny hole in the toe. Before leaving home, he had slipped upstairs and taken it off his mother's workbasket, where she had laid it to mend, "to remember her by."

At half-past ten o'clock the next morning, all the people on the farm went to church, about three quarters of a mile from the house. It was a beautiful day, and already quite a crowd of people had reached the spot ahead of them. Most of the women had gone into the church, but the men sat about on logs, or the wagon-seats, talking over the events of the week. Farmer Slaten was heartily welcomed by everybody, and he soom made William acquainted with several of the country-boys about his own age, with whom he quickly got on very friendly terms.

With one eye out for the Parson, who was conversing with a little group of parishioners, William slipped away, took three or four of his new friends around back of the church, and proceeded to show them his hawk's feet, giving an exhibition of how they worked, and telling what he should do to one of his school-mates when he got home.

SHOWED THEM HIS HAWK'S FOOT.

His auditors of course grew deeply interested, and in a little time one of them proposed to swap a couple of ounces of large shot for one of the hawk's feet. Having two of them, William agreed to this trade, and it was quickly consummated. Then having nothing to contain the shot, he finally put them into the stocking which had so comforted his lonely hours the night previous. No sooner had he tucked them away in his pocket, however, than Parson Flint stepped around the corner, and when he saw William's occupation, looked at him in solemn rebuke. The abashed youth hastily thrust the remaining hawk's foot into his pocket, and at a backward nod from the Apostle, followed him meekly around to the front, and into the building. In order to keep the wayward youth under his eye, the Parson marched him up to the pulpit, and seated him upon a bench near the altar rail.

Then the services were opened. The interior of the building was oppressively warm, and as the sermon progressed William grew very drowsy and uncomfortable; the bench was hard, and so high that only the tips of his toes reached the floor. It had no back, either, and the restless victim could assume no position that would ease him.

For some time he amused himself by looking over the congregation, and when this ceased to be interesting, he tried to pass away the time by watching two flies that sailed back and forth in the air above his head, playfully butting each other as they met.

To sit still for any great length of time, and especially in hot weather, is certain to make any ordinary boy itch intolerably; and William was not an exception to this rule. He squirmed about, relieving first one tickling spot and then another; finally, as the perspiration had gathered on his freckled nose, he reached absent-mindedly into a pocket after his handkerchief.

Alas! Instead of that useful piece of linen, he drew out the stocking with the shot instead. He had forgotten all about it, and never knew that it had a hole in the toe! The shot streamed through this hole and fell upon the floor with a clatter that could be heard all over the church. Aroused by the strange racket, the drowsy congregation stirred curiously and craned their necks to see what was happening. William sat as if paralyzed; but the Parson paused in his vociferous sermon, fixed a lurid eye on William and said in his most sepulchral tone: ·

"William, leave the room!"

Then with white face, knees knocking together and his heart trying to get out of his mouth, William rose blindly up and staggered down the aisle, thinking it must be a mile in length. But at last he reached the door, and with face working, hands clenched and a sense of overwhelming calamity in his breast, he picked up his heels and flew like a wild thing down the road in the direction of the farm. He knew the way and ran until his breath gave out; reaching Brother Slaten's in a reek of sweat and almost in a state of collapse, he went into the barn and hid in a stall, wondering in his daze what on earth would happen to him next.

When the services were over and the congregation was dismissed, a man who had gone out ahead of William to look after his team told the anxious Brother Slaten what direction the boy had taken, and of course it was at once surmised that the fugitive had gone back to the farm. The family returned and when the Parson found that William was safe, his face set and he said never a word. To William this ominous silence meant far more than appeared to Brother Slaten and his good-hearted wife.

When time for the evening service arrived, Brother Slaten and the Parson went to church alone. Mrs. Slaten said she would remain at home and keep William with her for company. This lifted a great load off the boy's mind; for he felt certain that everyone would stare at him and wonder what kind of an animal had come among them.

Sister Slaten was as loving as she was big; and when alone with the depressed urchin she began to talk cheerfully to him, finally drawing from him the entire story of his mishap.

"Ye see I swopped one of them hawk's feet fer some shot," he blubbered between his sobs, "an' I did n't have any paper to wrap 'em up in, so I hed to put 'em in this here stockin'," drawing it out of his pocket. "I did n't know there wuz any hole in it; I went to git out my handkerchief, and mistook the stockin' fer it, and the shot run out of this yere hole in the toe."

The memory of his mother the article awoke in his heart, mixed with the recollection of his awful mishap entirely overcame him, and he fairly choked in his unbearable grief. Mrs. Slaten listened with amused sympathy: finally she reached over and took the article out of William's hands, and unrolled it full length with an expression of intense astonishment:

"Why, my son, what is this, and where on earth did you get it?" she asked.

"It's one of ma's stockin's," sobbed William bitterly. "I went an' got it out of her work-basket to remember her by."

Suddenly Sister Slaten reached out her great arms and snatched William into her lap. First she laughed, and then she cried; and all the time she was nearly squeezing the breath out of him, patting his back and kissing him furiously, taking on in a manner wonderful to see.

"Why, My Son, What Is This?"

"You pore lonesome child!" she at last exclaimed with a catch in her voice. Then she set to work to soothe his sore heart, telling him stories about her own boy that had gone to the war. Occasionally she interrupted her narratives by hugging her interested auditor close and kissing him with a tender violence that made William wink.

Finally when it came time for him to go to bed, she knelt down to pray, and William knelt comfortably by her. Thus holding him to her motherly bosom with loving arms, she prayed so earnestly and sweetly that a great peace stole over the lonely boy's heart; and he felt that if he did n't already have the dearest mother in the world, his next choice for that relative would be Sister Slaten.

The good woman's motherly talk and sympathy brought a great rest to William's strained nerves, and by the time Parson Flint and his parishioner got back from church, all the boy's troubles had been swept from his mind by the soft wings of slumber.

About ten o'clock the following morning the Parson hitched Daniel to the buggy and got ready to go home. Mrs. Slaten gave William a peck of luscious Bellflower apples, for himself, and sent along two fine, fat chickens as a present for Mrs. Flint. William parted from the farmer's wife with a hearty hug and kiss.

For a long time during the homeward journey Parson Flint maintained a dismal silence, and seemed to be wrapped in the maze of his own gloomy thoughts. At times he would heave a deep groan or sigh, as if the burden of the world lay heavily upon his shoulders. Once or twice William ventured a few timid questions, seeking to find what manner of temper the Apostle was in; but receiving only short answers or more often none at all, he finally gave up his attempts and sat in a greatly depressed state of mind, wondering what more could possibly happen to him.

Presently he found out. About two miles from town, in a place where a long stretch of straight road showed no one in sight, the Parson drove Daniel out to one side of the highway, tied him to a tree, and ordered William to get out of the carriage and follow him. Then he took his knife and cut a long hickory sprout. When the Parson had directed William to come with him, the boy thought his father was halting for one of his numerous seasons of prayer, but the familiar rod of correction quickly undeceived him. Without any preliminaries or useless explanations, the Apostle at once began to administer to William a liberal dose of Solomon's remedy for "foolishness," after which his comments were very few.

During this hearty exercise William did a ghost-dance in the dead leaves which rivaled that of the great Pau-puk-keewis described in Longfellow's Hiawatha. And at the same time the penitent youth was proclaiming in a loud voice, and with every degree of emphasis that he would ever afterwards lead a different life. When the Parson had completed his familiar task he said:

"Now, take that hawk's foot out of yer pocket and throw it away; and see if ye'll ever be caught disgracin' me when I take ye anywhere again."

With this admonition he turned to retrace his steps, not presuming that after what had happened, William would dream of disobeying But that weeping youth took from his pocket, and threw away with a great clatter among the dead leaves to deceive his father— *a ten-penny nail!*

That hawk's foot was the one compensation he had left for the terror and misery of the past two days. He just could n't part with it.

CHAPTER XXIV

THE LAST STRAW.

"Saw Nathan Coming."

WHEN the Parson and his chastened offspring reached Bluff City it was nearly noon. Daniel was stabled, and by the time William had put off his Sunday attire and donned his every-day clothes, the school-bell rang taps for dismissal. During the afternoon a mass meeting of the citizens was to be held in the school-building. Mr. Leckrone and the Parson were expected to address the gathering, so there was a half-holiday.

William was on the lookout, and in a short time he saw Nathan coming home. But he was not returning in a direct line as usual. For some mysterious reason he took a roundabout way, evidently making for the barn. Upon meeting him, William was astonished to find his brother's coat split up the back, his face a stormy red with swollen eyes, and an appearance very much dilapidated in general.

Nathan was not inclined to talk much, and occasionally

293

looked with apprehensive eye toward the school-house. After a few hurried questions to which he got little reply, William also gazed in the direction Nathan was looking, certain that something untoward was about to happen, and very anxious to know what it was.

In a little time Mr. Leckrone was seen to come from the school-house and walk with rapid strides toward the parsonage, evidently bent upon some important mission to the Apostle. As he entered the gate, Nathan shook a vengeful fist at him, and then suddenly turned more gloomy than ever. But full of his own woes, William began a bitter recital of the incidents of his trip already related, and tearfully exhibited his hawk's foot; yet interesting as it all might have been under other conditions, just then neither boy was in a state of mind to dwell upon such past history

"What 's 'e come for?" asked William finally, referring to the strange visit of Mr Leckrone.

Then Nathan's story came out, and William found that he was not the only one who had cause for grief.

It seemed that on his way to school that morning, Nathan had passed a neighbor's premises, and found a small, dead pig which had died during the night, and been tossed over the barn-yard fence Boy-like he stopped to examine the dead porker; and finally in obedience to some vagrant impulse tied a string around the animal's neck and carried it with him to the school-grounds

Here he and his odd play-thing were received with shouts of laughter, and for several minutes the rollicking scholars amused themselves by throwing the pig at each other until it was a bunch of broken bones. Finally tiring of this rude sport, Nathan had flung the carcass aside and forgot all about it; but later it caused him trouble.

Mr. Leckrone scarcely ever reached school until the last bell rang, and never entered his room until he had seen all the scholars file before him on their way in. This morning he was a trifle later than usual, probably being engaged on the speech he was to make that afternoon.

Behind the platform on which he sat during school hours was a small black-board, and above this was a hook upon which he always hung his hat. When the school was seated, it was seen that a sheet of newspaper hung from the hook, covering half the board. Mr. Leckrone strode to his place upon the platform, and jerked down the paper. Then a great gust of laughter broke out in the room; for there, hanging to the hook by its string was the pig, and underneath it, scrawled in mis-spelled words was the legend:

"Lectroon's diner."

Now the teacher was not at anytime a man noted for his self-control. His temper was quick and fiery, and in moments of excitement or sufficient provocation he would act very inconsiderately. When he grasped the meaning of the trick played upon him, he whirled upon the scholars with face black as a thunder-cloud, and in a voice that rang threateningly through the room asked:

"Who put this pig here?"

But of course the miscreant was a coward, and no one responded to the pointed question. Next time it was altered slightly:

"Who brought this animal here?"

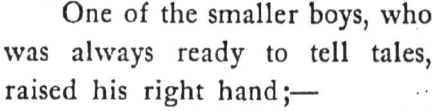

One of the smaller boys, who was always ready to tell tales, raised his right hand;—

"Well!" exclaimed Mr. Leckrone savagely.

"Nathan Flint brought the pig," was the reply.

"Nathan Flint," demanded the teacher, "did you bring this beast here and hang it up behind my desk?"

"No sir!" bawled Nathan indignantly. "I brought the pig to the school-grounds, but I never hung it up there."

"Who Put this Pig Here?"

Much as he would have liked to find the offender, it seemed to dawn upon the teacher's mind that he would fail to do so. And after Nathan's positive denial, he said surlily:

"Well, as you brought the vile thing to the grounds, come and take it down, and throw it out of the window."

But this did not at all please Nathan. Conscious of his entire innocence in the matter, he had no mind to be made a laughing-stock for the entire school by obeying such a humiliating command; so he settled down in his seat, frowned resentfully and did not move.

"Did you hear what I said?" demanded Mr. Leckrone sharply.

"Yes, sir, I did," rejoined Nathan in a much louder tone than was polite or necessary; "but I did n't put the pig there, and I ain't goin' to take the nasty thing down."

For a moment the teacher was dumfounded. The reply was so utterly contrary to Nathan's usually obedient habits that he could hardly believe what he heard. However, such impudent obstinacy only added to the flare of his temper. He snatched a tough hickory lying handy, strode from the platform and seized Nathan by the collar. But the boy clung tightly to his seat, and not until Mr. Leckrone had put the rod between his teeth and used both hands to break his grip did he succeed by lifting the culprit into an aisle between the rows of benches. Then snatching his rod again, he began to dust Nathan's jacket at a tremendous rate.

But the boy was not idle; he squirmed about and made a grab for his chastiser's person. His curved fingers caught in the waistband of Mr. Leckrone's trousers, and as the irate teacher kicked his victim's feet from under him, Nathan came down throwing his whole weight upon the article he had seized. There was a sound of ripping cloth and flying buttons, and the result came near being as humiliating to the teacher as to Nathan. However, the boy's hands were torn loose, and he was thrown face downward over a desk and fanned with all the strength of Mr. Leckrone's good right arm.

By this time the school was in an uproar; the girls were crying loudly, and mutiny was hot in the air. Just as some of the big boys were about to make a rush and rescue Nathan, the teacher jerked him to his feet, slammed him into a seat, and said between his angry gasps for breath:

"Now, see that you don't give me any more back talk, and do as I tell you next time, or it will be the worse for you."

But despite this admonition he seemed to realize that it would be useless to carry his commands any further just then; so after rearranging his disordered clothing, he took the pig down, threw it out of a window and sat behind his desk very pale and much exhausted by the reaction from his anger and exercise

It was some time before he proceeded with the school routine, and as out of the tail of his eye he saw Nathan sitting with clouded face, knuckling the hot, angry tears from his eyes, there came an uneasy conviction that he had gone too far in the matter In his mind there arose an important question; what would the Parson think of it?

Nathan, too, had been putting this inquiry to his own thoughts; but no doubt of what the Parson was likely to do troubled him; his numerous experiences on other occasions settled the question for him

By the time Nathan had briefly sketched these incidents, William had entirely forgotten his own troubles, and his eyes stuck out in admiration for his reckless brother and fear of what was to follow He summed all his feelings up in one significant question:

"What d've think pa'll do?"

"What does he always do?" returned Nathan gloomily.

"I never done anything wrong, but that won't make no difference."

"You stay here," exclaimed William eagerly, "and I 'll go to the house and see what I kin find out!"

With this he set off on a run, arriving in time to see the satisfied Mr. Leckrone depart, and hear the Parson say doggedly:

"Ye did jist right, Mr. Leckrone, and I 'll tend to his case. I believe in meckin' boys behave theirselves. If Nathan cuts up any more sich shines send him to me, and I 'll dress him down ag'in after you 've done with him."

This was enough for William. He hastened back to the barn and told Nathan all he had heard. Both the boys remembered that in his firm determination to carry out discipline, the Apostle had sternly said he would duplicate any punishment they received at school with another and harder one at home; and experience had assured them that such promises on the Parson's part were always sacredly fulfilled.

"Whachu goin' to do?" asked William nervously.

"I 'm a-goin' to hide till he gits off down town," said Nathan, after a moment's hard thinking

Then without stopping to think how foolish this trick would be, both the boys climbed into the barn-loft, and burrowed under the hay, on the side next the parsonage, so that they could see anything that transpired through a crack in the boarding.

It was not long before the Parson issued from the kitchen door and made for the barn, holding a tremendous hickory in his fist. He strode into the stable, looked all about and called the hiding urchins several times; but they lay breathless, and finally concluding that they were not there, the Parson returned to the parsonage. Presently he strode rapidly out of the gate towards the school-house, where a group of scholars could be seen at play. Evidently he thought the boys had aggravated their case by going to join them.

Seeing the enemy retire, William crept from his hiding place and ran to the kitchen; he was already quite hungry, and determined while the opportunity offered to secure something to stay his stomach during the afternoon. Ruth met him and learned all that the boys had done. Her hearty sympathies were with them; so she furnished plenty of provisions for the siege, exhorting William to retreat at once, as the Parson would return quickly when he found they were not at school.

William acted upon this timely warning and flew back to the barn; but alas! he did n't remember that the Parson was a woodsman with a keen, far-seeing eye. The returning avenger caught a glimpse of the fugitive as he shot into the barn. Instantly the trick dawned upon him, and he came back hot-foot with full vengeance in his heart and the formidable rod of correction in his hand.

This time he made straight for the boys' ambush. Opening the lot gate he strode into the barn, climbed up the ladder until his head and shoulders were in the loft and called out in his hardest voice:

DODGED INTO THE BARN.

"Young men, see if ye kin crawl out from under that hay and come down here, or I 'll give ye an extra dose that 'll warm the wax in yer ears."

Then the silly boys knew that there was no escape. They slowly obeyed the harsh summons, and a great load of shame was added to their grief and dark prospects.

When they had reached the lower floor, the grim Parson first selected Nathan as perhaps the more guilty culprit, and opened the exercises with all his accustomed zest. It might be surmised that his seance with William a few hours before had taken the edge off his strength, but not so. In the way of duty he had the endurance of a martyr, and as this particular occasion seemed to warrant extra energy, he summoned all his reserve forces and performed with a vigor of arm and determination of soul that did him credit.

But as William had already taken an allopathic dose of the remedy for "foolishness" that eventful morning, the part he was required to undergo was something less than usual, though quite enough to fulfill all Scriptural demands. When the Parson had completed the affair to his satisfaction he took a long, deep breath and said:

"Now, ye 'd jist as well learn it fust as last; ye 've got to behave yerselves; and I 'll see that ye do, if I hev to wear out all the second-growth hickory on the hill out there!" Then, as memory of, their impudent trick returned to his mind, he gazed at them, overpowering rebuke in his eyes, and remarked, "Ye 'll try to *hide* from me, will ye!"

That was all, and surely enough. He did not even feel

22

like praying over them this time, but walked away to the house, and soon went down town to the meeting of the afternoon.

The Parson's punishments were always severe enough; but although the boys had this day received double measure, their bodies were less hurt than their feelings. Never had such a dark storm of revolt and recklessness filled their hearts. They climbed back into the loft and lay down upon the hay, believing that the very limit of endurance had been reached; and indeed their cups were full. The fatigue and reaction of double distress stole over them both; the afternoon was warm, and presently deep sleep came to relax their quivering nerves

For more than two hours they slumbered, and then they were aroused with a start by the voice of the Parson calling them. Rubbing their swollen eyes, they sat up wondering if something else had happened to bring them under the frown of his wrath. Upon following him out of the barn, however, they found that he had saddled Daniel and was about to take some unusual journey Before mounting to ride away he said in a tone that still rang with menace and rebuke:

"I want ye to git and cut some wood. I 'm goin' away to be gone over night; and do you both stay at home and tend to your work Do n't let me hear of any shines out of ye when I git back, or what I 've already given ye won't be a circumstance"

Then swinging himself into the saddle he rode away.

When he had disappeared Nathan sat down on a log and said bitterly:

"I ain't goin' to stay here an' be licked to death any longer."

"Whachu goin' to do?" asked William, startled by his words and unusual determination.

"I 'm a-goin' to run away; an' I 'll go to-night!"

The last straw had broken the camel's back.

CHAPTER XXV.

"TRAMP! TRAMP! THE BOYS ARE MARCHING."

IF anyone had charged Parson Flint with cruelty, it would have much surprised him, and he would have indignantly denied the accusation. And if his harsh treatment of the boys had been cited as proof of the charge, he would have all the more repelled it.

There was but one standard of conduct which he recognized, and that was the Bible. To him "total depravity" was a terrible fact, and the means of overcoming it seemed to his mind perfectly plain. As may often be seen in really sincere people, the Parson's convictions only served to strengthen and confirm the naturally stern temperament with which he was born. Having been brought up by strict and old-fashioned parents, whose cherished means of reforming wayward youth was "the rod of correction," he simply followed with his own offspring the ideas and manners inherited from his forebears.

In reality, however, there was a very deep streak of tenderness and parental pride in his makeup, only it was often overborne by his all-pervading sense of religious duty.

Above all his natural instincts towered his fervent religious faith, and Solomon's dictates were his sole authority in matters of family discipline. He punished the boys because he thought duty and Scriptural commands required it, not because he particularly enjoyed the whippings. And for all these reasons it would have been hard to convince him that he was not doing right.

If it ever occurred to him that he had given the mischief-loving youngsters a whipping they did not really deserve, probably he excused himself with the reflection that if they happened not to have merited it just then, they would certainly deserve it often when he had no time to attend to the duty. Therefore, in general, the boys got but little pity or sympathy from him.

But it is very easy to do wrong under mistaken sense of duty, and especially when that feeling overbears all the kindliness of soul which makes life happy and sweet. Himself, he often said that "all men are poor miserable sinners;" but perhaps he forgot the further and just as needful thing to remember:

"The mercy I to others show,
That mercy show to me."

For their own part the boys could not at all appreciate the Parson's point of view; and hence as he rode away, leaving them sore and sullen to work upon a hateful task, their hearts were brimming with bitterness and rebellion. Endurance of such woes seemed out of the question, and so arose that wicked purpose to run away from home and go to the war as several of their boyish acquaintances had already done.

If their mother had been at home to comfort them with

her love and sympathy, no such wild scheme would have entered their minds; but she was gone and her stay was indefinite, hence the only restraining influence that could have held them was absent.

From the talk of the girls at supper-time they learned why the Parson had left home. He was summoned to attend a parishioner who was ill with a malignant attack of typhoid fever, and was not expected to recover. To the plotting boys this was good news; it left the coast clear, and firmly fixed in Nathan's mind the resolve that he would be missing when the Apostle returned.

The long nap of the afternoon, together with intense excitement kept the boys wide awake that night; and after going to bed they discussed their plans in cautious whispers until everything was arranged to their satisfaction. When the girls had retired, and sundry muffled snores told the plotters they were sound asleep, Nathan and William crept noiselessly out of bed, dressed themselves and made ready for flight. First they sneaked cautiously down stairs into the kitchen, where Nathan secured a huge loaf of bread and a beef-bone that had been boiled for dinner, but which yet had a considerable quantity of meat left on it. These provisions he tied up in an apron, not finding anything else to carry them in. Next he sought a candle and some matches which he stowed in one of his pockets. Then cautioning William to wait and make no noise, he tip-toed back to their bedroom, got a heavy quilt, his gun and ammunition, together with the Parson's sword, and made his way quickly back, where his brother anxiously awaited him.

With this plunder they softly opened the kitchen door and let themselves out, closing it after them.

Once safely out of the house they hurried to the barn. Here the quilt was rolled up as they had seen the soldiers' blankets, and Nathan tied it with a piece of rope, leaving a loop to go over the head, so that it could be swung upon the back, marching fashion.

Having got everything into shape, Nathan hoisted the roll of bedding over his shoulder, and picked up his gun. William took charge of the sword and their bundle of provisions, and then they climbed over the fence, and struck out across the commons, bound for the war.

BOUND FOR THE WAR.

The night was without a cloud, and no breath of wind stirred. Everything seemed ominously quiet; a shred of moon hung low in the West; it gave but little light, yet the stars glittered brightly all over the sky, and furnished light enough for them to march by.

Away to the North the low hills gloomed against the horizon, looking like the backs of some huge animals lying prone on the ground. From far off down the river the hoarse toot of a steamboat sounded once or twice, but the little village seemed to have gone to sleep, and only a faint light or two shone from a drug-store down the main street.

Everything seemed perfectly safe, but fearing lest they

might meet some belated traveler, the boys worked their way with stealthy steps across the commons, keeping a sharp look-out for the enemy. Opposite the school-house Nathan stopped for a moment, jerked the gun from his shoulder and took aim at the hated place, heartily wishing Mr. Leckrone was in sight; how he would blow him to Halifax, or some other world-distant port!

In a little time the fugitives reached the main highroad which led out of town to the east, but soon turned south, the direction in which they intended to go. The last house was quickly left behind. About a quarter of a mile from the village the road swung sharply round a long, low ridge,

LOOKED THEIR LAST.

with which it ran parallel for nearly a mile, and then stretched through a creek-bottom. At the turning of this ridge the boys both paused, and looked back upon Bluff City, bidding it good-bye, and secretly wondering if they should ever see it any more. Then straightening up they stepped out bravely, Nathan the while repeating in a low voice to time their steps a doggerel formula which had been used among the school boys in their mimic drills:

"Right! Right! Right mit the left foot,
Two by dern!"

Upon hearing the scholars chanting this one, Mr. Leckrone had very severely tabooed the last word of the rigmarole; so the ingenious boys had substituted "Two, by-cracky," for the offensive word. It was not so terse nor did it make as good rhythm, but the purpose was served just as well. However, having cut loose from all irritating authority, Nathan returned to the original form of the thing with much satisfaction, giving it extra emphasis as he marched along.

By the time they had gone a mile, the commissary department was becoming quite burdensome to Wiiiiam. For several rods he had been changing it from one hand to the other; and once when he swung the bundle from right to left it suddenly came open, spilling the contents in the road.

"Daggon the luck!" he exclaimed in disgust; "the apron's come undone, and now all our grub is-ruined!"

A halt was made for repairs. Picking up the scattered provisions and dusting them as well as he was able, Nathan replaced them in the apron, this time tying its knots more securely. Then, as William complained of the weight, his brother slipped the sword under the knots and showed him how to carry the thing across his shoulder, which was easier and much more satisfactory.

Again they took up their march, and a mile further on crossed a long bridge that spanned a deep, still stream, whose surface reflected the spatter-work of stars overhead. Here they entered a straight stretch of road through bottom lands that ended in a steep hill, up which the new recruits toiled, becoming short of breath and wondering if the ascent would never end. Upon reaching the top at last they felt quite leg-weary, and sat down at one side of the road to rest.

"What d' ye suppose pa 'll do when he finds we 've run away?" asked William presently.

"If he know'd where we are goin' he 'd take after us with a, fist full of hickories," returned Nathan bitterly. "But he do n't know, and he could n't even guess which direction we 've took."

"What are we goin' to do?" queried William anxiously. He had no plans of his own, trusting entirely to his brother.

"Why, we 'll go on a piece," replied Nathan, "and then we 'll find a place to sleep. Tomorry we 'll strike out fer Alton, and mebbe we kin git to be drummer boys among the soldiers there."

This idea pleased William mightily, and he sighed with great satisfaction. In a little time Nathan said they had rested enough and had better be moving along. Scarcely had they gone a hundred feet, however, when something happened that sent their hearts jumping into their throats and brought them to an abrupt halt.

On ahead somewhere, and apparently not very far away a scream was heard that sounded as if someone was in mortal agony So keen and unearthly did it rise in the still night that both the boys began to tremble, and shrink out into the bushes lining the road. William cowered down in hiding and Nathan feebly cocked his gun; neither of them could guess what terrible thing was likely to happen.

Presently the scream sounded again, and a little later once more This time Nathan recognized it, and got up with a grunt of disgust

"Shucks!" he exclaimed scornfully. "It's nothin' but a

lot of hogs. I know where they are now; they're at Borden's
old slaughter-house a little ways ahead. I've been by it with
pa when he's took me with him on the circuit. There ain't
anything to be skeerd of."

This assurance was an unspeakable relief to William, and
saved him from a fit of ague. He had been muttering a snatch
or two of prayer, and had a great desire to go back home.
But the familiar sound pierced the air once more, setting all
possible doubts at rest, so they got up and marched on, feeling
very brave.

About two hundred yards from the hill-top they came
abreast of the slaughter-house, which stood back a hundred
feet from the road. The bushes were tall and thick about
it, but the noise of the hogs guided them and they found their
way to the door. . Pushing this open they entered, and Nathan
lighted his candle the better to direct their steps, and enable
them to explore the place.

The building was a mere shell, about eighteen feet square
and built of rough boards. It was raised nearly three feet from
the ground on underpinning, and faced the road by which the
boys had come. Back of it were two pens divided by a partition between. They were made by lines of fence running from
the corners of the slaughter-house to a sharp bluff, at the base
of which and through the pens flowed a small stream which
served to slake the thirst of the animals confined within the
enclosures waiting the butcher's time.

When the candle burned up Nathan and William looked
around. On one side of the room, and within two feet of the

wall was a pile of dry hides from the slaughtered cattle. This stack was about four feet high, and around the room were other scattered pelts, among them half a dozen sheep skins.

Across the building overhead ran several heavy joists, and to one of these, at the end of the structure opposite the pile of hides already mentioned was swung a heavy iron hook. On the floor underneath this formidable hook lay a great blotch of dried blood; it was the place where butchered cattle were suspended to cool. Both the boys shuddered as they gazed upon the sinister sight.

"We 'll stop here and sleep till morning, I guess," said Nathan finally. "I kin make a good bed out of them sheep-skins; we 'll put it behind the pile of hides there, and they 'll keep the wind off of us that 's blowing through the cracks."

"I 'm hungry," suggested William dolefully. The long tramp had given both of them an appetite.

"So 'm I," rejoined Nathan. "We 'd better go around to the branch above the hog-pen, where we kin git some water. But we must n't eat too much; what we brought has got to last us clear to Alton."

Taking their provender they wound around through the bushes until the stream was reached, and then they sat down to eat. Nathan scraped most of the dirt off the loaf of bread, but it was not so easy to clean the meat. Even when it had been washed in the stream the sand clinging to it made their lunch disagreeable. William said the grit of it in his teeth sent cold chills down his back.

They ate hungrily, however, but at last concluded to throw

away the remaining meat. The greater part of their loaf was left, and after tying this carefully in the apron again, they lay down on their stomachs and filled up with long draughts of water.

On their way back to the slaughter-house, they stopped to peer over into the pen. It contained twelve or fifteen lusty fat hogs that had been fed for several months, not only on corn, but upon the offal from the slaughtered cattle. Some of the unwieldy brutes were nosing about their quarters, while the rest were piled up in a wallow they had made next the enclosure for the cattle.

After going into the building again and lighting his candle, Nathan took a couple of sheep-skins and made their bed. This space between the pile of hides and the wall was rather narrow; barely wide enough for the boys to lie down, and then they had to "spoon" closely. To keep off the draught that came through cracks in the wall, they stood up a dried hide in front of their bunk, and after pushing to the door, crawled into the sleeping place.

Nathan tucked his gun and sword carefully under the edge of their pallet of skins, and William, missing his usual head rest, seized upon the loaf of bread in its apron wrapping for a pillow. Then pulling the hide across the opening of their den, both boys stretched out under their quilt, feeling very tired from their tramp, and the excitement of the nefarious enterprise.

"I wonder what the girls ur doin'?" said William presently, for somehow his thoughts would travel back home.

"Sawin' gourds, I reckon," Nathan responded; "anyhow Eunice is, I bet. She always snores like a harrycane."

"My! What do you suppose they 'll do when they git up in the morning and find we 've run away?"

"They 'll raise Cain, and tell all the neighbors; but by the time anyone starts to find us, we 'll be out of reach."

William lay silent for a minute; none of this was what he really wanted to ask, and he was only leading up to the real question. Presently it came out:

"But what 'll poor ma say when she hears?" he asked ruefully.

This thought had been worrying Nathan's conscience for some time, but he had kept it to himself. Even now that it was put so plainly he had no ready answer for it.

"We 'll write to her, and tell her all about it when we git to Alton," he said after a long pause. "But we 'd better git to sleep now; we must hike out early."

Nothing more was said for several minutes; but during this interval William turned restlessly, seeming to be very uncomfortable.

"Gosh!" he broke out presently. "This bread is hard as a rock," and he raised upon his elbow to pound it soft with his fist, hoping thereby to make a more comfortable pillow of it

But despite the novelty of their surroundings, the unpleasant odors, and the uncertainty of their prospects, the boys soon began to feel drowsiness stealing over them. They snuggled up to each other for warmth, yet just as they were on the verge of slumber one of those ear-splitting screams came from the hog-pen, and brought them both wide awake in a second.

Notwithstanding his ferocious greed and love of dirt, the hog is very sensitive to cold. It was now after midnight, and the air had grown decidedly chilly. Most of the porkers had bestowed their unwieldy carcasses in the general bed, and like the boys, were lying close for warmth. But occasionally one of those that had been foraging about the pen would get tired, and wish to follow his companions. He would then waddle up to the sleeping drove that were packed closely together, and begin a series of tactics to secure a place already warmed by some slumbering grunter.

After sundry meditations and rootings he would raise a fore foot, plant his sharp hoof upon a snugly placed member of the drove, and begin to bear down. This would raise a growl of protest. Presently the intruder would mount with both feet upon the victim's broad back, and the growl would rise to a yell. Finally when the tactician took two or three steps along the fat spine of his victim, the yell would turn into an agonized scream, one of which had frightened the boys some time previously. Then the tortured animal would make the whole sleeping community heave with his struggles, and uttering savage, angry barks, would plunge out of his place, while the intruder that had disturbed him would settle down in the vacant warm spot with grunts and sighs of great satisfaction.

Now observant farm life had thoroughly familiarized the boys with the habits belonging to swine, and they quickly understood what was going on among the noisy brutes near by.

As some unusually vehement screech announced the success of a bed-hunter's maneuvers, the listening youngsters laughed heartily. Such homely sounds recalled many incidents of their recent life in the woods, some of which were not only funny, but pathetic as well.

Finally, however, the quarreling hogs seemed to have placed themselves to their mutual satisfaction, and gradually everything became quiet. Then sleep again stole over the tired boys. But for a long time it was neither so deep nor so comfortable as they were used to; and only their extraordinary exertions, together with the reaction from a long day's excitement could have sunk them into such heavy slumbers as at last wrapped their waking senses.

Even then the cramped quarters of their bed, and the strange conditions about them wrought upon the sleepers. They were followed by visions unheard of before, and in the land of nightmares struggled with calamities born of guilty consciences.

CHAPTER XXVI.

"THE TERROR BY NIGHT."

FOR nearly three hours the boys slept the sleep of the weary and conscience burdened. In his uneasy state William had wriggled up against the dried hides, and their flinty points pressed against his spine. He struggled with a vivid vision in which a monstrous hawk's foot held in the Parson's giant fist had seized him by the back of the neck. Nathan dreamed that he had reached the army and was in the midst of a fierce battle. A cannon ball had taken off his head and it was rolling down hill, he and William in hot pursuit. Just as he reached out to pick it up, suddenly both urchins were brought to startled consciousness by a grand charge of the hogs, which, somehow becoming frightened, had dived under the slaughter-house in a rushing, barking body.

THE BOYS' DREAM.

The contact of the plunging brutes shook the shell of the building as if some sudden wind had struck it; but when the last fugitive had reached the safety he sought all was quiet again.

"What is it?" whispered William in a shaking voice.

"I dunno yet," replied his brother softly; "but do n't make a bit of noise; we 'll find out what it means purty soon."

The same thought clawed at the heart of each boy; namely, that the vengeful Parson had somehow discovered their purpose and come after them. They listened breathlessly, and presently the gate of the cattle-pen creaked complainingly. Peering through a crack the watching youth saw nearly a score of horses being led into the enclosure by as many shadowy forms, which in the dim light looked very spooky.

"Be keerful now," they heard a low voice say. "No use makin' any great noise; ye can't tell what it might stir up."

When the horses had been secured to the fence the shadowy forms filed out of the pen, and softly closed the gate after them. The boys lay down quickly, and putting his lips close to William's ear Nathan whispered warningly:

"Let's keep still as mice. This thing looks mighty skeery; if they ketch us, we 'll have to go back home again."

Presently they heard the door of the slaughter-house pushed open, and then the sound of numerous cautious feet were detected coming into the building. When the last one had entered and the door was shut all stood still, and one who seemed to be the leader of the gang scratched a match; as it blazed up he cast a hurried glance about the room, saying as the match burned out:

"Ye kin pile yerselves down here anywheres; there 's nothin' to set on, and we 've got an hour or so to wait before the job comes off."

Then as the men sat down upon the floor, two or three leaning their backs against the very pile of hides behind which the boys were hidden, one said with a whistle:

"Pheww! This smells wuss than a glue-factory!"

"Cork yer smeller and breathe through yer mouth!" muttered the leader. "It ain't half as bad as some places I've seen; that battle field down Yazoo way, fer instance, the next day after the fight."

When the men were settled in their various places, there was a general lighting of pipes, interrupted once by a remark from the leader:

"Do n't make too much of a glim with yer matches! Shade 'em in yer hands; I ain't certain that we ought to smoke anyway."

"Why, there 's not likely to be anybody comin' along the road at five o'clock in the mornin', Cap," said one of the number.

"Ye can't tell anything about it. Might be; and besides we were told not to take the least chance of bunglin' what we 've come to do."

But even the captain's desire to smoke overcame his caution, and for half an hour there was a silent pulling at pipes. During this interval one or two of the gang dropped asleep, and presently disturbed the company by long drawn snores.

"Wake them fellers up!" growled the captain. "We do n't want their bazzoos goin' till ye could hear 'em a mile."

Some of their near by companions poked the sleepers awake, and for their trouble were rewarded by a few choice oaths.

"Shet up, and keep your eyes open," snarled the captain, who seemed to be over full of caution and ill temper. "Ye kin sleep all ye want to when we 've finished our business; and git back across the river."

There was some muttering and then a long silence. At last the strain on William's nerves became awful; he turned his head very softly and whispered to Nathan:

"I 'm a-shakin' all over."

"What 's that?" suddenly asked a voice in startled tones. Nathan laid his hand across William's lips, and both the boys held their breath

"What d' ye mean?" asked the captain fretfully.

"I heard some one whisperin'!" said the first speaker.

It was one of the men that leaned against the pile of hides, and he was seated right opposite the boys' heads. A thrilling silence fell upon the crowd at his words, and they seemed to be listening intently. Presently some of the pigs beneath the floor stirred uneasily and one or two emitted long sighs

"Ye heard them brutes down below, I guess," remarked the captain gruffly. "What else should there be?"

"That is more than I can tell," returned the man addressed. "What I thought I heard did n't sound like hogs."

The speaker's voice seemed very familiar to the breathless boys, but just at that moment they failed to identify it. In a short time the captain again got to his feet and lighted another match. This time he gazed keenly all about the room but saw nothing to arouse his suspicions. Before darkness fell again, however, his eyes alighted upon the formidable iron hook that dangled from the joist above his head.

"That 's just the trick, and no mistake," he said in tones of great satisfaction, holding the match aloft the better to see.

"What 's the job to be, Cap?" asked one of the men near by, who seemed not to have understood the leader's grim remark.

"Chokin'!" was the terse response.

"Why, ye do n't mean ye 're goin' to hang the man, Cap!" exclaimed another of the gang. "I understood the thing we wuz to do was only to trap him, and give him a good cowhiding. Remember old, Flint is a Methody preacher!"

"Yer understandin' needs a new in-sole," was the scornful reply. "I got my orders, and I 'll obey 'em. It 's to be hangin' and a plenty of it."

"Let him hang; he 's no relation or friend of mine," drawled the voice whose familiar tones had puzzled the boys previously. Instantly they recognized that it belonged to Jordan Blake!

"And he 's no friend of mine either," said the man who had begun the discussion. "But he 's a preacher, and besides he 's got a family."

"What's the matter with ye, Stoper?" snarled the leader in a rising rage. "Is he any better than Grigsby that we let the blood-hounds tear to pieces over yander in the swamps? Does he deserve easier than Simmons or Craig what we hung up by the heels to dry after they'd been howlin' for abolition?"

"Mebbe not," replied the man thus addressed. "But I do n't like the job of hangin' a preacher; and I say we'd ought to have knowed what we wuz about when we come over here."

"Ye kin take the back track right now if ye want to," said the leader with a ring of threat in his words. "What you bound yerself to do when ye jined us was to obey orders. The boys 'll give ye a lively welcome if ye show the white feather and desart us now."

"I 've no notion of desertin'; but honest, Cap, d' ye mean to hang the man like ye say?"

"That's jist what I 'll do. He 's been yawpin' long enough, and I 'd 'a' fixed him long ago, if I 'd had my say. The d——nigger-lover! I 'll not only hang him, but I 'll do wuss!"

"What 's that, Cap?" queried an interested listener.

"Why, when I 've stretched his infernal neck, I 'll bury him whar they can't dig him up and identify him!"

"Where 's that; in the river?" asked the man.

"In these damned hogs' bellies," returned the leader brutally

"Great God, Cap! Ye do n't mean to say ye 'd feed a man to the hogs, do ye, especially a white man?" exclaimed the listener whose protest had so aroused the leader's anger.

"That's jist exactly what I'll do," was the savage reply.
"Hev ye got anything to say ag'in it?"

"Ugh!" was the shuddering response. "It fairly makes
me sick, even t' hear ye talk about it!"

"Well, ye'll git over that mebbe some day. I'm mighty
sorry yer stomach's so weak. Ye'd ought to take somethin'
fer it; the thing may kill ye 'fore long."

This sarcastic menace brought no response, and presently
the heartless leader went on as if to excuse his proposed outrage:

"That snortin' pulpit pounder hez been at large too long.
He's hed warnin's enough; more 'n we ginerally give his stripe,
and all he's done is to blow an' make fun of 'em. Hangin' 's
too good fer him. If I hed him tother side of the river, I'd
pour a can of coal-ile over him and touch a match to his coat-
tails."

A profound silence followed this burst of brutality, and
the men seemed to be pondering what their leader had said.
The sluggish brutes under them had lain down, and only an
occasional grunt or snarl from them could be heard, like an
emphasis to the captain's horrible details. Presently one of the
gang who had not hitherto spoken asked with lively interest:

"How d' ye expect to trap yer meat, Cap? What's the
program?"

"I've kep' track of the abolition hound fer a week, through
Blake here, lookin' to carry out this job," replied the captain.
"Last night the blame fool went to set up with Guthrie that's
got the fever. The place is not more than three or four mile

from here. Tom Scranton left us when we'd landed from the boat; he's to go over to Guthrie's and tell old Flint that Borden, the man that owns this slaughter-house an' lives a mile beyond here is hurt bad, an' wants him to come over at once. He'll take the bait easy enough. When he leaves Guthrie's, he'll strike the main road here down in the bottoms jist this side of the bridge, and when he gits this fur we'll be layin' fer him. He'll not be lookin' fer any trouble an' 'll walk right into the trap."

"Suppose he do n't come this way," suggested the listener.

"But he will; there's no other road fer him to take," said the captain.

"The captain's right; I know the lay of the land; he'll come this way. I wonder what th' price of side-meat and sausage 'll be in town fer a month or two," drawled Jordan Blake with a lazy laugh.

"Oh, shet up! You'd make a dog sick," snorted the man who objected to hanging a preacher. "I kin never eat any pork ag'in as long as I live!"

The breathless boys had heard it all, and they lay in a stupor of utter terror, bathed in a cold sweat. They knew only too well the character of the savage men near them, for Bluff City had long been full of rumors about their horrible doings. They recognized a band of raiding guerrillas from the state across the river; probably the same merciless gang that was responsible for the outrage upon the farmer who had lived but a few miles distant. The story of his misfortunes had stirred every heart in town.

Even if the intended victim had not been called by name, the horror-stricken urchins would have recognized who "the nigger-lover" was that these men were after. He had been called by this name very often in the anonymous, threatening letters he had so rashly scorned.

Taking care not to move a finger, and scarely daring to breathe the boys lay listening to the hideous details of the plan they heard, quivering in every nerve. And as the dreadful tragedy was unfolded by the talk about them, their very blood seemed to turn cold, and the tobacco-tainted darkness appeared to close down upon them like some dank, slow, smothering hand.

Their hearts had been full of rebellion and bitterness. They had run away from home and the cruel rod, bent on escaping from their stern father's rule and discipline. Only the day before, they had thought that no fate could be worse than that which dogged them; and as they set forth upon this wandering journey both of them would have declared that nothing could make them forget the cause that urged them to the great undertaking. But as the villainy and unspeakable horror of the thing they had overheard soaked into their bristling heads, an utter revulsion of feeling came over them. They no longer remembered the numerous griefs and mountainous woes that had driven them away: they forgot the double punishment of the day before, and the hundred other whippings of other days. Every stroke of the rod seemed nothing; for in their terrorized imaginations there arose but one picture that grew in dread and lurid savagery until the very breath seemed about to fail their lips.

In this dark fancy they saw that stern face that had so often chilled their warm impulses with its heavy frown growing black and ghastly as the cruel rope choked out the life of its victim, while he was dangling from that iron hook above the hideous blotch of blood. And they clung desperately to each other as imagination painted a more destroying sight. They beheld that hard, strong face, and the hands that had so often wielded the avenging rod over their backs, torn and mutilated among the growling, fighting, storming brutes that now lay so quiet beneath them.

And as the full terror of it gnawed at their very hearts, and strained every nerve almost to breaking, not a single stroke of the rod was remembered, but a great resolve began to grow and glow in their sickened hearts.

They could not think how to escape, nor what to do; yet if it could be done, if it were possible, they would save him, even if they died in the attempt!

CHAPTER XXVII.

DANIEL TO THE RESCUE.

WHILE the incidents we have last related were transpiring, the dawn was slowly coming. Gradually the gloom melted, and the old slaughter-house began to lose its darkness, a wan gray light soon making the interior faintly visible in the chill coming of a new day.

Silence had fallen upon the motley group of bandits sitting about in grim discomfort and waiting. Doubtless the vicious threats of their leader had impressed their minds, and perhaps some of them less hardened than others wished in their hearts the job was over.

Presently the rattle of a horse's hoofs was heard upon the road, and all of the men pricked sharp ears to learn who was coming.

"That's Tom Scranton, I guess," exclaimed the captain with fierce eagerness. "I told him to come on here and let me know after he'd give old Flint the yarn."

The horse turned from the highway and dashed through the bushes up to the slaughter-house door. Directing his men to remain within and keep still, the captain hurried out to meet his messenger.

"Well, what news?" he asked of the rider.

"It's all right. He was just going to breakfast as I got there. I gave him the message and then told him I'd ride to town for a doctor. He said he'd come over as soon as he'd snatched a bite to eat. By this time he's on the way, and you'd better get your trap ready."

"Ride straight for the river," returned the captain hurriedly, "and see that everything is ready to cross without a minute's waitin'. It may be we'll want to go in a hurry, though 't ain't likely."

The messenger turned and galloped away to carry out this order, and the captain hastily re-entered the building. As he did so the hogs, wakened by the noises, began to fight, grunt and squeal, digging each other with snout and sharp tusks.

"WELL, WHAT NEWS?"

"The critters 're gittin' hongry, Cap; they wants breakfast," suggested one hardened wretch with a gutteral laugh.

"And we'll give it to 'em purty soon, I guess," returned the captain with a hoarse chuckle. "Git ready, men. String yerselves out now as I told ye, on each side of the road about ten foot apart. Stay close to the edge, but keep hid. I don't want any shootin' except as a last thing, and then I'll be below you, so that if he should start to run I kin drap his hoss. Ye know what to do. Blake here 'll holler to him when he gits opposite where we are, and make him stop. Then four of ye jump for the hoss's bridle and the rest nail the old skunk."

"First, Blake, you go down nigh.the top of the hill, and when ye see him comin' hurry back an' let us know. Dave an' me 'll stay here and fix the necktie fer the onery galoot, and take our places a bit later. Let there be no bobblin'! We 'll shut one mouth that 's done more harm by his fool blather-skite than ary dozen. Go now."

In obedience to these hurried directions, the men filed out of the door and disappeared in the bushes. When they had gone the captain said to Dave, who had remained with him:

"Got the rope?"

"Here it is, and glad to get rid of it," was the reply, as the aid unwound from about his waist ten feet of clothesline.

Peeping out between the hides and wall, the boys watched the captain deftly form a hangman's noose in the rope, and then after a toss or two succeed in cast-ing the cord over the iron hook.

"There; that 's all ready," he remarked with grim   "GOT THE ROPE?" satisfaction.

"I guess several of us 'll have to pull on it," laughed his companion. "The old rooster is pretty heavy, Blake says."

"We 'll pull hard enough," rejoined the captain with an oath. "Then I 'll pry up a couple of plank in the floor, and drop the dog down under them out of sight."

"Lord!" exclaimed the aid, rubbing his sides tenderly. "This stuff in my belt feels as if it weighed a hundred pounds; I 'm fairly rubbed raw with the heft of it!"

"Me, too, with mine," responded the captain. "Six or seven thousand dollars in gold gits derned heavy after a man hez carried it a few hours on horseback. But I did n't dare to leave it in camp. I 've picked it up in half a dozen states, and risked my neck to get most of it; so I take no chances of losin' it. However, we 'd better lighten ship till this job 's over. We may hev to hustle purty lively. Give me yer stuff and I 'll hide it until the picnic is done with."

Saying this he unbuckled from about his own waist a heavy belt, and taking the one handed to him by his aid, they both left the building.

Nathan glued his eyes to a crack, and presently saw the men come in sight about thirty paces from the door. Here the captain dropped the two belts into a hollow stump, and covered them carefully with a few handfuls of dead leaves. Having thus secreted their treasures, the guerillas disappeared in the bushes, going to their ambush by the road.

"Oh, good Lord! What 'll we do?" whispered William, trembling violently with the excitement and danger.

"We 've got to run," replied Nathan in a strained voice. "Now 's the time, 'fore any of 'em come back. Be keerful, an' do n't make a noise a cat could hear."

They abandoned gun, quilt and sword; these would only be a burden to them, and they could not afford to carry any extra weight. Tiptoeing to the door, Nathan peeped out with pounding heart, but seeing the coast clear he motioned to William, and together they dodged out of the building, around the corner into the bushes that lined the stream flowing through the pens. The grunting hogs made a rush towards that side of the enclosure, under the impression that some one had come to feed them as usual. With a last glance at the pushing, crowding brutes, and a mental vision of that horrible feast the captain had sworn to provide for the ferocious animals blighting

DODGED ROUND THE CORNER.

their very hearts, the boys hurried away down the stream.

In the far East the glorious sun had just climbed a hill-top, and he was smiling broadly over the land, as if no scene of savage barbarism had been planned to greet his coming. The air was cool and fresh, and the brook babbled some story of its own, as it purled along on its hurried way to the great river.

The boys remembered that this stream made a turn, crossing the road by which they had come about two-thirds of the way towards the long hill they had climbed the previous night. Hurriedly, yet making scarcely any noise they scudded along the bank, stooping so that the rank undergrowth might hide them from any chance enemy.

In a few minutes they reached the curve of the stream, and knew that the road must be near. Slackening their pace they approached the highway cautiously, and anxiously scanned it from behind a bush. A dozen yards off they saw Jordan Blake. True to his lazy habits, he had stretched himself out face down on a log beside the road, where he could just peep over the crest of the hill by which the Parson was expected to come. His chin was resting on one fat arm, and with the other hand he was slowly scratching himself, evidently very sleepy and uncomfortable.

For a minute the boys watched his recumbent form fearfully; then slipping off their shoes and holding one in each hand they stole softly from the bushes for a few feet, suddenly put on a wild burst of speed and ran by the unsuspecting spy, disappearing over the brow of the hill in a trice.

As they flew by him, Blake gave a sudden start and rolled off the log. Scrambling heavily to his feet he drew a revolver and hurried to the brow of the hill in pursuit; but already the boys were a quarter of the way down, going ten feet at a jump. Blake caught sight of them just as William stumbled, falling headlong and rolling over and over, his two shoes flying in opposite directions. But whether hurt or not, he sprang up quickly and sped on all the faster.

The discomfited lubber had recognized both of the fugitives and he handled his pistol nervously. But the captain had forbidden any use of firearms, so, as the only thing left to do he turned and ran for the slaughter-house faster than his legs had ever carried him before. When yet he was a hundred yards away the captain, who had been eagerly watching for his approach saw him coming, and quickly surmised that something unforeseen had happened. With a muttered oath he

24   *Ran by the Unsuspecting Spy.*

rushed from his ambush to meet Blake, and between his gasps
for breath that worthy managed to say:

"Sold, Cap! Parson's boys. They must ha' been hid behind that pile of hides; knowed I heard somethin' last night.
They 're on the road and 'll meet the man you 're after!"

With a roar of profanity the captain jerked himself about
and rushed for the slaughter-house, calling loudly for his men
who at the sound of his voice swarmed into the road filled with
alarm.

"The horses, quick!" cried the furious captain. "Not a
minit t' lose; stir yerselves or the job 's lost!"

Running at full speed the gang reached the pen, tore open
the gate and were quickly mounted, galloping after their leader
who was foremost in the hurried stampede.

Meantime Blake had made for the slaughter-house, where
he found the boys' bed and traps, thus confirming his first sur-
mise. As the captain swung into his saddle Blake yelled to
him:

"They 've been here all right, Cap; I 've found their outfit!"

The crowding gang broke through the bushes into the
road, and one of the bewildered men called out:

"What 's the row, captain?"

"The Parson's brats were hid in the house; heard all we
said; gone to meet the old man; they passed Blake at the hill;
ride!"

"What 'll we do with the kids?" yelled the questioner.

"Pups make dogs; shoot the whole breed," returned the

captain with an angry oath. "No more talk; use yer spurs!" and the astonished band set off at breakneck pace after the luckless fugitives.

Meanwhile the boys had reached the bottom of the hill, and at their utmost speed flew along the quarter of a mile of straight road through the bottoms, leading to the bridge. Terror barked at their nimble heels and urged them to greater effort than otherwise had been possible. But this fright had strained their nerves, too, and already their breath was coming in hot, short gasps. Nathan was straining his eyes toward the bridge, near which he knew that the road by which the Parson must come debouched into the highway; and as he ran, not seeing the Apostle, a great sob bubbled up in his throat fairly choking him.

But when yet within two hundred yards of the by-road, to the inexpressible relief of both urchins they caught sight of the familiar head of old Daniel, nodding through the trees, and turning into the highway ahead of them. With a tough, fresh-cut hickory sprout in his hand the Parson was riding along easily, not in the least dreaming of any danger lurking in that bright morning.

When he caught sight of the flying boys the old horse threw up his head and came to an abrupt halt. The Parson stared in a state of alarm, for he recognized the runners instantly What on earth were they doing here at such a time; and what ailed them!

As they rapidly drew near, Daniel snorted and made as if he would whirl and run; but with a kick and jerk of the reins the Parson brought him to a standstill; then with dropping jaw he glared at his offspring in a trance of stupefied amazement.

The appearance the two urchins presented was enough to bewilder anyone who had no knowledge of their mission or what had led up to it. They were both bareheaded, having lost their hats. They were wild-eyed, unkempt, dirty and reeking with sweat from their desperate speed. William was almost past speaking, and Nathan but little better; but as the latter reeled up, he seized his father by the leg and in a gasping voice whose very prickle of terror stirred a tremor of alarm in the Parson's stout heart, he dropped out the words:

"Oh, pa—!—gueril's—run, run! They're right back yander—run, run! they're goin'—t' hang ye—they're comin'—they're goin' t' feed the hogs! run, run, *run!*"

And as if to emphasize his terrible though incoherent warning the thunder of beating hoofs sounded through the still morning air from the hill, over the crest of which poured the now infuriated bandits who were after the Parson's life.

"Oh Pa! Guer-i-ls!"

But the Parson was sharp-witted and very quick to act. He did not fully comprehend the real nature of the peril until much later; but there was enough in the wild horror of the boys' faces and words to make his own heart leap, and cry that flight meant possible safety, not only for himself but the panting urchins.

Slipping a foot from its stirrup, he held out one of his powerful hands and said sharply, "Up behind me, Nathan!" And when the boy had instantly climbed to his place, with one mighty sweep of his other arm the Apostle caught up William and held him in front, close to his breast. Then whirling the horse in his tracks, he laid on the hickory in hard, stinging blows that roused the animal to frenzy.

Fly, Daniel, fly! Three lives are depending on your speed! It is a race between safety and a dog's vile death! There is no mercy in the tiger hearts behind you! They mean cruel destruction! What would mother say if she knew! Fly, Daniel, FLY!

Stung by the cutting gad the old horse stretched himself to the uttermost; he thundered over the long bridge which shook under his passage, and took the road beyond with a wild gallop that even Black Bess might not for a time have rivaled. Nathan bounced about upon the croup, holding to his father's waist with the tenacity of a squirrel, and William, grasped by the Parson's sinewy left arm, burrowed his tow head into his father's breast to hide the dreadful world from his frightened eyes

As they thundered over the bridge, the guerillas who were by this time coming down the long hill caught sight of them, and with a keen yell bent low in their saddles, digging spurs into their horses to overtake the fleeing victims. The leader unslung his rifle and the others imitated his example, but no further word was spoken; they strained forward as fast as horseflesh could carry them.

"Fly, Daniel! Fly!"

Meanwhile old Daniel was tearing along the highroad, putting every atom of his strength into his strides. With heels and hickory the Parson kept him to the mark, and even tried to urge him into faster pace, but the gallant old charger was already doing his level best.

A growing fear began to chill the Parson's breast; the horse was old, and his sinews somewhat stiffened. He had never been put to such a terrible test before. Already the sweat started from his sides and neck; his breathing was loud and hoarse. He was trebly burdened, and the load must utterly exhaust him in a brief time at the rate he was going. Safety was yet nearly two miles away; would they ever reach it!

On! On! The sun-flecked road seemed to fly backwards beneath them, and the heart-breaking stride was never relaxed; but behind them the rumble of pursuing feet grew near and menacing, while the savage riders raked bloody spurs into the sides of their straining horses. At last Daniel turned a slight bend, reaching the stretch of road which ran parallel to the ridge that shut Bluff City from sight. Across that bluff-fronted ridge it was but a scant quarter of a mile to safety, but by the highway there was yet nearly three times that distance to go. Daniel's breath was coming loud and hoarse; he could not hold out long. He stumbled. The Parson brought him to a quick halt and said in a shaking voice:

"The horse is falling! Jump, Nathan, and run! Take that trail over the ridge; the bushes 'll hide ye Run and raise the alarm!"

Nathan understood instantly. He was familiar with the

trail, having often crossed it with his mother in their evening walks. Sliding from his perch, he dodged into the bushes like a frightened rabbit. He had got his breath again, and fled up the slope, crying in very terror for the Parson and poor William who had been left behind. Oh, if he could only make his voice heard in town!

As Nathan dived into the bushes overhanging the trail, the Parson again started Daniel on his mad race. It was but half a dozen breaths the distressed old horse had got in his pause, but they helped; and besides some of the burden taxing his strength had been taken off. He stretched away, the Parson's arm rising and falling as he plied the frayed hickory. But the blows served only to keep the straining charger up to his former speed; he was doing the best he could. They had gone perhaps a hundred and fifty yards when the pursuers swept around the bend behind them, and a clattering volley of shots rang out on the still air. But they went wild, and seemed not to reach the mark Frightened by the strange noise, Daniel aroused himself, and putting all his scared wits into one wild burst of speed he seemed to fly.

The Parson was straining William close, and had his eyes glued upon the end of the ridge around which the road turned. How far it yet seemed to be! Yet Daniel was drawing toward it, nearer and nearer. Suddenly William uttered a squeaking cry

"What is it, my son?" asked the Parson in a strained voice as his arm rose and fell

"The saddle-horn's a-hurtin' me!" gasped William.

Pounding Daniel's sides with his heels, the Parson placed the switch between his teeth and reached down to lift William to an easier position. The boy's legs were flying wildly about with the lunges of the horse, and just as the Parson lifted him another crash of shots rang out behind them, sending the Parson's heart into his mouth, while one bullet all too close lifted the hat from his head. Zipping of bullets was heard all about  them, and a shot grazed one of William's tossing legs, making it feel as if a hot iron had been laid across it. The terrified boy gave one eldritch screech, and clung to his father with both hands.

With a groan and muttered "God have mercy!" the Parson swung William astride in front of him and bent low, completely shielding the boy with his own great body. Then snatching the switch from his mouth, he rained such a shower of blows upon Daniel's withers as made the straining old horse groan, and put his last remaining strength into his flight.

"We 're gittin' nigh town, Cap!" called one of the pursuers to the leader after the last shots. "There 's danger ahead! How fur ye goin' to chase the man?"

"D—n the danger! Chase him to h—l, and see that he gets there!" was the furious reply.

With neck and head stretched forward, his nostrils flaming red, Daniel galloped toward the end of the long ridge, and finally swung round it with a deep groan. Then from the Parson's straining heart burst a fervent "Thank God!" For there, not a hundred yards ahead, was a body of the home-guard cavalry, thirty in number. They had been out on early morning drill, and in the midst of it had heard the volleys fired at the fleeing Parson; at a word of command from the leader, they started in a swinging gallop to see what was the matter.

"Guerrillas, Men!" shouted the Parson as he neared them. "Ride! ride! You 'll get them!"

And as if to confirm his words some of the band behind him dashed into sight at the bend of the road. But seeing the danger ahead they quickly wheeled their horses and started on the back track.

"Forward!" shouted the home-guard captain; and un-slinging their carbines as they rode, the guard set out in hot pursuit of the daring bandits. In a few moments a fusillade from behind the ridge told that the guerrillas with their blown horses had fallen into the trap, and were likely to pay for their temerity.

The early risers of Bluff City were now treated to a strange sight. Bareheaded, and holding William in his arms, the Parson galloped through the street and made straight for Dr. Parker's office.

A STRANGE SIGHT.

CHAPTER XXVIII.

THE PARSON'S ANGUISH.

DOCTOR PARKER'S office stood in his yard, a little to one side of his residence. The doctor himself was at breakfast, when, glancing through the window, he saw the Parson with his strange burden at the gate, and he hastened forth to see what was the matter.

Swinging from his saddle, and not even stopping to throw the reins over the hitching-post, the Parson pushed open the gate and went with long strides toward the office. When left to himself Daniel stood still with his trembling legs wide apart, head bent low, sides pounding and panting, while the sweat trickled and dropped from him in numberless streams. He did not move until one of the neighbors who had run up took the saddle off him, rubbed him down and led him away.

When Doctor Parker had opened his office door the Parson carried William in and laid him down upon a sofa.

THE HORSE STOOD STILL.

"We've been chased by bushwhackers, Doctor," he explained hurriedly. "They shot at us twice; the boy's hit somewhere."

William was so scared he looked silly; and his exhaustion

341

was so complete that he had ceased even to tremble. He lay limp as a rag where the Parson had placed him, and stared about with big eyes in which the fright of his thrilling experience yet glared.

Doctor Parker hastily stripped off his clothing. A bloody smear across his trousers' leg quickly showed where the bullet had grazed him. Hurried examination showed that this was the only hurt the boy had received. Doctor Parker straightened up and said in cheerful tones to the fear-ridden Parson:

"It's but a slight scratch. No danger whatever. The clip will only be sore for a little time; that's all."

At these comforting words the Parson's nerves began to relax, and a sigh of intense relief burst from his heart. Laying one of his hands upon William's forehead he asked:

"Do you feel all right now, my son?" and the quivering tenderness so unusual to his tones made William cry.

By this time a buzzing crowd of excited people had gathered at the gate, and two or three men had made their way into the office All kinds of wild rumors were afloat. News had spread that the town was being attacked; that the Parson and his boys had been shot to death, and everybody was demanding more information

"You'd better go and tell them all about it, Parson," said Doctor Parker, glancing apprehensively through the window at the gathering neighbors. "They'll all be crowding in here to find out what's the matter if you don't. I'll take care of the boy. He's all right."

At this suggestion the Parson, followed by those who had

entered the office, went out to reassure the uneasy crowd. He explained in brief manner what had happened as far as he knew it; and told the gaping listeners that a little squad of the home-guards had already gone in pursuit of the daring guerrillas.

Meantime at the parsonage a little distance away, Eunice, Louise and Ruth had missed the boys, and were already bewildered to learn that they were absent from home. When a neighbor led Daniel wet and exhausted into the lot, they all rushed out, and learned some of the absurd rumors that were flying about, and were also informed that the Parson was at the Doctor's office.

Crying and distressed by great fear they hastened across lots, reaching the Doctor's premises as the Parson was telling his tale of escape to the thunder-struck crowd. The people made way for them, and after a few soothing words, the Parson directed them to go in and looked after William.

They then hurried to the office, but had not been there a minute before Louise ran frantically back down the path crying aloud with anxious face:

"Oh, pa! Where is Nathan?"

The Parson gave a great start, and his face blanched.

"Did n't he get home? The horse was failing, and Nathan started over the trail across the ridge yonder," he faltered in reply. Then as renewed fear gripped his heart he clenched his great hands and groaned as if to himself. "Could those butchers have caught sight of the poor boy and chased him?"

"WHERE IS NATHAN?"

At these words Louise uttered a frightened cry, and several of the sympathetic women gathered about her. But the Parson tore open the gate, and followed by a score of the startled crowd ran in the direction by which Nathan should have reached town.

Most of those who followed were directed to go along the highway around the ridge, and the few remaining followed the Parson along the trail leading across it. These were urged to scatter and search the ridge, while with a growing dread clutching at his heart the Parson hurried on the trail, going its entire length without seeing anything of the missing boy.

With a bitter burst of prayer upon his lips, he turned back at the highway to retrace his steps. Unconsciously the habits of his old hunting days took hold upon him, and he bent over, looking for any traces upon the narrow trail. Nearly at the top of the ridge his eyes caught sight of the boy's footprints in a space of sand; and with anxious heart he slowed his steps, scanning everything closely as he moved along.

Meanwhile, what of Nathan?

When he had slid from Daniel's back and taken the trail, the fleeing urchin felt no sense of peril for himself; and indeed there was none from the rear. The pursuers had not seen his movements. Nathan's clamoring fright was for William and the Parson, and as he fled along the bush-hidden path every nerve in him was strung with anxiety.

Scarcely had he gained the top of the ridge when a crash of rifles rang out from the road below, making his heart jump

Looking into the White Face.

into his throat. He stopped as if one of those bullets had stricken him, and listened with bated breath. Only the sound of hammering hoofs could now be heard, and this astonished him, for he supposed that the Parson and William might have been killed.

With hot tears stinging his eyes, he stretched away once more across the broad top of the ridge, scarcely able to see the trail. No doubt all would have gone well with him if only he had more closely watched his footsteps. But the trail ran alongside a steep ravine ten or twelve feet deep, and Nathan caught his feet in a trailing vine, pitching headlong over the gully and snatching frantically at everything within reach. The bushes grasped at gave way, and he rolled to the very bottom of the decline. Even then, however, he might have escaped with a few bruises, but his head struck a stone with a cruel thump and the boy lay still.

When the men who had followed him overtook the Parson, they found him kneeling in the trail, holding Nathan in his arms. The boys eyes were closed, and his hair matted with blood from a cut on the temple. He showed no sign of life, and his head hung limply upon the arm that held him; the Parson was looking stonily into his white face, and the iron lips were loose with growing grief.

Willing and strong arms took turns in carrying the unconscious boy hastily back to town. The crowd about Dr. Parker's office had dispersed, and after his leg had been bound up, William had been taken home, the girls sobbing and crying as they went.

Someone opened the gate, and the Parson hurried with
his limp burden into the Doctor's office. His voice was
cracked, dry and hoarse, as, laying the boy down, he said:

"Here is Nathan, Doctor; is he dead?"

When he saw the youth's pale, blood-smeared face,
Doctor Parker turned very grave. After closing and lock-
ing the door, he hastily stripped off Nathan's upper garments; then he felt for the boy's pulse, and finally laid his
ear over the heart.

The now overwrought Parson dropped upon his knees at
Nathan's head, and buried his face in his trembling hands. In
his heart there was a terrible, despairing cry, and his breath
came thick while the awful suspense seemed to weigh him
down as with a leaden cloud.

In a little time the Doctor turned one crooked eye upon
the bowed, shaken man, and said in a tone meant to be assuring:

"Don't give way so, Parson; the boy is not dead."

Then the Parson raised his grief-lined face and in a manner that might have melted the hardest heart prayed to the
busy doctor; and no petition he had ever addressed to his
Heavenly Father had in it more of fervor and heart hunger:

"Save him, Doctor; he must not die! You don't know
all that is in my heart, and I can't tell you now. I haven't
much of this world's wealth, but you can have all I own if
you save him for me!"

And the tender-hearted, cross-eyed doctor, who was suspected by many as being an unbeliever and an infidel, felt

his own throat constrict, while a lost tear wormed its way out of one ingrowing eye, and fell upon his grizzled beard. With mouth close pinched to keep his own lips steady, he sponged off Nathan's bruised head, and deftly dressed the ragged gash cut by the stone. Then forcing the boy's clenched teeth apart he administered stimulants, chafing his hands and occasionally holding aromatic salts to his nostrils.

With eyes glued upon his boy's face, the Parson sat by in silence, and presently the cordials administered began to take effect; with a sigh and weak murmur Nathan feebly moved his head. It was his first sign of coming back to life, and deep down in his heaving breast the Parson said "Thank God!"

Doctor Parker sat on the edge of the sofa, and for some moments watched the now restless boy, keeping steady fingers on his pulse. Then he greatly laid the limp arm down and said quietly:

"We may as well look at the matter sensibly, Parson. You want to know the truth. I think the boy has had a fall that may result in slight concussion of the brain. This blow on the head here, and the excitement he has gone through is likely to give him brain fever. His symptoms suggest that." Then, after a hesitating pause, he finished with, "I'd send for his mother. No one can nurse him as she will."

At these words, freighted with so much significance, the Parson's face went gray and he caught his breath chokingly, but his eyes were dry and burning. Together he and the doctor carried Nathan to the parsonage, and that afternoon's boat took a letter to Mrs. Flint.

Under the influence of a sleeping potion the doctor administered Nathan slept heavily all the rest of the day and night. But the next morning his face was flushed, his eyes bright and glittering, with pinched pupils, and he was muttering in the beginning of delirium.

"It is as I surmised, Parson," said Doctor Parker as he watched the boy's picking fingers. "He will have a spell of fever. You must keep him very quiet and watch him closely. Yet do n't look for the worst; he is young and strong for his age; that 's in his favor."

When the doctor had prepared his remedies and gone away, the Parson drew his chair up to Nathan's bedside and sat there all the long day, grudging it seemed any moment that he was called away.

The evening's boat brought Mrs. Flint home, and a neighbor drove her to the parsonage. The girls met her in a body, and took her up to her own room, where William had been put when brought home from Dr. Parker's office. Hastily removing her mother's traveling wraps Eunice began the story of the last three days; and as the terrible tale was unfolded to her they saw her face grow white, and her eyes become wide and haunted by the horror of it. Long before the narrative was concluded she was kneeling by William, the warm tears streaming down her cheeks, and her mother's lips kissing, kissing, kissing him, while he clung to her in a very frenzy of delight. And between his own sobs he told her over and

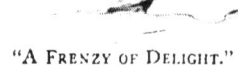

"A FRENZY OF DELIGHT."

over how much he had missed her; and how he loved her; and how if she had been at home he never would have run away, and never would do so again!

At last she arose from William's side, and said:

"Stay here, girls; I want to go down alone."

Softly she entered the sick room, and found the Parson sitting silent, and watchful by the bed. All her heart filled with tears at sight of the stricken man. She walked straight to him, knelt by his side and put her arms about his neck.

As she approached him the Parson looked up with a world of woe in his eyes, and his firm lips quivered; but he said never a word. When she knelt at his side, he wound his great arms about her, and kissed her very tenderly, holding her to his breast in silence. The girls stole to the door a little later, and saw the Parson folding her close to his heart, her face resting against his.

After a time she arose and bent over Nathan. He was in a troubled sleep, but perhaps some dream of that tender kiss she pressed upon his fevered brow stole like balm into his darkened brain. He stirred slightly, and whispered the one dear word,—"Mother!"

Then side by side she and the silent Parson began their long, anxious watches together.

CHAPTER XXIX.

LINGERING SHADOWS.

ANXIOUS days and sad nights fell upon the Parson's household. The black cloud of terror that had so suddenly swept down upon them yet made them shudder, and the lingering shadows of it still darkened their hearts with a chill foreboding.

William's slight wound quickly began to heal, and beyond making him a trifle stiff and lame for a few days, resulted in no serious consequences. All the family were very tender to him; and when in his growing loneliness for want of Nathan's company, he would steal into the sick room to see his brother, the Parson would gaze at him with such a loving look upon his rugged face, and speak to him with such a note of love in his tones, that William was actually embarrassed.

A sharp and swift vengeance had overtaken the guerrillas. Upon realizing the great danger with which they had suddenly come face to face, they abandoned the chase of the Parson and strove to flee; but their horses were already jaded and breathless from the desperate speed to which they had been spurred, and the mounts of the home-guards were fresh. Memory of the outrage upon that helpless farmer up the river, to-

A Swift Vengeance.

gether with this daring attempt upon the Parson wrought the pursuers to a pitch of instant fury, and they determined to show no mercy.

Scarcely had the fleeing bandits gone a half mile before the cavalry were in short range of them and opened up a running fire. At the first well-aimed volley the tiger-hearted captain, his aid and three others of the desperately riding marauders were killed; and a little later another hail of bullets reached others of them.

Realizing that the fight was against them and flight along the road impossible, the remaining members of the band dashed into the woods and hills, several of them sorely wounded. Those that remained unhurt found that progress on horseback was too perilous, so abandoned their animals and escaped on foot. Only a half dozen of their number reached the boat in' waiting and crossed the river again.

Jordan Blake, who had not followed the main body, was one to get off unharmed; but a few weeks later the news came to Bluff City that he had been caught stealing horses in Missouri and was hanged. No regret was felt for his merited fate; and when the towns-people learned how he had betrayed the Parson's movements to the outlaws, and was among them in their murderous attempt, the popular feeling against the remaining members of the Blake family became so violent that they left the village, and were never afterwards heard of. This was the last of any guerrilla raiding on the Illinois side of the Mississippi.

Though sharp enough, Nathan's attack of fever was not

so severe as had been expected; and it was fought stoutly and well by Doctor Parker. He came several times a day, and would sit watching every symptom with a care and anxiety that could not have been greater if he had been attending one of his own family. Always he had some word of cheer and comfort for the Parson and his faithful wife.

And the Parson was utterly tireless. Seldom speaking, but with a secret burden upon his heart, he sat ever at the bedside, observant of each movement the sick boy made and hanging with a dumb sort of longing on the words and ministrations of the doctor.

In the midst of his special care of Nathan, that good friend kept an anxious eye on the Parson, too; though how he managed to do so might puzzle an optician. He observed and dreaded the evident condition of the Parson's mind; and one day said to him brusquely:

DOCTOR PARKER.

"Come, Mr. Flint; I 've got enough to do just at present; and first you know you 'll be putting yourself on my hands. You must not be unreasonable. The boy is in no special danger yet, and I think there won't be any. But if you keep up this constant worrying it will break you down. I want you to go to bed, and get some sleep."

The Parson would listen gloomily to these well-meant exhortations, but they seemed to make little impression on him.

He would turn his tired eyes upon Nathan's flushed face, and say in a dry, hard voice:

"Do n't pay any attention to me, Doctor; save the boy!"

Then Doctor Parker would grow more vexed than ever, and sit frowningly looking at the bridge of his nose, evidently very dissatisfied that his warnings fell upon heedless ears. When Mrs. Flint followed him out of the room one day he said to her very earnestly:

"Get the man to bed if you can. I know he has the strength of a horse, but flesh and blood can't stand up forever under his load. I do n't like the looks of him. Make him take some sleep."

And then lovingly urged by his secretly anxious wife, who assured him that she would call him at the least hint of change, the Parson, fairly exhausted, would consent to lie down for a little time. But he would never go away from the sick room; he would stretch himself upon a sofa near by and sometimes for two or three hours would fall into a restless, unrefreshing slumber. His dread evidently haunted even his deepest doze; for suddenly he would come wide awake again, and with a sigh or groan get up and seat him- self by Nathan's bedside, seeking anxiously for any favorable change that might have taken place while he slept.

During eight days Nathan tossed and twitched, in his eyes the dull fires of fever, and his mind

"THE PARSON WAS TIRELESS."

wandering in the byways of delirium. But strange to say none of his sick fancies ever seemed to touch upon the happenings immediately leading to his illness. It was an odd medley of imagination, mixed and muddled by the wayward kaleidoscope of dreams.

Most of his vagaries took form in low mutterings to himself; but occasionally towards night his fever would rise and then sometimes he would rave aloud. And it was during these worse attacks that the Parson seemed to feel remorse whipping him with cruel blows.

In his delirious struggles the boy would cry aloud, "Do n't whip me! It was n't my fault! I did n't put the pig there; I do n't know who did; do n't whip me! Please do n't!" and then after a few panting breaths he would turn stubborn and defiant, crying in a high, cracked voice, "Lick! Lick! Beat me! Kill me if ye want to! Ye never did love me anyhow; I want to die!"

Then the Parson was piteous to see. His face would blanch and seem to shrivel: his breath would catch, coming with great gasps, and he would put out both hands, groping blindly toward the boy's bed, while his great body would shake as if with an ague. Such scenes nearly broke Mrs. Flint's heart. And to quiet the boy she would sit upon the bedside, the tears blinding her own eyes, and lay a soothing palm upon the struggling invalid's forehead, saying in her calm, gentle voice:

"Nathan, my darling child; mother's here!"

Then the restless boy's eyes would open in a vacant stare;

but somehow, somewhere in the tangled maze of his thoughts he seemed to hear an echo of her words; for he would cease his raving, and with a faint moan say plaintively, "I'm so tired!"

After he had grown quiet again, the broken Parson would get up despairingly from his chair and walk the room, dragging with him the burden of a sorrow that had no tear, but whose dreary heat burned his eyes almost to blindness. During these heavy-footed pacings he would sometimes lift his arms and groan "God forgive me!" in a little time kneeling by the sick bed and burying his face in his hands.

Very early on the morning of the eighth day, Doctor Parker paid the sick boy a visit, and he came again before noon. His skilled observation saw signs of a change in the fever, and he announced the cheering news that every symptom appeared to be encouraging. That afternoon the sickness began to abate, and Nathan grew very quiet, a grateful moisture breaking out on his hot forehead. By night his temperature was almost normal, and he fell into a deep slumber.

"It is the best of all medicine for him," said Doctor Parker as he stood watching the regular breathing. "His brain needs rest. Let him sleep as long as he will, and see that nothing disturbs him."

The good news lifted a mighty load off the Parson's weary heart, and for the first time in all these trying days, his nerves began to relax and he could breathe again. During the day a man came in to say that Guthrie, the sick parishioner with whom the Parson had sat up during that memorable night, was dead, and the Parson was required to attend the funeral services the next day. He would have demurred, but Doctor Parker urged his compliance with the request:

"Do n't hesitate to go, Parson," the anxious physician said; it fell in with his wishes with respect to the worn out man. "The boy is not in any danger, and it will do you great good to ride out"

The next morning Nathan still slept soundly, and the Parson reluctantly tore himself away to preach the funeral of his dead parishioner With what feelings he again rode over that stretch of road along which the wild pursuit had followed him may be better imagined than described. His heart swelled in his breast, and frequently he raised misty eyes to the great blue vault above him, while words of immense thankfulness burst from his lips.

It was late in the evening when he rode home again; and all the journey his father's thoughts traveled fast ahead, sometimes even winged with fear, as imagination clouded his mind with dread of accidents to the sick boy he had watched so faithfully

"He was awake at four o'clock, pa," said Mrs. Flint softly as she and the Parson again stood by Nathan's bedside. "He ate some and drank a glass of milk The doctor says there is no danger any more, and tomorrow he 'll be clear headed again"

The Parson stood silent for a little time, and then turned to kiss the lips that told him this good news. And that night he slept; slept the deep, dead sleep of great exhaustion, But somehow he looked old and sallow, and the lines of his face seemed to have deepened and grown sharper by reason of the long strain.

It was nearly ten o'clock the next morning when the Parson wakened from his profound lethargy; and even after so much rest a strange lassitude clung to his nerves, and seemed to make his powerful frame feel heavy and lifeless, despite the fact that the mental dread which had weighed him down was vastly lightened. For this much of relief, however, his heart throbbed with gratitude, and he felt happier than for many days. Strange for him who had always been so hearty, his appetite was small, and after a brief pretense at breakfast, he went straight to Nathan's room.

"It is all right now," said Mrs. Flint hopefully as the Parson stood and looked down upon the quietly slumbering boy. "He woke up again last night, and was very hungry. The eating will give him strength; he 'll soon be up and around once more."

"Did he know?" asked the Parson in a hesitating voice.

"Yes. He knew me at once, and in a little time everything came back to him. His agitation made me tremble for a while; he tried to cling to me, and fairly shook until I told him that you and William had escaped without harm. I dared not excite him, and in a little time he dozed off again. Just as he was about to fall asleep again he whispered, "I 'm so glad!"

The Parson sat down upon the side of the bed, and as he
26

gazed upon the wan countenance of his boy, his rugged face melted into a look of infinite tenderness. Who could tell what thoughts and emotions were storming his heart?

Presently Nathan stirred uneasily, and then all in a moment his eyes came wide open, and he was looking full into the Parson's face. The misty veil of sleep thinned away, and very soon recollection shone clear in his wondering eyes. For a little space he was silent, and then a shudder passed over him, while one faint cry escaped his lips.

"Oh, pa!" and a weak hand crept across the coverlet to rest upon his father's knee.

Then the Parson's great shoulders began to heave; his broad breast rose and fell convulsively, and lo, the long-sealed fountain of his tears gushed forth again! The Parson wept! Reaching down with his strong arms as tenderly as to a babe, he slipped one of them under Nathan's head, and the other about his waist, raising him gently and holding him closely to his bosom, as if the boy had come back from the dead. Nathan sighed in great content, and curled one weak arm about his father's neck

Like rain upon a thirsty land were the Parson's tears. They softened all the hard, dry soil of his nature, and melted his harshness into a tender love that was never more to grow cold. The boy lay very quiet, and when the Parson could see again, he found that sleep had come once more to the tired brain which was soothed and strengthened by the emotion of joy that had fallen upon it

The Parson laid Nathan softly upon his pillow again,

and with a touch light as love's longings could make it, smoothed back the hair from the sleeper's forehead. Then suddenly bending down he pressed upon it a kiss, as tender as a woman's and as heart-felt as a prayer.

As he sat up again Mrs. Flint's hand crept into his own; and with a great grip of it he turned his face toward her and exclaimed:

"Oh, Dolly, thank God! Thank God!"

It was the sweetheart name by which he had used to call her when life was young and love was warm. She had not heard it before for several years.

That afternoon Doctor Parker came in: not that there was any pressing need for him to do so, but he always liked to know that his work was fully accomplished.

"God bless you, Doctor, for what you have done!" said the Parson with deep feeling. "You have been a faithful friend; I shall never forget it. Make out your bill now, any time."

For some moments Doctor Parker made no reply. Those marvelous eyes of his seemed trying to inspect his ears from opposite sides. He was never a fluent talker, but presently said diffidently:

"Never mind about the bill, Parson. Credit it up on your salary; I haven't paid my quarterage yet."

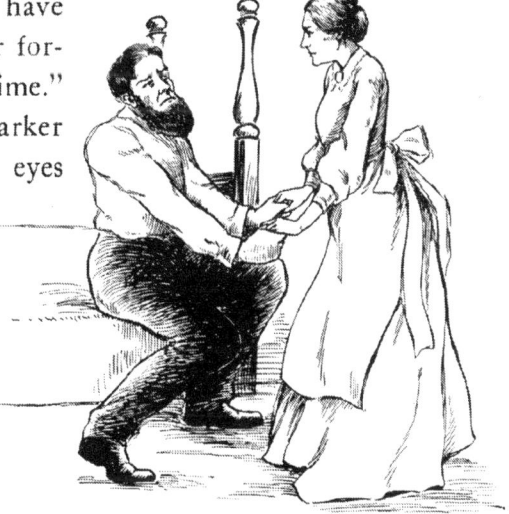

"OH DOLLY, THANK GOD!"

Then after an embarrassed pause he went on:

"It was a close shave at one time. I was interested in the case, and proud of the boy. My own youth was hard. The old man was very harsh with me. Never seemed to remember that he had once been a boy. And—Parson,—I 've wanted —a boy—all my life, but I never had one. It has been a great grief to me . . ." Then, as he hurriedly got up to go, he stumblingly added, "I 've heard some of the boy's talk while he was sick. . . . I can't say what I 'd like to; but perhaps it 's just as well; I guess you understand. . . ."

"I know, Doctor! I know!" faltered the Parson solemnly.

It was quite enough. The diffident doctor, and the now changed Parson had said very much.

CHAPTER XXX.

SORROW AND SIGHING.

IT was now the middle of September, the beginning of a prolonged and remarkable Fall. At times a faint blue haze seemed to creep over the low hills, and a smell like that of·burning leaves tainted the air. But the weather was yet hot and dry, as if the sultry August hours had forgotten to go.

Spurred by his religious zeal, the Parson again took up the routine of his duty with old-time energy, but somehow the depressing weight that had fallen upon him was not lightened. His face grew sallow and his frame gaunter. One day he rode to one of his preaching places, expecting to be gone over the Sabbath: but late in the afternoon the household was surprised by his returning home again; and as he dismounted from the horse he tottered dizzily.

"I 've had a chill," he said to his alarmed wife. "Something strange ails me; my head aches so that I can hardly see."

Mrs. Flint hurried him to bed, and bathed his dry forehead with tepid water, but by now the growing ache had spread all through his bones, and he moved restlessly, while his mouth was cracked, parched and dry from a rising fever.

Doctor Parker was sent for, but he was away on another call, and he did not come in until nearly bedtime.

"So! You are bound to give me a job, too, Parson," remarked the physician jocularly as he sat down by the Parson's side.

"It *does* seem so, Doctor," replied the Parson in a weary tone. "I 've hardly known what sickness meant before; but I 'm feeling very bad just now. Maybe it 's some passing trouble, though."

"Well, we 'll hope so," responded the doctor with an assumption of great confidence and ease.

After determining the patient's pulse, and asking a few questions, he prepared some medicine and went away, promising that he would come again early the following morning. But all that night the Parson tossed uneasily, and slept but little; and by the time the doctor arrived next day, something seemed to weigh the sick man down as with a leaden cloud. This time Doctor Parker examined into the case more thoroughly. He asked many questions; how long had the Parson been feeling this way? How had his appetite been, and when did the headache first come on? etc.

"Oh, I hardly know, Doctor; several days ago. Food has n't tasted right for two weeks, and during most of that time I 've had a dull headache; but the ride yesterday made my head nearly split. It seemed as if I should never be able to endure it until I got home."

The doctor listened keenly to these words; his face did not alter its expression, but he was thinking deeply.

"You sat up with Guthrie, and waited on him before he died, I think," remarked the doctor presently in an inquiring tone.

"Yes; I remained-with him over night; it was the day before that guèrrilla raid; you remember it," said the Parson weakly.

"Try to sleep, and do n't let yourself worry, Parson," urged the doctor earnestly as he took his leave. "You need rest very much."

It was not until twenty-four hours later, and after several more visits in which he narrowly watched the Parson's symptoms, that Doctor Parker rendered his final diagnosis. During this time there was no sign of improvement; but rather a steady increase of that strange depression, and those rising febrile symptoms that marked the malady.

"We 've got a little fight ahead of us, Parson," the doctor replied to the sick man's direct questions upon the subject. "You have contracted the fever, and must gather all your will and strength. Perhaps that visit to Guthrie's is the cause of it; it 's hard to tell."

At these words the Parson looked at the doctor with a strange shadow in his eyes. In his voice and manner was that which gave the physician more uneasiness than did the disease itself.

"I 've thought from the first that was it," said the Parson in a despondent voice "It has been creeping on me all the time, and I think it will finish me, Doctor."

"Come, come! None of that!" exclaimed Doctor Parker

loudly. "You must n't think of such a thing. There is too much to live for, and your family needs you, sir. . . . Do n't think of allowing such fancies to worry you. We 'll fight the thing through, and look for the best."

"The Lord's will be done," said the Parson very feebly.

In the presence of the despondent sick man, Mrs. Flint put on a brave cheerfulness; but this time she followed the doctor out of the room, and with new fear contracting her heart said:

"Tell me the worst, Doctor!"

"I am not going to look for the worst," was the kindly reply "We must none of us expect it. Do n't take his condition and fancies too much to heart. His somber notions are part of his disease. He is badly poisoned, and as a result very low spirited Watch him closely and try to cheer him all you can; but do n't give way yourself."

Though ever brave, tireless and self-sacrificing for those she loved, Mrs Flint read and felt in the doctor's kindly admonitions something more of his own thoughts and foresight than he had uttered, enough indeed to make her heart shrink with dread; and when afterwards she told the rest of the family what had been said, that threatening cloud which with Nathan's recovery had seemed to lift crept over them again, haunting their anxious minds with the weight of yet more grief and trial to come.

And indeed the Parson's condition seemed to warrant this dark foreboding As is the case with most strong, healthy persons whom serious illness catches in its relentless grip, he brooded over his situation in a deeply despondent frame of mind. For three days his spirits sank lower and lower, while the insidious poison that had crept into his veins gathered and grew, tainting his very blood and changing its vigorous red tide into the ferment of fever. In the waning of his strength, and the misery of his depressed nerves, the Parson had an over-powering premonition that he must die.

The doctor scolded him roundly for giving way to such unhealthy fancies, but he could not drive them away from the clouded mind. And fear has in it a vile contagion. So profound was the Parson's conviction that his end.was near, that the hearts of his household were touched and overshadowed by his own creeping dread.

One morning the sick man asked the children to leave him alone with his wife, and he talked with her long. What passed between them was never known; but after an hour Mrs. Flint came to the sickroom door and called the girls. Then the boys, who remained without in tearful waiting, heard the sound of many sobs, and murmurs of the conversation that came to them in indistinct fragments.

Again the door opened, and with the tears raining down her face, their mother came out and took both the boys in her arms:

"Come, boys," she said presently, "pa wants to see you."

And they followed her tremblingly, convulsed with sympathy for her grief, and the dread of what was yet to come.

The Parson was sitting drooped and feeble upon the bed-side, and Ruth knelt before him with her head upon his lap.

She had wept her penitence to him, and all her bitterness was gone. As the two boys entered the room, the Parson looked up at them with a world of grief in his hollow eyes. His strong chin quivered, and in a very passion of tenderness he put an arm about each, drawing them down on either side of him upon the bed.

"SITTING DROOPED AND FEEBLE."

"My precious boys!" he said; and his full heart seemed to melt within him, as a great flood of memory swept his mind.

They both clung to him closely, burying their faces upon his bosom, and between his violent sobs William jerked out fearfully:

"Oh, pa, don't you go and leave us! We jist can't live without you!"

The Parson pressed his sorrowful face down upon their heads, and presently said in a tone of quivering intensity:

"You saved your old father's life, my sons; and that when he least deserved it!"

"Don't! Don't, pa!" cried Nathan shrilly. "I'd a-died if them guerrillas had caught you! Oh," and he shuddered with the very memory of it,—"think of them awful hogs a-eatin' you!"

How their helpless grief swallowed them up! How their

sobs, tears and prayers mingled together as one! For a long time none of them could speak a word; then as they all knelt about the Parson's knees, the mother prayed aloud, asking God to spare the life of her husband, and the father of her children: and while the precious incense of her heart ascended to Heaven, the violent storm of their sorrow calmed into a gentle rain, and the wild gusts of grief died down.

Already the Parson's strength was taxed by his great emotions, and his wife persuaded him to lie down again; but still he reached out and held the boys, each by a hand.

"There is one thing I want to say to you, my sons," he quavered at last in a strong effort to restrain his tears. "I've wanted to say it always, only I forgot. And if you forget everything else I have ever done or said to you, I want you to remember this; I love you, and I always have loved you, no matter how poorly I have shown it!"

As he uttered these words with a burden of pathos and tenderness, a great sob seemed to swell in his throat and choke him. The boys clung to him desperately, and in a frantic return of his fear William raised his head and cried:

"Oh, pa, you ain't goin' to die, are you?"

"God knows, my dear boy," said the Parson chokingly. "But if it be His will that I shall not get well, I want you and Nathan

"I Love You!"

to take care of your dear mother." Then after a pause, "She has always shown her love for you, and I know you've always given her yours; she has deserved it far more than I have."

Having uttered these words, so full of bitter remorse and self-reproach, the Parson closed his eyes, and lay silent; and presently exhausted by this prolonged tax upon his strength, he seemed to fall into a restful doze. At a low word from their mother the children noiselessly left the room, praying in their very hearts that the life now so precious to them all might be spared.

Then followed thirty long days of fever; thirty days of slow, sinister dying. For at the time a change for the better had been expected, a sharp relapse came on, and the creeping poison seemed to spread with new vigor through the sick man's body. And when a second time the grim shadow of calamity took its grip, the last hopes of the stricken watchers seemed gone, although Doctor Parker still tried to encourage and cheer them in every way he could.

The gloomy days dragged along. Soldiers came home from the war, some wounded, some dying, and some with malignant fevers that affected many healthy persons in the little village

Doctor Parker was kept busy night and day; and the wonder of it was that he so well endured the long strain. He seemed to have nerves of steel, and endurance that knew no limit. When and how he managed to sleep no one could guess; for he ever went his dreary rounds, and fear-ridden hearts clung to

The Parson's Wife.

him as their last hope for the loved ones over whom their eyes wept tears.

Three times each day he visited the Parson, and would sit by his bedside, staring at him with those eyes askew, and searching for any and every symptom on which he might build a hope. The neighbors were tender and kind. Daddy Case, who lived nearest them, a dear old soul, together with others of the church came with loving services to sit up with the sick man, and attend his wants. For everyone felt great admiration and respect for the Parson, even though he had not won their deepest love.

But though everything was done that human skill could devise, the stubborn malady that had borne down the sturdy man would have its course. Little could be done but sustain his strength as far as possible, and await the results of time.

Rapidly the sullen tide of the fever gathered and rose, until finally its subtle undertow broke the Parson's hold upon his present, and swept him helplessly into the swamps of vagary and delirium. Then the tropic heat of it reached his rugged brain, and mazed his once clear mind in a tangled jungle of wayward fancies. Reason was lost in the thick darkness, and into the overwrought brain trooped numberless ghosts of bygone years. The strong man tossed and talked, muttered and raved He preached sermon after sermon, sang song after song, prayed prayer after prayer, and pronounced the benediction over a thousand spectral congregations.

Thirty long days the fever crawled and clung It flowed through his veins, wasted his great body, and crept a smouldering fire to his very finger-tips, until his skin was dry as dead leaves. In the slow fierce wasting of his strength, his voice took on a funereal tone of solemnity and pathos. And when in the fancied routine of his duties, he thought he was standing by some open grave, reading the services over the dead, his mighty wailing voice boomed through the silent house in awful distinctness:

"Earth to earth! Dust to dust! Ashes to ashes!"

None who heard him thus ministering to the shades they believed he must soon join ever forgot the solemnity of it, and hope died utterly out of the hearts of his weeping wife and children

Sometimes from very weariness of brain and tongue he would fall into an uneasy doze, lying supine, and often unconsciously picking at the covering on the bed. Then with his sunken eyes, and gaunt, sallow face, his look was that of one already shadowed by Death's dark wings. But the smouldering fire would flash up again, and the dreary round of dream and delirium go on anew

For thirty long, dark days he thus writhed and tossed, shouted and sang, preached and prayed. Then one evening as his faithful wife sat by his side, utterly worn out and nearly dead with the long strain of watching, and the anguish of hopes deferred, the stubborn fever burned itself out, flickered and died.

The Parson sank, collapsed, and gave one faint gurgling groan Aroused by the strange sound, Mrs Flint sprang to his bedside, calling loudly for help, which quickly came. At a word from her mother Eunice ran for the doctor, waiting neither for bonnet nor shawl. Mrs. Flint raised the Parson's head, poured brandy over his neck and chest, forcing some powerful cordial between his colorless lips.

The Parson whined in his throat, made one feeble effort and swallowed. But his face went white; his head rolled loosely upon the loving arm that held it; the ghost of a sigh fluttered between his bearded lips, and then there was utter silence. It seemed as if the sick man's premonitions had fallen true, and that the Parson was gathered to his fathers.

All that day Doctor Parker himself had been uneasy; for his long experience warned him that some kind of a crisis was near. As Eunice rushed from the house to call him, he was already approaching the parsonage on his nightly visit. Seeing the flying form of the girl, he hastened his own footsteps:

"Oh, Doctor, run!" cried the frantic messenger. " He is dead or dying!"

"Oh, Doctor, Run!"

And even Doctor Parker who had seen so many die, and who had looked upon death in numberless forms, drew his breath hard, and his countenance fell as he stood by the Parson's side, and saw the mask-like face of the unconscious man.

His fingers quickly sought the pulse, and then he bent his cheek over the silent man's lips for any sign of breath that might be left in him. Suddenly he stood up and spoke sharply to the sobbing wife and girls about him.

27

"There's a flicker of life left! Warm water and hot cloths quick! We must fight to save him!"

Flying feet and willing hands soon brought everything that was accounted needful; and all that long night the faithful doctor sat by the Parson's bedside, steadily and stubbornly battling for his patient's life. With cordial and heat, and gentle chafings he guarded and nourished the feeble spark of vitality that lingered in the wasted body that it might not be extinguished. Little by little he loosened the icy fingers that strove to drag the utterly helpless man into the shadows of the tomb. And never did anyone get so near the land of the leal and yet return. It was not until the sun was well up on the following morning that the doctor breathed a sigh of real relief and hope. Then in a voice that trembled with the joy of his own victory he said:

"I think we'll win. It was the closest call I ever knew. But if something unforeseen does n't happen, you may yet have him with you sound and well, Mrs. Flint. He has come back from the dead!"

And oh, how the streams of sunshine warmed the hearts of the Parson's household that glad day!

CHAPTER XXXI.

SUNSHINE AFTER STORM.

IT was nearly six weeks after the Parson's illness described in our last chapter, and the time lacked but a few days to Christmas.

When that anxious night had passed, in which by infinite care and constant watchfulness Doctor Parker had kept alive the expiring spark of life left in the Parson's exhausted frame, the sick man slowly but surely crept back into the land of the living. Weak as water, and for several days helpless as a babe, he was nursed with untiring tenderness and vigilance. Always a man of clean habits though, and endowed by nature with an iron strength of constitution, just as soon as the vital tide set in to flow again he began to make rapid progress towards recovery of flesh and vigor.

But after all, what a blessing that fever had proven to him! When his mind cleared, and the light of reason again illuminated his thought, the very nature in him seemed to have undergone a change. All the hard crust of his disposition had been burnt away; all the harshness and stern fibre of him had been softened and rendered sweet by his near approach to death. So close had he come to Heaven that some of its warmth and love had enriched his heart with a patience and loving kindness that never again died out of his life.

373

The Parson was truly a new man. And as day by day his lost strength returned, the mellow light of a great love transfigured his face with an expression of indescribable sweetness and joy. Everyone about him felt the wonderful change, and rejoiced.

Love always has an irresistible drawing power in it: and as the Parson's newly awakened affections grew and twined about the members of his responsive household, who so happy and light-hearted as they!

Mrs. Flint quickly recuperated her strength, and went about her duties singing those sweet old hymns that bubble up in the glad heart like echoes from heaven. The girls vied in petting and caring for the convalescent; Ruth in particular was always hovering about his chair, trying to make him more comfortable. She would brush his hair, bring him warmer wraps, and always insist upon carrying him his meals before he was able to sit at the table. And as to Nathan and William, the doting father for a long time could hardly bear to have them out of his sight. Every barrier between him and them was gone forever; all the loving father in him was glowing, and never again while he lived did the Parson lay the rod across their backs. He seemed to have drifted far away from Solomon's old time methods, and reached a newer inspiration, where "Love endureth long, and is kind." No longer were the boys afraid of him, dreading and shrinking from his stern frown of rebuke. And the natural love in their own

CONVALESCING.

Happy Greetings.

hearts sprang up and flourished in the glowing warmth of their father's affection.

But this was only a part of it. Not only did the members of his own family feel this renewed awakening of his love and tenderness, but when he preached in the old church six weeks after the fever left him, the whole congregation was touched as never before; feeling their hearts melted by the simple words he spoke, and the marvelous new fire that seemed to emanate from him. It was like a pentecostal season, and the happy tears and glowing responses to his thrilling message showed that the people were warmed by the fires of his own soul.

"It's a good thing for us all to get religion again, is n't it, Parson?" said Daddy Case, as with a hundred others he shook the preacher's hand after the services closed.

"Ay, Brother Case, it is. And it is a far more blessed thing for religion to get hold of us once more," replied the Parson.

※　※　※

On the day after he had preached this stirring sermon, the Parson's family were all gathered in the cozy sitting-room, early after dinner. The Parson was reading his paper by a window, and the girls were all busy on various little articles they were making as gifts for the coming holiday.

"And to think it is only five days to Christmas!" exclaimed Ruth. "What do you want for a Christmas gift, pa?"

The Parson laid down his paper and looked at her with a slight shadow in his eyes. Presently he said tenderly:

"None of you must think any more about me. I've had

enough joy to make all the rest of my life bright and happy."
Then after a pause he went on regretfully, "I 'm very sorry
we can't make the coming Christmas as sweet as I 'd like to
have it; but the little means your mother and I had saved up
were sadly eaten into during the last two months. However,"
he broke out more cheerfully, "the Lord will provide, and we
shall see what will happen when Christmas day comes."

"Do n't you worry, pa," cried Ruth, going to him quickly
and patting him on the cheek. "We have got you, and that
is worth everything else."

"Bless your dear heart, daughter; do you think so?" faltered the Parson, drawing her glowing face down with both
hands and kissing her tenderly.

"Well, I just do!" exclaimed Ruth earnestly, and then
after cuddling him awhile she went back to her sewing.

The Parson fell into a brown study for a time, but looking up suddenly he said:

"I saw Mr. Borden to-day, boys. He told me he had
found your gun, and daddy's old sword in the slaughter-house.
Forgot to bring 'em in, he said, but we can get them any time
we go by "

"Oh, pa!" exclaimed William scrambling up from the
floor where he had been lying at full length; "let 's go an' git
'em to-day We might find some squirrels on the way back,
and have a pot-pie!"

"Yes, do, pa," chimed in Mrs. Flint "The day is so
bright and lovely. It will do you good to drive out and get
the fresh air."

"Mebbe you are right, Dolly," said the Parson cheerily. Then turning to the boys he added, "Fly around, my sons, if ye want to go. Give the old charger some water and harness him up for your daddy."

Away the delighted boys ran, and in an incredibly short time the old two-seated family carriage was waiting at the gate. As the Parson drove away he found Doctor Parker leaning on the fence before his office, seemingly with nothing to do. Halting Daniel the Parson hailed the good physician with warm friendliness:

"Good day, Doctor! You don't seem to be very busy just now."

"No; for a wonder, I ain't," replied the doctor, scanning the Parson through the bridge of his nose, with head on one side. "I 'm trying to take it easy for once."

"Then come git in here and take a drive with us," rejoined the Parson insistently. "We are going out to Mr. Borden's to git some of the boys' traps he has in keeping."

"Well, now, you are very good, Parson," said the doctor with some hesitation, and after a moment's thought he added, "The fact is, I feel very lazy to-day, and I guess I 'll go. Then no one will come and make me go to work again."

Over the old familiar road Daniel jogged once more; and it might be that some memory of his wild race lingered in his brain too; for when he came round the end of the ridge, his flopping ears arose and he looked sharply at the road which lay ahead.

"You know I never did get the straight of that story,

Parson," said Doctor Parker, who evidently felt like being entertained. "As we drive along you must tell me yourself just how it happened, and point out the interesting places."

And the Parson did so, graphically relating the incidents one by one. "Here is where the last shots were fired. This is the place where Nathan jumped down and took that trail over the ridge; and it wasn't two minutes before the guerrillas came flying around the bend here and tore loose at us. Yonder is the bridge. And there is the place where I struck the road on the way from poor Guthrie's; and when I had got about here, just by that big tree on ahead I saw the boys coming. I was completely upset; and they met me just here, so short of breath it was all they could do to speak."

Among these familiar landmarks, the whole scene became so vivid that the Parson could fairly see it again; his tones hoarsened with kindling emotions, and his deep voice faltered.

He looked at the boys with glowing eyes. "Ye'd come to save yer daddy, hadn't ye, my sons? And only the day before he had treated ye like some old animal!"

"Good boys!" exclaimed Doctor Parker heartily. And then to put down his own feelings that caused his slanting eyes to look more crooked than ever, he said loudly "All's well that ends well, Parson But what strange and unexpected things do happen to us in this common-place old world! The thing would make a wonderful story; you ought to write it out."

"I'll leave that for the boys when they grow up," rejoined the Parson with a smile "They did most of it; they and the old horse here"

To lighten the load for Daniel, Nathan and William walked up the long hill, and then getting into the buggy again, they were soon at their destination. In response to the Parson's hail Mr. Borden came out, and when he saw who it was, brought the gun, sword and quilt, together with the very apron in which the boys had carried their bread and gritty beef-bone. Then declining a very cordial invitation to get out and stop awhile, the Parson turned Daniel about and started for home. As they approached the slaughter-house on their return, Doctor Parker suddenly exclaimed:

"Let's go and see the place, Parson. I must look at the stage setting, where the tragedy first began."

To humor his whim the Parson halted, tied Daniel to a sapling and together they all made their way through the bushes toward the half-hidden building.

The slant afternoon sun was shining brightly, and streaks of its golden light shot through the cracks, barring the dusky interior with a steady glow. Nothing had been changed. The pile of dry hides had not been moved, and the great iron hook hung sullenly from its heavy support. Most of the hogs that had disturbed the boys on that eventful night had fallen under the butcher's ax, and had swung from the hook but a few days previously; and one golden bar from the wintry sun fell aslant the hardly dried blood beneath it.

In the presence of these sinister surroundings, the memory of their terrible night made the boys shudder anew. Doctor Parker was full of interest, and at his request Nathan related most of the incidents that occurred, terrible to recall even though long weeks had elapsed since they were enacted.

"We was behind these skins here," he concluded; "and when the captain had sent his men out to hide and watch for pa, that fellow he called Dave handed the captain a rope. He made a loop in it and flung it over the hook up there. Then he swore, and said they'd all pull hard on it, because Jordan Blake thought pa was so heavy. Then when they'd got that done they took off their belts——"

At this point in his recital, Nathan stopped as if he had been shot. When the Parson looked at him the boy's eyes were opened widely, and he was beginning to tremble. Thinking it was the disturbing memory of the scene that ailed him, the Parson laid an assuring hand upon his shoulder and said:

"The danger was all over long ago, my son. You said that they took off their belts—go on."

"Pa," faltered Nathan presently, clinging to his father's hand, "was all them guerrillas killed?"

"Not all of them, my son. A few of them scattered into the hills and got away   The guards got most of them, though "

"Did they kill the captain?"

"Yes; he and several others were dropped at the first shots the home-guards fired "

"And did they kill that man he called Dave?"

"That I don't know "

"Did any of 'em come back here?"

"Not one of them, Nathan   They didn't dare, and besides that they did n't have time. They took short cuts to the river after crossing the bridge down in the bottoms there."

As this conversation proceeded Nathan's excitement became more and more intense. Suddenly he exclaimed:

"Come with me, pa; ther's something they left behind."

Wondering and excited themselves by the boy's strange emotion the two men and William followed him out of the building. He made straight for a stump about thirty paces distant. Leaning over he looked into this and started back with a shrill cry:

"Oh, pa, here's a whopping big snake!"

"What!" exclaimed the Parson in astonishment; for it was the time of year when all reptiles should be denned up for the winter.

Seizing a stout stick, the Parson hurried forward and peered over the edge of the hollow, touched the reptile with his club and then said with a smile:

"It won't hurt you, my son."

But there it lay, coiled into frozen spirals, ugly and menacing, a ghostly guardian of the guerrilla's gold—stone dead. Doubtless it had descended from above, and the receptacle being wider at the bottom than the top, it could not escape from its prison.

When assured that the scaly monster was harmless, Nathan reached in, plucked the dead reptile out and threw it away. Then he stooped again, clawed aside the matted leaves upon which the serpent had lain, and in an instant straightened up with the belts of the dead bandits in his trembling hands

"They took 'em off and dropped 'em in here when they left the slaughter-house to hide for pa," he gasped. "There's lots of gold in 'em, they said!"

The Parson stared in speechless amazement, and it was Doctor Parker who took the belts from Nathan's outstretched hands. When he felt their weight, and fingered the çanvas sides, he raised a great shout, and threw his dignity to the winds:

"Who-o-op-pee!" he yelled, swinging the articles wildly above his head. "The spoils of war, Parson! The spoils of war! All's well that ends well! I said that before!"

How the Parson's hands did shake as he felt the weight of these sudden riches. How the gleeful boys did caper and shout and turn cartwheels until the few hogs yet in the pen seemed to catch the infection of their excitement. They plunged awkwardly about, relieving their frisky feelings in those piggish barks the boys knew so well:

"Boo! Boo! Boo-uh-wooh!"

And finally when the joyful four started for town again, Daniel striding along with a vision of corn in his mind's eye, what a different trip it was to that of coming out! When they arrived at the parsonage there were Daddy Case and another parishioner on a visit, and full of rejoicing over the Parson's recovery. The great good news was quickly told to the wonder-struck family and friends, but they could hardly believe their own ears until the yellow treasures were lying in a beautiful heap before them.

When emptied from the greasy belts, piled up and counted,

"Whoop-pee!" yelled the Doctor

the sum was but a trifle under thirteen thousand dollars, all in solid disks of gold, which at that time was at a high premium. Daddy Case made a hasty calculation, and announced that the real value, of the amount was somewhere near fifteen thousand dollars.

"But have we any right to keep it?" suddenly asked the Parson in a pause of the excited comments.

"Why man alive!" exclaimed Doctor Parker astonished at this unheard-of question; "Keep it! Why should n't you keep it?"

"I should say so, Parson," chimed in Daddy Case warmly. "It is prize money. Who ever heard of a ship giving up its prize money?"

"We might be able to find the owners or their people," faltered the conscientious Parson.

"Nonsense!" shouted the Doctor. "Why man, if you should advertise for an owner, there 'd be a thousand thieves try to claim the stuff. You 'll never find any more rightful owner of it than yourself; and do n't you be foolish about it now. That 's my advice."

Just here Nathan broke in with his recollections of how the guerrillas had said the gold was picked up in a hundred places, and the visitors declared that this only showed how futile it was for anyone to seek those who had owned the money in the past. The opinion was all one way, and it finally appeased the Parson's scruples. He thought it over for a few moments and then said significantly:

"This stuff all belongs to my boys."

28

"No, pa!" cried Nathan, taking his hand. "It's all yours; we'd never 'a' got it if it hadn't been fer you."

The Parson reached out a big hand to William and drew him up by his other side.

"And what do you say, my son?" he asked with a twinkle in his eye.

"Why uv course it belongs to you, pa," William said eagerly, "but we kin have things fer Christmas now, can't we? You'll buy me a brass cannon, an' some marbles, an 'a rubber ball, an' somethin' to shoot it with, won't you?"

William doubtless meant something to shoot the cannon with, but in his great excitement his words naturally got tangled.

"You just see if I don't!" said the Parson laughing, while the others, ha, ha'd uproariously.

It would take too long to tell all that was said before the visitors left the parsonage; but it was the Parson who finally decided on what should be done with the money

"I shall place ten thousand dollars of it out at interest, so that the boys shall have a good start when they grow up," he said "The balance of it we can make mighty good use of at present. There are some things we want to do without any delay, and one of them is to pay your bill, Doctor Parker; that is, as far as money will go The immense debt of gratitude we owe you, and the rich friendship we can never wholly re-quite"

Thus suddenly addressed the good doctor blushed, and actually looked embarrassed When pressed to it he named a ridiculously low sum, and the happy Parson completely flabbergasted him by crowding double the amount into his hands, saying "God bless you" besides. Then the tender hearted fellow looked queerer than ever, and his eyes actually seemed trying to revolve on their axes. He strove to say something fitting, but like those dodging optics, his words turned inwards and he finally had to gulp and swallow them.

Royal old Doctor Parker!

In all the land there was no happier household than the Parson's on that memorable night. The wonderful fortune that had so strangely fallen to them seemed too good to be true. When the visitors had gone home, the family sat and talked about the matter for hours, going over every detail, and dwelling with sad or loving delight upon each incident of all those eventful weeks that had brought so much of sorrow, but in the end such an overwhelming joy.

"And now my dear ones," said the Parson at last, while his eyes grew humid, and his wondrous voice mellowed to a cadence of love that was intensely thrilling and impressive, "we must not forget the marvelous lesson which the blessed Father of us all teaches us in what has happened. There is a fragment of Scripture that keeps ringing in my ears, over and over, 'All things work together for good to them that love God.'

"And it is that word 'together' which means so much. Think of all that has happened in the last three or four months! How full of threat and dread some of these things seemed to be at the time! Taken separately they didn't always seem to be working for good; but 'together!' Ah, that is the great fact we must look to for the explanation. Surely the good Lord ordereth all things well! He maketh the wrath of men to praise Him, and the remainder of wrath will He restrain. How wonderfully He has done this all along! In a strange blindness I had almost forgotten the one thing worth remembering above all others,—that Love endureth long and is kind. May the good Lord never suffer me to forget it again!

"Then when my error had borne its evil fruits; when the boys suffered unjustly and rebelled; when they ran away, and got to that slaughter-house where the Devil had his trysting place; when those misguided men laid their foul snare; when the boys came to warn their daddy who was blindly riding into the awful danger; and when the brave old horse was flying from it, while our lives hung upon his feet and speed; when afterwards the clouds grew black and the way seemed leading down into the valley of death;—oh, looked at singly, and at the very time, none of these heart shaking incidents seemed to be working for good! But taken 'together!' See how out of all the maze of danger the great Guide has safely led us; and each incident was but a step of the way, a part of the purpose 'working together for good!' My heart is overrunning with measureless gratitude for all the good Father's forbearance and tender mercies toward us!"

Here the Parson's love burdened tones faltered, and he caught his breath audibly, while glad tears of sympathy and recognition glistened in the eyes fixed upon him in reverential interest in his words.

Suddenly Ruth sprang up, walked to the Parson, flung her arms about his neck and kissed him furiously.

"Oh pa, how I love you!" she exclaimed.

The Parson folded her in his embrace, and returned her impetuous caress with indescribable tenderness and affection.

"God bless you, my precious girl!" he said earnestly. "I love you too; and I know what love means now, as I never knew it before."

Ruth returned to her chair with heart aglow. Suddenly the Parson reached out his great arms to the boys and said,

"Come here, my sons."

They went to him, and he took one of them on each knee, holding them close to his heart, while he repeated from memory the twenty-third Psalm, "The Lord is my Shepherd, I shall not want."

As the words began to fall from his lips, Mrs. Flint, the girls and the two boys joined in to the very last. And what unutterable meaning it had to them! "Yea, though I walk through the valley of the shadow of death, I will fear no evil; for Thou art with me!" and so on to the triumphant climax of the noble thought, "And I shall dwell in the house of the Lord forever!"

Then the Parson knelt for family prayer, and in a circle of welded hearts and embracing arms, the household knelt close about him. Never did such sweet incense rise from grateful souls as from theirs that glorious night! For sorrows may fall, terrors may threaten, and sickness spread its sable shadow over loving hearts, but these uplifted ones had truly found that "joy cometh in the morning."

The tender prayer ended, and after a sweet silence the Parson arose to his feet. But to the great surprise of all William still remained upon his knees, his tow head buried in his arms upon the chair, and he weeping with some convulsive emotion

"What is it, my son?" asked the Parson in a concerned voice, as he knelt again by the shaking urchin, and put one loving hand upon his head

"Oh—pa,—" snuffled William between his sobs, "I—I—think—I—I 've—g-go-got re—religion!"

"Praise the Lord!" ejaculated the Parson fervently; for he believed in early conversions. "It seems to me you 've always had a good share of it, my son. But what makes you think you 've got religion just now?"

" 'C—c—c—cause I 'm s—s—s—sor-rry I d-d-did n't throw away that haw-haw—hawk's foot when ye told me to!"

With a sudden sound in his throat, between a laugh and a sob, the Parson reached down and gathered William close to his heart.

THE END.

Lightning Source UK Ltd.
Milton Keynes UK
UKHW021841190321
380653UK00006B/1330